in
search
of
wisdom

Also by These Authors

Alexandre Jollien

In Praise of Weakness

Christophe André

Feelings and Moods

*Looking at Mindfulness:
Twenty-Five Paintings to Change the Way You Live*

Happiness: 25 Ways to Live Joyfully Through Art

Matthieu Ricard

The Monk and the Philosopher: A Father and Son Discuss the Meaning of Life
coauthored with Jean-Francois Revel

The Spirit of Tibet: The Life and World of Khyentse Rinpoche, Spiritual Teacher
coauthored with Khyentse Rinpoche

*The Quantum and the Lotus:
A Journey to the Frontiers Where Science and Buddhism Meet*
coauthored with Trinh Xuan Thuan

Happiness: A Guide to Developing Life's Most Important Skill
coauthored with Daniel Coleman

Motionless Journey: From a Hermitage in the Himalayas

Why Meditate: Working with Thoughts and Emotions

The Art of Meditation

Bhutan: The Land of Serenity

Tibet: An Inner Journey

*On the Path to Enlightenment:
Heart Advice from the Great Tibetan Masters*

Altruism: The Power of Compassion to Change Yourself and the World

*A Plea for the Animals: The Moral, Philosophical,
and Evolutionary Imperative to Treat All Beings with Compassion*

Enlightened Vagabond: The Life and Teachings of Patrul Rinpoche

Beyond the Self: Conversations between Buddhism and Neuroscience
coauthored with Wolf Singer

Matthieu Ricard
Christophe André
Alexandre Jollien

in
search
.of
wisdom

A Monk, a Philosopher, and a
Psychiatrist on What Matters Most

Translated by Sherab Chödzin Kohn
Trois amis en quête de sagesse

SOUNDS TRUE
BOULDER, COLORADO

Sounds True
Boulder, CO 80306

Translation © 2018 Christophe André, Alexandre Jollien, and Matthieu Ricard

Originally published as *Trois amis en quête de sagesse*
© L'lconoclaste et Allary Éditions, 2016
Published by special arrangement with Allary Éditions
in conjunction with their duly appointed agent 2 Seas Literary Agency

Sounds True is a trademark of Sounds True, Inc.
All rights reserved. No part of this book may be used or reproduced in any manner
without written permission from the author(s) and publisher.

Published 2018

Cover design by Jennifer Miles
Book design by Beth Skelley

Printed in Canada

Library of Congress Cataloging-in-Publication Data
Names: André, Christophe, author. | Jollien, Alexandre, 1975- author. |
    Ricard, Matthieu, author.
Title: In search of wisdom : a monk, a philosopher, and a psychiatrist on
    what matters most / Christophe Andre, Alexandre Jollien, Matthieu Ricard ;
    translated by Sherab Chadzin Kohn.
Other titles: Trois amis en quête de sagesse. English
Description: Boulder, Colorado : Sounds True, Inc., [2018] | Includes
    bibliographical references.
Identifiers: LCCN 2017048476 (print) | LCCN 2017049836 (ebook) |
    ISBN 9781683640257 (ebook) | ISBN 9781683640240 (pbk.)
Subjects: LCSH: Spirituality. | Self-realization.
Classification: LCC BF637.S4 (ebook) | LCC BF637.S4 A6213 2018 (print) |
    DDC 170/.44—dc23
LC record available at https://lccn.loc.gov/2017048476

10 9 8 7 6 5 4 3 2 1

Contents

Preface

The house where we worked on this book is in the middle of a forest in the Dordogne. Not far away is a small road where we often went for walks between our discussion sessions. At a fork in the road is a wooden road sign indicating the direction of the nearby village, with these words on it, painted by hand: *Coeurjoie, voie sans issue* (literally in English, "Heartjoy: Dead End"). But we weren't swayed by this message. During the two weeks of work and camaraderie we shared, the joy in our hearts was far from being a dead end!

This is not intended to be a book of moral lessons but rather an opportunity to share our views and our experience with you. It seemed to us that our very different paths in life, our three "trades"—philosopher, monk, and psychiatrist—might perhaps lead to a fertile exchange of ideas on the big subjects that we human beings all must reflect on in considering how to lead our lives.

The three of us have known each other for a long time. Before meeting in person and eventually becoming friends, we were introduced to each other through our writings. Occasionally reuniting over a period of time, publicly or privately, we began to notice our common values and shared views, and the idea of doing a book together was born.

Each of us has a role in this book. Matthieu is the elder brother, generous and solid, who travels the world advocating for the causes he really cares about (humanitarian projects, Tibet, altruism). His intellectual and physical vigor and strength compel the admiration of his two mates. Alexandre is the younger brother, joyful and affectionate, with a brilliant, creative, poetic mind. He loves to laugh and make others laugh; he adores being pampered and is very loving. Christophe is the middle brother, calm. He is always trying to be helpful, to explain, to comfort his patients and his readers, and always happy to be in the company of the "companions for good," as we nicknamed ourselves.

The days of discussion and personal exchange that this book is made of took place in a very simple house on the valley of the Vézère. From there we could admire the rising winter sun as it emerged slowly from the mist and gradually illuminated the countryside. It was a house where we were treated like princes. Our meals were taken care of—we were provided with succulent vegetarian cuisine—and so we had nothing to do but reflect and sit together by the fireside and have our discussions. To clear our heads, we took long walks in the natural surroundings, shared chatty meals with visiting friends, and visited the Buddhist community at the Chanteloube Study Center, whose temples, stupas, and retreat huts surrounded us.

We had a lot of laughs trying to hit on a title for this book. Here are some of the titles you escaped (though we hope you can catch a glimpse of what prompted them in the chapters that follow): The Three Men in a Hamlet; The Cobblers of Compassion; The Ego Terminators; The Lumberjacks of Altruism; The Plumbers of Gratitude; The Chatterboxes of Perigord; The Garbage Collectors of Me, Me, Me; The Earthworms Who Could Listen; The SWAT Team for the Optimization of Compassionate Activities.

During these days of work, we were surrounded by well-wishing friends, long term or of the moment, without whom we could not have carried out this project. Our three names are on the cover, but an entire band of fairies and angels bent kindly over the cradle of this book. At the end of the book, we express our thanks to these traveling companions of ours.

This book is made up of exchanges concerning the experiences and views of three friends whose life paths, personalities, and professions have led them to think about and work on what benefits human beings. But we don't pretend to be experts on the subject matter or models in accomplishing the work or overcoming the obstacles involved in it. Our discussions were on the themes we had chosen before our time together, and we decided each evening on the particular subject for the following day so we could sleep on it. Our wide-ranging discussions were recorded in their entirety, then transcribed. We and our editors worked on the transcriptions in order to give some form to these many hours of conversation and debate. We hope you will find in these pages something of the thoughtful and joyous atmosphere of our discussions and of their spontaneous spirit, but also a sense of the care we took to be coherent and communicative.

Now come and take your place beside us, in a regular chair or, more like us, on a well-worn and comfy couch. Other friends are here with us in the room who a little later on will regale us with their valuable comments on the discussion we've just had. The fire is crackling on the hearth, the breadth of the valley can be seen out the window, the winter sun is gradually fading, the tea steaming in our cups warms our hands and stimulates our brains. Alexandre takes on his impish air and tells a joke. Matthieu adjusts his glasses and claps his hands to bring the session to order, and Christophe has a last look at the notes he took last night in his little notebook (he knows that his tricky pals often turn to him to get the conversation started).

So the discussion is about to get under way. You were all that was missing.

Introduction

MATTHIEU Clarifying our motivation here is a little bit like deciding what direction one is going to travel in when one gets up in the morning. Should one go north, south, west? In beginning these discussions, which are meant to supply the content of a book, it might be helpful to spend a little time asking ourselves what direction we want to give our discussions. First, we have to ask ourselves if our purpose is mainly to help other people or to pursue our own personal interests?

Our Motivation for This Book

CHRISTOPHE As far as I'm concerned, it seems to me that my motivation is threefold. First, I want to be helpful. I'm a doctor who writes psychological self-help books and who tries to help people with them. Knowing that I can be useful to other human beings without necessarily meeting them in the flesh gives me a great deal of pleasure. I don't think I've ever written a book with any other motivation than to do that. I think that's true of all three of us. I want to help my readers suffer less and develop further as human beings. Spending a couple of weeks with two friends I love and admire is a second motivation!

But I see a third aim for this book with three voices: to bring the image that people have of us more in line with who we actually are. We are sometimes wrongly perceived as sages, as though we have achieved a kind of knowledge and a way of being that makes us quite different from other people. Obviously, at least in my case, that is an illusion. In talking about our own journeys and the difficulties we have had in becoming better human beings, I think we can help our

All humans are alike: we have to work hard to be better.

readers a little more by reminding them that we are not their superiors. It seems to me that it is comforting for readers to know that there are not two categories of people: those who float ten kilometers above their heads and those who are floundering around like themselves in the muck and mire of everyday life. All humans are alike: we have to work hard to be better.

ALEXANDRE Beginning this exchange, I have the feeling of entering an immense spiritual laboratory to explore life's great areas of endeavor with you. Taking up this heady challenge in the company of you two happiness experts both gives me pleasure and intimidates me a little. Most of all, what is important to me is that our remarks be helpful. There are books that have saved my life. So I would be happy if our discussion—without presenting any recipes, because there aren't any—could encourage those who are struggling and transmit to them the desire we share to engage ever more deeply in the spiritual journey. Even the greatest spiritual progress is meaningless if it does not make us feel more closely connected with each other, if it does not bring us closer to our neighbor. And work on oneself can quickly begin to smell moldy if it does not open into genuine generosity. The ego is so talented and so twisted that it appropriates everything, or almost. There is certainly such a thing as spiritual egotism. If we forget about others, we inevitably end up crashing and burning ourselves; we turn the very means that could save us into a trap. That is why it is of the utmost importance that we stay free from this pitfall along the way. Friendship heals a lot of ills; it gives us wings and it comforts us. Friendship is what initiated our coming together. It is what makes ever deeper the bonds that unite us, which nothing can demolish. It is essential never to forget that we are all shipmates, sailing on the same ship. To cross the ocean of suffering we have to work together. It is to this dynamic of solidarity that I would like to dedicate this book.

MATTHIEU   This book was born, to begin with, from our friendship and our recurrent desire to spend a few days together in open conversation about the subjects that we hold most dear. The idea here is not simply to lump our mental fabrications together in one place in order to produce yet another book. There are people who get a kick out of inventing new concepts and then promoting them as much as possible. But our aim here is to share what we have learned from our masters, spiritual and otherwise; from our studies; and from our practice, meditative or therapeutic.

As far as I'm concerned, it is only due to the wisdom and kindness of my spiritual masters that I have been able to transform myself even a little bit and place myself at the service of others. Now it is my turn to attempt to share what they have taught me, doing my very best always not to betray, distort, or dilute their message.

ALEXANDRE   There is only one really urgent thing, and that is to engage fully in one's practice, to cultivate in oneself a burning desire to make progress, and to realize that we are capable of escaping from the prison of our conceptual mind. People can theorize all they want about practice, but what really counts is living it day by day. I was attending a conference for members of a popular movement that protests the social injustice prevailing in today's world. But I soon found myself protesting against the protesters. After all the beautiful speeches, I found myself standing alone in the pouring rain and had to make my way home on foot. It is meaningless to condemn the system, to blame everything on the world. What really matters is deeds, actually doing something to help. We shouldn't hesitate to follow Nietzsche's advice for the best way to start our day. The moment we wake up we should ask ourselves if we can make "at least one person happy" today. Everything begins with one's "neighbor," with "the first person who comes along," as Christian Bobin puts it. How can I be wholeheartedly open toward the person I run into on the street or the people I rub shoulders with every day? How can I genuinely love a person who gets on my nerves?

CHRISTOPHE   We might all be like those protesters who make speeches about altruism and don't help you get to the station, because we're caught up in our concepts, because as soon as the conference is over we're right back into our own problems and concerns. Fundamentally, the essential message is not "Altruism is a beautiful thing" but rather "What can I do for other people right now, today?" A concept by itself doesn't cure anything. It might be comforting, illuminating, satisfying, but sooner or later the cure always has to come through action; it has to come through the body. It's through trial and error in real circumstances that we finally find out if an idea has power and meaning. It's when we put it into practice that we can learn what the consequences are for ourselves and other people.

> A concept by itself doesn't cure anything. It might be comforting, illuminating, satisfying, but sooner or later the cure always has to come through action; it has to come through the body.

MATTHIEU   The point you are making is right at the heart of Buddhism. We say that the value and sense of any teaching is measured by the extent to which it becomes an integral part of oneself. All the rest is just pointless. Getting a lot of prescriptions from the doctor without following the treatment he prescribes does nothing for your health. Ideas are useful for clarifying our thinking, for helping us know where we're going, for determining the principles of our actions, but if we don't put them into practice, they're not good for anything.

There's another important question that is worth clarifying. It again has to do with our motivation here and the possible use of this book. It's about the ambiguity of what is known as *personal development* or *self-help*. If this development takes place solely within the bubble of our ego, it will feed the ego, polish it, ornament it with reassuring ideas, and so on. But all this will be within a very limited and narrow framework, and it will totally miss what we are aiming for—because the only way to achieve fulfillment is through compassion and openness toward others. At all costs, we must avoid having the exercises of mindfulness and meditation become havens where we can hang out full-time in the world of ego. As Alexandre often says, "The inside of the bubble of ego, it feels rather stuffy." Either you try to transform yourself for the sake of serving others and everybody wins, or you stay inside the bubble of ego and everybody loses. Because by desperately trying to be happy just for your own sake, you don't help others or yourself.

CHRISTOPHE I have the sense that the dimension in which my development is happening is a little different from the one you two are working in. I'm a caregiver who has to deal with the expectations and problems of my patients, who often lack self-esteem. As a result, I tend to have a less critical view on this question of ego. In my work, I find that the first step often consists in comforting the ego, restoring it, reinforcing it. Many people have a relationship with themselves that is characterized by self-hate. It seems to me I have to take a two-step approach. If I start by encouraging them to be concerned for others, that will certainly do them some good but I won't have done my work in the right order. I do know that eventually you have to let go of the focus on self, or at least you have to let go of the excessive aspect of this self-centered interest. But you mustn't do this too fast. I see it this way all the more because in my own development, this is the way I was able to make progress.

There's something else that has always obsessed me in my practice. What is known as "the self-disclosure of the therapist" occurs at the moment where the caregiver, in coming face-to-face with the suffering of the other, speaks a little of his own suffering. And by the way, this is the approach we are taking in this book. This phenomenon has been studied and theorized about because it's a powerful factor, like a condiment in cooking. Without it, a therapeutic relationship is too dull and bland, but with it, a sense of complicity and humanity comes into play. What does self-disclosure consist of in a therapeutic relationship? At a certain point, the caregiver hears in his patient a suffering that echoes a suffering he has experienced himself. And he decides to talk to his patient about some of what he has gone through himself because that might help the patient. The patient realizes that he or she is not alone. This self-disclosure has to be dispensed in very small doses. There can be no question of filling the whole space of the consultation with our own story, no question of trying to "relativize" the patient, because you don't want to devalue the patient's right to suffer. You just want to allow the patient, through his suffering, to join the vast group of humans around him. Which reminds me of another phrase of Christian Bobin's, in his book *The Ruins of Heaven*: "Whoever you're looking at, know that that person has been through hell several times." When they come to see us, patients are in the midst of going through hell. They feel alone and lost. Knowing that others have also been down the road of suffering can sometimes bring them solace and relief.

Our Paths

ALEXANDRE   The idea of a calling is very liberating. It can serve as a compass on days where everything is going badly, as an encouragement to respond once more to the deepest summons of our lives. In times of trial as in times of joy, one must continually ask oneself, "What is my existence calling me to, here and now?" As for me, I think life has entrusted me with three vocations. First, my disability, which I have to experience fully. Infirmity, far from being a burden, can become a fabulous practice ground. If I consider it purely as an onerous load, I might as well put a bullet in my head. From that point of view, I'm better off looking at it as a possible path to wisdom. But be careful—it's not suffering that makes us grow but rather what we make of it. I distrust like the plague any talk that is too quick to justify suffering. Such talk forgets that pain can bring bitterness; it can kill a heart. Although it doesn't mean that I accept my disability entirely, once and for all, nonetheless, some days I discover in this calamity a chance to become more joyful and more free. And I see clearly that without a spiritual practice, I'm a lost cause. In short, my disability makes me feel the urgent need to convert on the spot and take refuge in the fundamental ground of all grounds, far beyond labels and appearances, and enter a new learning situation every day.

The profession of writer is also a path, an answer to a summons. This passion, this need, made itself felt very early on. In my time of struggle, I realized that one day I would have to bear witness to the legacy bequeathed to me by my comrades in misfortune. They transmitted to me a taste for what is essential: the desire to improve, the thirst for unconditional joy, and the experience of solidarity with others. At the institution for the disabled where I grew up and spent seventeen years of my life, the path of bearing witness was born. Without doubt it was a survival mechanism, but a very fertile and creative one. In my suffering I felt with all my being that I had to make something of it.

> In times of trial as in times of joy, one must continually ask oneself, "What is my existence calling me to, here and now?"

Lastly, the path of being a father and a husband calls on me to unlearn a great deal, to heal from fear, from reflexive responses, from deficiencies, and always to move forward and improve.

These three life paths are with me constantly, hour by hour, particularly when things are difficult—that is to say, often. They go beyond the notion of a personal objective that ego should be trying desperately to accomplish. Here there is no promotion in rank to be won—it's just a matter of going forward and loving ever more deeply, without clinging to any fixed reference point. Someone who confines himself to a particular identity will never know an end to suffering. If, for example, I persuade myself that my happiness depends on being a writer, the day that I can't write anymore, I will lose my joy.

At present I draw my nourishment from the great spiritual traditions, in particular from the practice of Zen and from a life of prayer. These enable me to experience more profoundly the three challenges to which life has summoned me.

Everything began from being disabled at birth. All it took was a misplaced umbilical cord to make me cerebrally motor-incapacitated for life. From the age of three, I grew up in a special institution, a rough and raw school of life. The main thing I discovered there—and it was a very heavy direct impression—was how precarious our condition is. Since then, I have been saddled with a feeling of insecurity and a fear of being abandoned, no doubt because of the wee-bit overdramatic beginning of my career in life and because of being separated from my parents. What this institutional life left me with was a sense of wonder with regard to the world and the need to keep moving forward.

Along with my companions in misfortune, some of whom were very seriously disabled, I also had to deal with death. One of my best friends, Trissia, was a hydrocephalic. When I was eight, one of my teachers took me aside and said, "Go take a look at Trissia. She's down at the end of the hall; look and see how beautiful she is." I went into the dimly lit room and saw my comrade lying in a coffin. I hadn't even known she was sick. This premature encounter with death and suffering both made me grow up and traumatized me. I will never forget this little girl lying there with her arms crossed as though she was praying. In that gloomy room I experienced a very basic call, which oriented me toward the spiritual life. I felt in my flesh that without an inner quest, I would be a total loss, finished.

The struggle to get into a so-called normal school was a long one. I had flunked the psychomotor tests. I wasn't fast enough. But thanks to my parents' perseverance, I was finally able to get a place in a school. The reason I insist on everyone's right to be included is precisely because I escaped being excluded by the skin of my teeth. When I was allowed to leave the institution, it was like landing on another planet. I knew nothing of the social codes: who I should kiss, who I should shake hands with. I'm still learning this social game.

From my childhood I've retained a certain sense of the tragic as well as a persistent naiveté. Through being in the company of people who couldn't talk, I learned the sweetness of a friendly gesture, a smile, a glance. It took me a long time to find my ground in society and to reconcile myself to adapt to it. I hugged the first girl I fell in love with so hard that her reaction still upsets me today: "Hey, what's your problem!" This first contact came very close to condemning me to a life of holding back. What brought us joy at the institute was just the opposite of that—point-blank transparency. When we were happy, we said so. When we were sad, we also made that clear. But in the outer world, I soon discovered, we frequently have to mask our feelings, disguise our intentions. Lesson number one was not to let everything show.

From a very young age, being in the company of helpless people transmitted to me a sense of solidarity. Some people say that human beings are bad, selfish, that they think of nothing but themselves. That is exactly the opposite of what I experienced with my comrades in misfortune. What we had together was natural solidarity, spontaneous compassion, a wish to find our way forward together. In a word, it was a living altruism. Face to face with a merciless destiny, we stood shoulder to shoulder. I want to take this idea that humans are selfish by nature and wring its neck. In your book *Altruism*, Matthieu, you quote a passage from the correspondence of the father of psychoanalysis that makes me laugh. In that passage he says that he has found very little "goodness" in people, that for the most part they're pretty much scum. But what I've found is the opposite. I've found naked goodness, devoid of self-interest, in the heart of many practitioners and especially in children. Why have we let ourselves unlearn this innocence?

It's true that the spectacle of everyday life and the most rudimentary self-observation reveal a thousand faults, such as jealousy, bad-mouthing, mockery. These are defects that are hard to root out. But all of that isn't enough to make me lose my belief in the grandeur of being human. That just means that we must double our efforts to reunite with the fundamental ground of all grounds, the profound nature of our being that is beyond these emotional mechanisms.

As I went along my way, one encounter, one lucky bump in the road, gave me a decisive shock and made me leave the beaten path. One day I asked the priest at the institute, "Why are there disabled people? Why, if God exists, does he abandon us here, far from our parents?" Father Morand had the decency not to try to placate me with some pat explanation where there really wasn't any. The goodness of this man, who had devoted his life to others, blew my mind and won me over. I remember his words to me: "You are a philosopher; you are like Socrates." That started me off. Even though nobody at the school took much interest in the nature of the mind, I ran out and bought books on Plato and Socrates. I found in them an endless supply of healing content and, more than anything, an invitation to live better rather than to live perfectly. The adventure could begin. A defenseless teenager started out on the road to improvement and dared to explore the depths of the inner dimension. Before that, I sought happiness only on the outside. I took refuge in the hope of a better life but without changing the way I looked at the world. The barefoot philosopher of Athens brought me a cure, spurred me on, gave me a therapy for the soul. From then on I had the desire to enter into philosophy the way one enters priestly orders. That was the only step I could take.

Along with being disabled, it was the lack of affection that had the heaviest lasting effects. Too many teachers have seen as their duty to preserve a supposedly therapeutic distance that seems to preclude all human warmth. I found myself surrounded by nuns who were rather on the cold side. They smelled idolatry everywhere, and when I said that I adored cake, they dryly replied, "One adores only God." Fortunately Father Morand made up for that. His extreme goodness and his great erudition gave me a taste for the spiritual life. His good sense, his unreserved generosity, and his wisdom touched me deeply.

He preached by example, and thus he converted me to the way of philosophy. During the war, he had provided shelter to a Jewish family. One day he told me this story. In the distance he saw coming a car belonging to the gestapo. Without hesitating, he turned his house upside down. He broke the plates, tore the clothes out of the wardrobes, and more. When the SS people arrived, he simply told them, "Your colleagues have just been here. They ransacked everything. Just look at the mess they made."

In short, this was a man of God, and it is to him that I owe my passion for philosophy. It took me quite a while to realize that wisdom is rooted in an art of living, in spiritual exercises that are practiced in the midst of daily life. Very soon I experienced the rather bitter fact that philosophy doesn't heal everything, at least not in my case. No matter how much I read and reread Aristotle, Leibniz, Spinoza, Nietzsche, and the rest, my negative emotions still gave me no peace. Along the way, I met the Zen master Jacques Castermane. Thanks to him, I experienced the peace that was already there in the fundamental ground of all grounds, and I learned that the body, far from being an obstacle to it, could lead you there.

At that point it became absolutely necessary for me to have a spiritual father who was both a Zen master and a Catholic priest—to explore further the faith in God that had always been with me as well as meditation. Thus my wife and I, and our three children, moved to Seoul to be initiated into the school of detachment and liberation. The diagnosis had become clear: I had lost the joy of my childhood, that simplicity, the spontaneity I had had then. My apprenticeship in South Korea pretty well stripped me to the bone. Far from the protective super-papa that my psyche was craving, what I found was an authentic spiritual master who showed me day after day that unconditional love was beyond anything I could imagine. He taught me to love more freely—basically, to leave my prison. Since then, I have been committed to meditating an hour a day. Devoting body and soul to practice is what really saves us. We are masters of very little in our lives, and that is why it is necessary to give ourselves over without reservation to the spiritual life that sets us free, one step at a time.

> Wisdom is rooted in an art of living, in spiritual exercises that are practiced in the midst of daily life.

Every day I rediscover with joy what really liberates us: contact with others and devotion to spiritual practice. Thanks to my master and my family, along with Bernard Campan, Joachim, Romina, Christophe, Matthieu, and so many others, I can give myself over to my vocations and make progress in the job of being human. Oh yes, a thousand helping hands reaching out to me every day enable me to live with my wounds. In the end, I am the opposite of the so-called self-made man. Without my companions in the good, I wouldn't be able to get around in Seoul. From moment to moment, I have to die and be reborn, and unlearn a great deal.

When I come to the point of cursing my disability, I remember the infinitely compassionate words of my master, which wake me

> From moment to moment, I have to die and be reborn, and unlearn a great deal.

up on the spot: "Bless obstacles; without this disability and these repeated tortures, you would probably be the king of imbeciles." Such electric shocks teach me to stop demonizing that which at first glance seems to hinder me.

CHRISTOPHE   I very much like the three vocations you talked about—father, disabled person, and author. For me too, being a father has been a revelation and a motivation for further development. I wanted to provide the best possible example for my daughters, and I saw right away that that was going to take a lot of work! My disability is simply being structurally and psychologically an anxious person, very much inclined toward unhappiness. My efforts not to slide down that slippery slope are a constant factor in my everyday life. As for the vocation of author, basically it is an extension of my vocation as caregiver. I very much like to help, to comfort, and to heal. When I read other people's books—yours, Alexandre, Matthieu's, Christian Bobin's, and those of many other authors—I find that I am very sensitive to whether or not they have a therapeutic or enlightening aspect. I assess in my head the amount of good this is going to do the reader. As I see it, there are two kinds of books: those that provide help and those that are only there to entertain.

My path? I was not born completely equipped to be a caregiver or to talk about suffering. I encountered all kinds of obstacles—infinitely smaller ones than yours, Alex. For a whole slew of reasons, I am a person who is profoundly ill at ease, pessimistic, and introverted as well. I really only feel capable of thinking when I am by myself. At the same time, I need other people. I often say that I am a gregarious loner. Whenever I have been able to talk about this dimension of fragility in my books and make clear how important it is for me to work on it, I think it has brought some comfort to my readers, because it has made them see that having to work on this dimension is the lot of every human being. My big fear is to be idealized by my readers. Although the people I'm close to might like me, occasionally admire some of the ways I do things, they are also aware of my limitations. That is why I often talk about myself in my books. It's not narcissism; it's something I do to expose the efforts I have to make in life.

It was a matter of good luck that I ended up studying medicine and not becoming an engineer. When I was little, since I was a good student, I was directed toward scientific studies. And like all my friends from that time, I dreamed of building rockets or big buildings. At the last minute, I read Freud, who was part of the philosophy program. His writings completely carried me away, and I decided to become a psychiatrist. Not a psychologist, but a psychiatrist—which resulted in my studying medicine and coming to the realization that I really enjoyed being a caregiver. Being able to help and comfort people brought me great happiness. This was all the more a revelation for me because in my student days, I had without doubt reached the height of egotism. I had never been taught to be altruistic, and all I wanted to do was chase girls and party. Studying medicine little by little brought me in contact with real suffering, awful things. It taught me the importance of being there for people who are suffering. I realized that I had chosen the right profession because, along with the sadness I felt at the woes of my patients, being able to give them some relief made me happy and gave a meaning to my life that my other activities failed to bring. Giving care and comfort made me feel really good. Were my altruistic motivations ultimately selfish because they made me feel good? I thought so for a long time, and I was ashamed of this cloaked selfishness. Much later, Matthieu came along and opened my eyes. He showed me that the sense of well-being that comes from caring for others was one of the benefits of altruism, one that comes as a bonus. It is a fringe benefit of altruism that isn't necessarily the primary motivation for it.

After studying medicine, I continued on to psychiatry. I saw right away that psychoanalysis, which at that time was the dominant force in our discipline, was not for me. It required assuming a posture of detachment with which I was unhappy and uncomfortable. It made me feel limited in my spontaneity, constrained to assuming a distance that seemed to me inadequate in the face of people's suffering. As with the caregivers in your institute, Alexandre, who took it to be their duty to refrain from having an emotional relationship with the children under their supervision, it was then thought that psychiatric treatment was more effective if it was contained, marked by a sense of therapeutic distance. We were denied the immense power of emotion, compassion, empathy. We ignored emotion or tamped it down. I was tremendously uneasy with this approach of being distant with patients, not holding their hands, not giving them advice. I said to myself, "You're not meant to be a psychiatrist." I turned instead to surgery, emergency medicine, and obstetrics. I liked those disciplines too, but psychiatry continued to attract me. I came back to it by another route. I left the academic scene. I gave up any ambition to land a career position in the hospital hierarchy, and I began to explore my interests. I trained in hypnosis and in family therapy. I met my master in psychiatry, Lucien Millet, who was what was known as a humanist psychiatrist. With him and with an alternative approach to the discipline, I felt like a fish in water. He was kind to his patients; he called them by their first names, took an interest in their lives, and tried to involve patients' families rather than keep them at a distance. He practiced psychiatry the way I felt it should be practiced—with compassion and care for others. I began to feel at home. I acquired training in the behavioral approach to psychiatry that was the countercurrent to Lacanian psychoanalysis. In the behavioral approach, we teach and offer friendship. We explain to our patients how their problems are produced and what they have to do to counter them. We are warm toward them and we take an interest. We also ask difficult things of them. We ask them to confront their fears and anxieties. Everything I did with my patients I drew from myself—my own problems, anxieties, timidity.

When I discovered positive psychology, again I took full advantage of it to counter my tendencies toward negativity, pessimism, and unhappiness. Then I encountered meditation, and this was a whole new thing for me once again.

In working with my patients, I was rowing along with them in the same boat. They never knew this, but often I felt tremendous gratitude after these sessions. Bringing them to an understanding about something in themselves made it possible for me to understand something in myself. The patients were my teachers. I remember roughly ten of them who transformed my life without their knowing it.

When you and I met, Alexandre, you shared with me the idea of *progredientes*, a Latin word referring to people who are working on themselves. You even had a group at one time with that name, "The Progredientes." This is the process I am engaged in with my whole life—to improve, develop, and progress—and part of my work is to explain this approach to my patients and encourage them to adopt it.

It took me a long time to understand what Matthieu has been talking about all along: the supreme importance of altruistic motivation as opposed to self-centered motivation. I was so shaky that if it hadn't been for my medical career, my life probably would have taken a bad turn. I might have become a good engineer but a bad human being. And I think I could never have taken in this altruistic message in any kind of deep and meaningful way unless I had become a father and a doctor and been tenderized by my children and my patients. Since that took a fair amount of time for me, I am always careful to feel where my patients are with regard to this possibility and to show them this direction as something in the distance they can aspire to, without pressuring them to do anything they are not yet fully capable of. I encourage them to see, for example, that small acts of altruism can allow them to think less about their own suffering. But I never present this to them as a saving grace. I always forgive my patients for being too attached to their battered egos, and I push them to forgive themselves for their mistakes and their slowness. That is the path I have traveled myself.

MATTHIEU   What can I say after all those beautiful words?

As a boy and as a teenager, I was neither better nor worse than the others. I had the reputation of being a little cold—as Alexandre also said of me at the beginning of our relationship. I was not very outgoing. Starting in my adolescence, I became involved in writings on spirituality under the influence of my mother Yahne Le Toumelin, and her brother Jacques-Yves Le Toumelin, a solo sailor who during his sea voyages read a lot about Sufism, Vedanta, and the other spiritual paths, especially through the books of René Guénon. We had a circle of friends who talked a lot about those things. I also read a number of books on spirituality—nothing very practical. I was raised in a secular environment. I wanted to be a doctor, even a surgeon. But I listened to the advice of my dear father, who said, "The world is full of doctors. Research is the future." I was rather good in physics, so I chose to study physics. I wasn't a very good student. Then my father told me, "Biology is the future." So I studied biology. Through a fortunate turn of circumstances, I got into the Pasteur Institute, in François Jacob's lab, and I wrote a thesis on cell division.

It so happened that just before I started at the Pasteur Institute, I saw some documentary films, while they were still in the process of being made, by Arnaud Desjardins about great Tibetan masters who had fled from the Chinese invasion. I was twenty years old, and suddenly everything changed. I realized that this was something more than the mere writings of Meister Eckhart, Ibn Arabi, Ramana Maharshi, the Desert Fathers, or other people who were long gone. These people were still alive. Over there, there were still living beings like Socrates or Francis of Assisi, and there seemed to be something exceptional about them compared to the people I had met up to that point. Arnaud Desjardins and another friend, Dr. Frédéric Leboyer, who had just seen them in person, showed me photos. They told me, "The one who made the biggest impression on us is that one—Kangyur Rinpoche, who lives in Darjeeling." I decided to go meet him.

My father had had the excellent idea of having me taught classical Greek, Latin, and German. He said I would end up learning English anyway. So I set out for Darjeeling armed with a pocket English dictionary. When I got there, I was immediately able to see Kangyur Rinpoche. He became my teacher, not just because he was the first one I met, but because he was the one who touched me most deeply. During the same trip, I met other teachers, but I spent most of my time with Kangyur Rinpoche. I spent three weeks sitting at his feet without saying much. I couldn't speak English and still less Tibetan. But I had before me the exemplar, not of a particular kind of knowledge nor of an exceptional skill—for example, that of a piano virtuoso—but simply of the best thing that could happen to a human being. He was nothing like people I'd known before. It was his way of being, his presence, his kindness, his wisdom, that inspired me the most deeply.

I returned to France, where I continued with my thesis. But every year between 1967 and 1972 I went back to Darjeeling—seven times altogether. At some point I said to myself, "When I'm at the Pasteur Institute, I mainly think about being in the Himalayas; and when I'm in the Himalayas, I don't think about the Pasteur Institute at all. I have to make up my mind!" So instead of going to the United States to do postdoctoral work as François Jacob wanted me to, I studied Buddhism in the Himalayas! I stayed there pretty much without a break from 1972 to 1997. I had almost no contact with the West. I didn't read a single book in French during this whole period. No newspapers and no radio either. Moreover, there is still a gap in my knowledge regarding the international events that took place during that time. And because I neglected the French language a bit too much, I was hindered when it came to writing books. For twenty-five years I worked on my Tibetan and practiced the Buddhist path.

Regarding the three situations you mentioned—being a father, a disabled person, and an author—a father I have never been. Nevertheless, I have taken an interest in children through Karuna-Shechen, a humanitarian organization I founded with a group of friends. At present, it is responsible for educating more than 25,000 children in schools; and every year it cares for 140,000 patients in the health centers it has had built.

As for being disabled, without wishing to stretch the meaning inappropriately, it is clear to me that any person who is not completely enlightened is disabled. As long as one still has a trace of malice, greed, or jealousy, and one does not feel boundless compassion toward others, one is disabled. Whether the goal is the happiness you talked about or the altruism to which I aspire, I am perfectly aware of the mixture of shadow and light that still exists in me and of the immense progress I still have to make. I know that sometimes I am far from being perfectly compassionate. I have thoughts and I say things that I can only regard reproachfully when I measure them against the yardstick of altruism. But I keep with me the profound wish to remedy this and to transform myself a lot further still. That's what counts, and that's the direction I want to go in.

My return to the West was triggered by the dialogue I had with my father, which we turned into a book, *The Monk and the Philosopher*. I have no vocation to be an author. I have translated Tibetan texts, but I am not particularly talented as a writer. When that dialogue was proposed, I went to see the abbot of the monastery I live in, Rabjam Rinpoche (the grandson of Dilgo Khyentse Rinpoche, my second master, who died in 1991). I said to him, "Here's what I'm being asked to do. Frankly I can't see what benefit there could be in spending ten days in idle talk." To my surprise, he replied, "Oh yes, yes, you should do it." So it was partly because of his advice that I accepted. Without that, I would have continued on the same track. I would have stayed in the Himalayas practicing and translating texts. Obviously this brought about a big change. One day I was a total unknown, the next, having appeared over and again on television, people were coming up to me in the street wanting to offer me a lift or chat for a few minutes. On top of that, dressed as I am in a monk's habit, I can be spotted very easily. That outfit is like a walking flag.

> Without wishing to stretch the meaning inappropriately, it is clear to me that any person who is not completely enlightened is disabled.

So why should I have gone on like that? Wouldn't it have been better to stay in my retreat and try to become a better human being so that later on I could put myself at the service of others once and for all? That being the ideal, it shouldn't have seemed like a good idea to fiddle around and harvest the wheat while it was still just grass. However, circumstances led to my getting involved in all kinds of activities, notably with the Karuna-Shechen Association, which up to the present day has completed over two hundred humanitarian projects. I think the book we are working on here will be helpful. People tell us that our books help them in life. That's always somewhat surprising, but at the same time it's comforting.

I travel back and forth between the East and the West, between a purely traditional contemplative life and a life of interaction with the modern world with all the challenges that that involves. I try to find friends who want to do good, the people who are most likely to advance the cause of altruism that is dear to me. As for science, I have returned to that through my collaboration with neuroscientists. I never could have imagined that I would find myself in a laboratory again thirty-five years after having left the Pasteur Institute. There are numerous other areas—politics, economics, the environment—where we can attempt to find common ground, with the idea that a hundred blades of grass, each by itself, cannot accomplish much, but if you put them together to make a broom, you can do some housekeeping. By housekeeping, I mean trying to remove the obstacles to a better world, to a more just humanity, doing away with inequalities, progressing toward a more altruistic view of the world, helping people find meaning in their lives, contributing to the welfare of society. When you meet people with whom you feel you share a common outlook and with whom you can knit the bonds of friendship, as has happened with you two, you cannot help but think that together we can do more than we each could alone. We can learn from each other, enrich our thought, and find better ways to help others.

Now as to being a writer, I really am not one. Mainly what inspires me is ideas. I am sometimes asked if I have a mission in the West. None whatsoever. No particular agenda. When I'm asked on television, "So, in the end, what are you doing here?" My answer is, "You asked me to come, so I came. But if you don't invite me, I won't have lost or gained a thing." If I can share some ideas, I am happy to do so. If not, there's nothing I would like better than to stay in retreat. I'm not going to keep saying to myself, "So what is your next book going to be?" Time is precious, and I have explored the subjects that interest me the most. After altruism, there is no other big subject matter that has to be dealt with. However, if together we can produce something that brings a further dimension, something beyond what each of us could do on his own, I will be very happy about it.

What Are Our
Deepest Aspirations?

MATTHIEU What really counts in life? What can we identify in our deepest selves that is essential? There must be something within us, something that motivates us, a direction that manifests and gives meaning to each step we take. Living is not being content with roaming around aimlessly at the whim of chance encounters and circumstances, just getting through each day as best we can. I don't mean that we have to decide when we get up in the morning that we are going to change the world, but it seems we need to see a certain continuity, a line of progress toward what we want to accomplish in our lives. Some people don't like the idea of perpetual self-development. Nonetheless, it is possible to work on ourselves month after month, year after year, not to satisfy our ego but to become a better person, a more altruistic and wiser person. You can't make a decision all at once to become 100 percent devoted to the service of others. You have to take the time that is needed to acquire the capacity to achieve this ideal.

What Motivates Us

ALEXANDRE Along with the wholesome aspirations that invite us to go forward and constantly improve, we have a whole host of egotistical ambitions that alienate us from ourselves and make us suffer. In his *Ethics*, Spinoza speaks of suitable desires (those which arise from the fundamental ground of things, that flow from our basic nature) and unsuitable desires, which we import from *outside* of us. Advertising, which arouses a thousand cravings, provides the perfect example. Distinguishing within oneself what is connected with suitable desire from what is not is a very liberating exercise. If I look at the expectations that shape our lives, I immediately flush out of its hiding place a fierce need to fit into the mold, to do everything possible, to the point of exhaustion, to imitate others. Thanks to a certain

> Every moment of life can become the occasion for liberation—because we are not born free, we become free.

ascesis, to spiritual exercises, I am beginning to glimpse the influences, the mechanisms, that weigh on me. It's more or less a game of considering every desire that goes through one's mind and seeing what its origin is. Freedom can be found in this exercise, and every moment of life can become the occasion for liberation—because we are not born free, we become free.

CHRISTOPHE At the moment, the question of my deepest aspiration makes me feel a bit ill at ease. For a long time it seemed to me that I was more or less on a path aimed at survival, trying to go in the direction that meant the least suffering for me, while at the same time trying hard not to make others suffer either. It was more an intuitive principle that guided my way of being than an aspiration or a conscious ideal. That being the case, it is rather logical that I became a doctor, since, fundamentally, this business of lessening the suffering of others put me in a kind of social position that corresponded with what I unconsciously was after. With time, I am becoming capable of more discernment. For a long time my life was a quest for security. I wanted my family not to be in material need, a fear I probably inherited from my parents, who came from poor circumstances. I wanted to protect those close to me and probably to protect myself. But these were not very noble aspirations, and doubtless the profession of doctor helped me go beyond this sole motivation. Today it is very difficult for me to say that my profound aspiration is really and only to help others suffer less. I don't have the ability to see whether this motivation comes from myself or from the outside, but it's important to me that I don't pass myself off as some kind of a pseudosaint.

ALEXANDRE Humans have a mysterious ability to deceive themselves and supply the necessary delusions. It is super-honest to recognize that our desires are not always very clear-cut, and sometimes, with the pretext of saving others, we are mainly seeking recognition and gratitude, something to bind our wounds with. A whole host of influences shape our actions and our behavior, and even the way we view the world. If I look back over the path I've traveled, I see many moments in which, while thinking myself completely free, I was only deluding myself. Looking more closely at my interest in the spiritual life, the main thing I discover is an immense fear of suffering. In the beginning I was a bit like a shipwreck survivor trying to get hold of a life preserver. Over the course of time, this mainly self-centered motivation has become more diffuse, and I am beginning to open myself toward others.

MATTHIEU When I was at the Pasteur Institute, I had a classmate, Ben Shapiro, with whom I shared a desk, and from time to time we'd talk about life. We didn't know what we really wanted to do in life, but we knew what we didn't want: a lukewarm existence that was without meaning or use.

It goes without saying that the primary goal of every person is to stay alive. There are moments or particular places in the world where this is even the absolute priority, because people have to face war, famine, epidemics, and natural catastrophes. But when we don't feel immediately threatened, even though the fact of impermanence is always there and we never know what is going to happen tomorrow, we have to make up our minds to not just kill time and waste our lives. We must have some growth, some form of accomplishment in our sights. Personally, my own thoughts were something like,

"Being happy, what's that? Having pleasurable experiences? Finding more profound satisfaction? Understanding how my mind works? Learning how to relate with other people better?" For me it comes down to asking myself, "What matters the most in my life?" Also, like Alexandre, I believe in asking which desires come from the deepest part of me and which come to me from the outside, which are imposed on me or insidiously suggested, as is the case with the glittering come-ons of consumer society. I remember one of my Tibetan teachers saying to me one day in Times Square in New York, in the midst of the neon signs constantly demanding to be looked at, "They're trying to steal my mind!"

At any given moment, independent of any external influence, we have to be able to ask ourselves, "What is really worthwhile? What will make it possible for me to think at the end of the year that I didn't waste my time?" We can ask ourselves this question regularly. And when twenty years later we look back, we should have the same feeling as a farmer who has done his best to cultivate his fields. Even if things don't always happen as we hope they will, we should still be able to say, "I have no regrets, because I did my best within the limits of my ability."

CHRISTOPHE When Patrick Modiano received the Nobel Prize in Literature, in his acceptance speech, he said in effect, "I was quite surprised, in reading the articles about me, that people outside me saw some coherence in my work; whereas as the author, I was like someone driving his car at night who doesn't see beyond the beams of his headlights. His goal is just to stay on the road, not to go over the speed limit, and not to run over any deer that might cross the road." That's pretty much the way I see the way I function myself—do the best you can for others and do them and yourself the least possible harm. Beyond that, it seems to me that at certain crossroads I have made deliberate choices about which way to go: It was not just chance that made me turn left or right; for me it had nothing to do with some ancient vision or any worked-out and structured life plan.

The Path and the Goal

MATTHIEU   I remember meeting in Canada a group of young people who were just graduating from university. For six months they had been seeing professional counselors and filling out questionnaires. No stone had been left unturned to help them find their direction. But how can you find direction in your life by filling out questionnaires and following the advice of people you hardly know? My own advice to them was, "Why not go sit by some lakeside by yourself or with someone you really like? Stop filling out questionnaires, turn off your computer, and ask yourself what you really want to do in this life; let the answer come from deep inside you."

The length of the journey and its difficulties are not a problem. When you travel in the Himalayas, things are not always easy. Sometimes the weather is beautiful; sometimes it's horrid. The landscapes might be sublime, but you could also find your way blocked by a ravine, or you could find yourself wading through a marshy jungle at the bottom of a tropical valley. Nevertheless, every step brings us closer to the place we want to go, and that is an inspiration. By the way, the definition of perseverance, one of the six "perfections" of Buddhism, or *paramitas*, that you are studying in Korea, Alexandre, is "the joy of doing good." "Good" here is not simply a good action; it is something that inspires us deeply. It is joy in the form of effort. Even if the journey is sometimes hard, our enthusiasm lasts if we keep making progress toward the place where we really want to go. On the other hand, if we stray and lose our reference point, we lose courage. Disorientation and a feeling of helplessness are added to fatigue. We lose our will to keep walking and we just sit there, beaten and in despair. That is why the direction we choose in life plays such an important role.

Psychologists of happiness, such as Daniel Gilbert, say that effort itself is what brings satisfaction. Once we have attained the goal, we are a little bit disappointed. In a discussion I was having with him, I put it this way: "If, for example, I want a Maserati, I'm going to be very

25

excited about it and basically 'happy' while I make a thousand efforts to make the money I need for it. But once I have my car, I'll be afraid it's going to get scratched or stolen, and in the end it won't bring me the happiness I was counting on." As long as there is confusion about what ultimately brings happiness, it's a fact that you're going to be disappointed once you achieve your goal. But if the goal is a worthwhile one, such as, for example, if I want to cultivate wisdom or altruistic love, both the path *and* the goal will be satisfying. The trouble is that we often delude ourselves by pursuing illusory goals, such as wealth, fame, physical beauty, more possessions—all of which is just smoke and mirrors and does not truly contribute to our development.

ALEXANDRE   Progressing without being bound to a particular goal, that's the challenge. What helps me is to ask myself what life is calling me to, here and now. When I am passing through zones of turbulence, this question invites me to take action but without haste. It helps me focus, to find my way through confusion. In the Gospels, Jesus says, "The Son of Man has no place to rest his head." Similarly in Buddhist practice, the practitioner must dwell nowhere. As soon as there is fixation, suffering appears. In a sense, mockery and trials can be liberating for us when they have the effect of jarring us loose and preventing us from fixating ourselves on one emotion or one projection. In the subway, when people snigger as I go by, I take advantage of the occasion to remember that I am not reduced to appearances; my basic being lies beyond the sight of the people looking at me.

I am not reduced to appearances; my basic being lies beyond the sight of the people looking at me.

I prefer the idea of vocation to that of goal, which reminds me that it is not me who makes the ultimate decision. Call it the will of God or the call of life or any number of other things—let's simply note that my little ego is not the master of the ship. An infinitely deeper reality has control of the rudder. That doesn't mean, however, that one should not be engaged, that one should not take action. Let's always go forward, without either falling into fatalism or giving up on our goals. The teaching of Zen on this subject is clear: do everything impeccably and remain detached from the result.

MATTHIEU   The goal that I'm talking about is that which inspires me. I'm not talking about a goal that obsesses me and that I attach all my clingings to. The idea of a direction or an aspiration is more satisfying and is not something that is subject to limits. In Buddhism we mistrust all fixations, including fixation on a noble goal, because such fixations produce effects contrary to the ones we are seeking. We can certainly say that we aspire to liberate ourselves from the causes of suffering—from selfishness, ignorance, jealousy, pride, and such—but the idea is not to score points. The idea is to define what we want to strive for, and decide if that is worthwhile.

ALEXANDRE   I am fascinated by the distinction between the social ego—that is, the set of roles that we play every day—and the fundamental ground of all grounds, our most intimate nature, which unfolds beyond all labels and remains indefinable. All ascesis, spiritual practice, ultimately consists in descending into and dwelling in that, instead of stagnating in the superficial ego that is always changing and continually suffering. This distinction goes a long way toward satisfying me. It brings into view an extraordinary path that smashes all labels and can be invoked by very simple questions: What am I really? What are the basic choices in my life? What influences have shaped me up to the present time? I am struck by the extent to which we compensate for our weaknesses and imitate others to build ourselves up. Spinoza supports this view in his *Ethics*, where he urges us to identify all the causes that drive us to act, and often to react. Freedom is born moment by moment from this act of awareness.

MATTHIEU   The question of doubt is also important. A few years ago I translated from Tibetan the autobiography of Shabkar, a yogi who lived more than two centuries ago. It so happened that a biography of St. Thérèse of Lisieux appeared at the same time as my translation. *Le Monde* published an article on the two works. It basically said that the life of Shabkar was not very interesting because the path of this great Tibetan yogi seemed so clearly delineated in advance. He went from ignorance to enlightenment just like taking a walk through the woods. He did undergo certain physical trials, but no "dark nights of the soul," no agonizing doubts. In the life of St. Thérèse of Lisieux or that of St. John of the Cross, however, there were moments of total faith, and then the next day that was replaced by complete nothingness; God seemed to have disappeared.

Asking myself what the difference was between the two paths, I came to the conclusion that for the Christian mystics what matters most is one's relationship to God, since they have abandoned all worldly concerns. Thus everything depends on their intense communion with God, and therefore on the existence of this God. Now this existence is a mystery, forever inaccessible. The idea of this mystery is magnificent. It is as though there is a huge mountain that is perpetually hidden behind clouds but which is the inspiration for our whole lives. There are moments in which one is intimately convinced that it is there, that one is in communion with it, and other moments in which one is preyed upon by doubt. Hence these great mystic flights followed by nights of darkness.

In Buddhism, enlightenment is a clearly defined goal, which stands before me a little bit like Mount Everest for somebody who wants to climb it. I have no doubt concerning the existence of this mountain rising majestically before my eyes, but I am uncertain as to whether I will be able to make the immense efforts it will take to reach its summit, whether it's worth it, and if I might not be better off just sunning myself on the beach. But after I think it over properly, it becomes clear to me that I do aspire to scale this mountain because I know that it is really worthwhile to liberate oneself from ignorance, hate, jealousy, pride, greed, and such, and I hesitate no longer. One might go astray in one's meditation, falsely imagine that one has attained spiritually profound states of realization, succumb to despondency, or fall into the duality of hope and fear. But these obstacles are without a doubt less dramatic than the alternation between total faith and total doubt described, for example, by Mother Teresa in her memoirs.

ALEXANDRE   Another reason I went to South Korea was to get deeper into the dialogue between religions. This path of dialogue is not a totally smooth one, even if it does encourage nonfixation and not absolutizing anything. Sometimes Buddhists give me little moral lessons, saying very politely, "Why do you believe in a personal God? This concept of a Creator is total hogwash." And when I turn instead to certain Christians, what I run into is not any better. They reproach me for looking elsewhere: "How can you do Zen when Jesus says in the Gospels, 'I am the way, the truth, and the life'?" But fortunately there are thousands of examples of possible reconciliation. I recently went to a Mass with a Zen master in attendance. And I saw him listening to the words of the priest like a child with infinite openness. As he was reading the psalms I realized that it is in practice that we come together. The crazy thing is that a Buddhist master, by his simple presence, transmitted to me the burning desire to devote myself further to a life of prayer. He was very far from theories and speculation—he was living in the inner heart. I am not denying that there are significant differences between Buddhism and Christianity, but I am happy to note that there are also links between them and experiences we can share. There's nothing worse than church wars, the result of a kind of dogmatism that in the end has very little that's religious about it.

As this dialogue progresses, I see that the notion of grace—that is, of a gift, divine help that comes freely—is essential in the Christian faith. And that is what turned me away when I was going through some really hard times. Giving oneself over, trusting, at a time when your whole situation is shaky and precarious takes enormous boldness, of which I was then incapable. Talking with Matthieu, I have somewhat understood that Buddhism offers a path, a way to attain enlightenment, a way to scale the Mount Everest of happiness. And that a person who wants to follow in Buddha's footsteps is encouraged to take up his pilgrim's stick, to transform his mind and practice the Eightfold Path to get that climb started. Simply put, as Matthieu says, Mount Everest is there, and it's up to us to climb it, even though the way up is an extremely hard one.

Reading the Gospels, I find a luminous ascesis that leads to a letting go of the self, an inner stripping away and total surrender to divine providence. In brief, to attain the summit of Everest, one must surrender oneself to God, count more on him than on our own strength. By way of a joke, I often say to Matthieu that in Christianity the path consists in taking the spiritual elevator that takes you to union with God. But it takes a whale of a lot of courage to believe, to get on the elevator and leave all self-will behind.

The essential is to move forward on a path without absolutizing it or denigrating the other paths. Living in contact with other religions, it's tempting to tumble into comparisons. As for myself, I find strength in Buddhism, which I think encourages me to become ever more Christian, to enter into a deeper union with Christ and to live the Gospels in everyday life. The wisdom of the Buddha also strips away the mental representations that I project on God. Meister Eckhart takes part in this same ascesis when he addresses the following prayer to the Supreme Being: "God, liberate me from God." How many times have I tried to exploit religion in order to find some kind of consolation in it, a crutch, rather than a source or a motivation? Seeing Christ chase the money changers out of the temple, I understand that there is a tremendous danger of co-opting religion for one's own purposes, of turning it into a market where you can buy peace at the price of sacrifices.

If the Buddha pacifies me, then Christ consoles me by his humanity. For me, believing in God and following Christ above all require faith, an art of living, an inner discipline, an ascesis. We can't help but notice that Jesus is less popular today than Buddha. One day when I shared a quote from the Dalai Lama on Facebook, I got a huge number of likes, but when I posted a video of Pope Francis getting out of his car to hug a disabled person on the side of the road, my post went almost unnoticed. The only comments I got recalled the painful history of the church: the Crusades, the Inquisition, the numerous cases of pedophilia, and so on. I think there ought to be prerequisites for interreligious dialogue: say goodbye to all apologetic partisanship, develop a real interest in the other, and drop the logic of "I'm right, therefore you're wrong."

The Buddha gives me strength every day, as Christ does. So why do I have to choose between them? It's as though I had two children, two friends, or two papas, and I was asked to renounce one or the other. No doubt we have to keep away from the relativism of people who practice spiritual tourism and make a big soup out of all the religions. I'm delighted that the Buddhists bring me closer to Christ. This is a magnificent ray of hope—as opposed to the usual thing of getting hung up on labels.

> The Buddha gives me strength every day, as Christ does. So why do I have to choose between them? It's as though I had two children, two friends, or two papas, and I was asked to renounce one or the other.

MATTHIEU We have talked about vocation, desire, direction, suitability, what is appropriate and what is not. The point is to find out what has meaning for a given individual. If, for example, I'm offered a job that doesn't interest me at all, it can have a meaning for me anyway if I need the money to feed my children. Wealth, power, and fame inspire some people and others not at all. Diogenes supposedly said to Alexander the Great, "I'm greater than you, Lord, for I have spurned more than you have conquered." In connection with finding an appropriate direction, the question is what helps us find meaning in every passing moment, in each effort that we make. Without meaning, life can roll by like an irritating film. As Pierre Rabhi has said, we go from one box to another: first the school box, then the entertainment boxes, then the business boxes, and finally the box we get buried in.

For the contemplatives, what has meaning is not building up a bank account but rather at the end of years of determined effort, liberating themselves from negative emotions such as anger, greed, or arrogance; and from confusion, inner conflicts, and distraction.

ALEXANDRE In your view, what is a contemplative?

MATTHIEU Contemplatives, at least in the Buddhist sense, are those who understand that their mind can be their friend but also their worst enemy, and therefore they have to transform it by meditation. They contemplate the fundamental nature of mind, and this practice has the effect of changing their perception of others, of themselves, and of the world. And when you change your perception of the world, in a certain way, you change the world.

Often we are content with finding little solutions to our daily problems, whereas the contemplatives I'm talking about try to radically change the way they experience the world and the way they translate their life circumstances either into well-being or suffering. They learn not to be trapped anymore by what torments and enslaves them but to free themselves from it. They become less vulnerable and thus more available to others.

They also familiarize themselves with the fundamental constituent of the mind, the primary awareness always present behind the movement of thoughts, and present even in the absence of thoughts, the pure luminous awareness that is never altered by mental constructs.

What Inspires Us

MATTHIEU   Whatever we do in life, we always need guides to learn from in order to further our development. When it comes to spirituality, the guide we choose must possess the necessary qualities. The danger is that when we are in a state of confusion or weakness, we might put our trust in a charlatan. A real spiritual master has nothing to gain or to lose. He has everything to give and to share. He couldn't care less about having a few more disciples. He's not looking for glory, power, or wealth. His only desire is to help others attain liberation. He himself must be the living example of this liberation. In my personal case, after meeting my first teacher, Kangyur Rinpoche, I went from confusion and aimlessness to a clear and inspiring vision of what I could accomplish in life.

ALEXANDRE   In trying to move in the direction of freedom, it's worthwhile to ask ourselves who our models, our exemplars are. Is it the victorious sports figure who keeps achieving new feats, the greedy CEO, the star actor? Or is it the neigh-bor from next door who modestly attempts to help others? Who is my reference point for learning how to live? What are the virtues, the quali-ties that I would like to have inspire me as I make my way through life?

> There is a discreet heroism of everyday life: getting up in the morning, being generous, facing difficulties without losing one's joy.

As for me, the people who touch me and help me grow are those who, day by day, radiate kindness and never let suffering make them bitter. There is a discreet heroism of everyday life: getting up in the morning, being generous, facing difficulties without losing one's joy.

MATTHIEU I recall a study done in the United States in which people were asked, "Between the Dalai Lama and Tom Cruise, who is the one you admire the most?" Eighty percent replied the Dalai Lama. The follow-up question was, "Which one of them would you rather be if you had the choice?" This time the majority answered Tom Cruise. I wondered what the reason was. They probably thought that if they already had the physical qualities, the fame, and the wealth of Tom Cruise, they would then be able to acquire the qualities of the Dalai Lama on their own, because that seemed easier to them than the other way around. In truth, it's not easier that way. Inner transformation is a labor that takes one's whole life to achieve. One day a Chilean journal-ist asked the Dalai Lama, "Thirty thousand people have come to this stadium to hear you—why so many?" He answered, "I don't know. Ask them." Then after thinking for a moment, he added, "Maybe it's because for sixty years I have been meditating on compassion every morning for four hours."

CHRISTOPHE I have had a problem with models for a long time. I grew up with a certain distrust toward adults. I saw their fragility so clearly that it probably made me develop a kind of caution or even revul-sion toward the idea that other human beings could be our masters. I was much more comfortable with taking all human beings for models, but in a passing way. The fact is that I am strongly affected by the lessons

I receive from my patients, from my children, and from people I don't know. I have never sought out a master; this kind of dependent relationship always frightened me. A master in passing could be a close friend who tells me a story that makes a strong impression on me because of the intelligence or strength that it portrays. Recently a friend told me about how he provided support for his dying wife. She had cancer, and little by little her physical condition deteriorated. He told me how he washed her, massaged her feet; how he managed to maintain and even enrich their love life. Listening to him, I felt I was dealing with something completely admirable, a model of dignity, of devotion, of altruism. Experiences like that make me think a lot, and when I run into somebody whose conduct is exemplary, I always ask myself, "Would I be able to do that?" and "What could I do right now to get closer to that?"

My daughters are also my masters from time to time. The second, for example, is an enthusiastic, joyous person, whereas I—if I don't make an effort—am a depressive type who can drag his feet and reason in a twisted way in order to justify his way of seeing the world. Before, I use to think that enthusiastic people were endangering themselves by exposing themselves to disappointment. Either they irritated me (I thought they hadn't understood the true nature of life) or they made me feel uneasy (I was afraid for them). I was afraid for my daughter for a long time, afraid of her enthusiasm, of her tendency to be joyful no matter what happened, afraid that she would be hurt or disappointed and that she wouldn't recover from it. And then a few years ago, in a period of renewed self-questioning, I realized that she was the one who was right! For two years she had been in intensive classes preparing for university entrance exams, and she was leading a hard life. She was getting up every morning at six thirty and her morning and evening trips on the subway each took an hour. And every morning I got up with her, made her orange juice, her coffee, her sandwich, thinking it was important for me to be there. She was practically always joyous and had a smile on her face, even in the cold and dark winter, even at exam time. Some mornings she would ask me how I was feeling, and sometimes I wasn't feeling that well but I didn't want her to see it, so I'd say, "Oh, I'm okay, doing okay." And she would scold me, saying, "Okay? Your 'okay' doesn't sound very convincing." Little by little I got the point. And one day it became clear enough for me to articulate: No matter what happens, you find every reason to be happy in the morning. The way you look at it, you wake up and you live in a democracy, you're going to live another day on this earth, you have people who love you, and even if you have problems, you're alive! So every morning I got a masterful but lighthearted lesson. I was face-to-face with a master of joy, enthusiasm, and confidence toward life, and I was extremely grateful.

ALEXANDRE   Following the teaching of a master is very far from meaning that you shouldn't distrust like the plague those gurus whom I consider the very height of insanity if they don't liberate us from our conceptual mind, and if they themselves don't live in a state of profound detachment. Handing over the keys to one's destiny to someone who has not been liberated through ascesis is abdicating one's own freedom, and we know what disastrous results that can bring. How can we avoid falling into idolatry and give up trying to find a super-papa who will pamper us? The vocation of spiritual father or master is precisely to awaken us to our freedom, to relentlessly expose all the tricks of ego, and at the same time to show us unconditional love. You won't find that on every street corner.

I had the good fortune to meet a Catholic priest who was also a Zen master. The instant our eyes met, I realized he was going to be my master. What touches me is that at no time does he lay claim to the title of master—just the opposite. He constantly throws me back on my own freedom. To this day I have never encountered anywhere along the way such kindness, such wisdom, and such faith in God.

A true master is free from ego. He has no desire to please, no need to manipulate others. He lives with flawless consistency. What I have uncovered in myself, thanks to my spiritual father, is my incredible ability always to delude myself. Only an enlightened and infinitely compassionate guide can bring us out of our illusions, which take us further away from what is really good for us. How difficult it is to keep a bit of detachment when from morning till night we are struggling through a jumble of emotions!

CHRISTOPHE   I have a nagging fear of adding to somebody's suffering. Nine times out of ten, this restraint is the right thing and it saves me from causing too much suffering. But every now and then, this fear of giving my candid advice is a fetter. I don't have the brass to look the person in the eyes and tell him, in so many words, "Enough! You have to stop making these mistakes!" And like you, I very much admire people who are capable of reminding us of the realities, that everything is not possible, all is not forgiven, you can't go on giving in to yourself indefinitely.

MATTHIEU   I'm reminded of when I was living with Dilgo Khyentse Rinpoche, my second spiritual master. While I could hardly imagine a more compassionate person, he was sometimes very severe with me. But after all, what would be the use of his indulging my faults and my ego?

ALEXANDRE   We have to make a distinction between two things. The vocation of the spiritual master is to pull us out of the prison of ego by bringing us closer to enlightenment or to union with God. The vocation of the therapist is to help us get through hard times, help us find the tools to accept and deal with great sufferings. If a psychiatrist tries to play spiritual master and make use of the electric shocks that are used in Zen, he might send his patient right to the graveyard.

MATTHIEU   This approach of Dilgo Khyentse Rinpoche's was not systematic. In fact, most people who met him would say that they had never seen anyone who was so kind, that he never said one word louder than another. But that did not keep him from being merciless with our faults when he saw that the moment was ripe. And when he also knew that the person he was dealing with had been around him long enough to know that he only wanted what was best for him.

ALEXANDRE   What touched you the most in your thirteen years with this master?

MATTHIEU First, at no time during these years was I witness to a single action that could harm others. I reached the point of total certainty that he never had even the shadow of a malicious thought, word, or action; that his sole desire was to guide other beings to inner freedom. I was also never witness to any ups and downs of mood on his part in the course of our everyday life. His way of acting and treating other people was always balanced and suited to the situation. He manifested perfect consistency between inner and outer. Sometimes he was extremely severe, but that had nothing to do with bad temper. I saw again and again that this severity was only there to help others attain liberation from their ignorance. Over time, that aroused total confidence in me.

ALEXANDRE Why total confidence?

MATTHIEU In the course of ordinary human relations, I am obliged to adjust to the dark side and the light side of each person. I know I can have confidence in some people and less in others. A skillful craftsman, an excellent chess player, or a great pianist can give me good advice on their specialty, but I don't expect them to be able to show me how to be a better human being. I am aware that, apart from the qualities that I look to them for, they might have all kinds of faults.

In the case of this master, experience showed me that I could trust him in everything. The thirteen years I spent continually in his presence only confirmed this. At no time did I see any chinks in his armor. And this confidence was of the essence for me. If I was going to ask him to liberate me from the causes of my suffering, I needed to trust him completely. At no point could I allow myself to doubt his advice.

The Ego, Friend or Impostor?

ALEXANDRE   Let's get into the major topic of ego without further delay. The story of Genesis provides us with a luminous diagnosis. It says of Adam and Eve after they tasted the forbidden fruit: "Then the eyes of both of them were opened, and they realized they were naked; so they sewed fig leaves together and made coverings for themselves." Shame, guilt, egocentrism—how can we avoid this infernal spiral? Losing one's innocence maybe means contemplating one's navel, beginning to cherish an image of oneself, a bunch of labels, a heap of illusions. It maybe means cutting oneself off from reality and trying to become the center of the world by demanding absolute independence.

This almost congenital tendency toward narcissism is the source of a tremendous amount of painful conflict. If I exile myself from the fundamental ground of my being, if I close myself off in my mental representations, if I continually play a role, how can I experience real joy? In concrete terms, if I cling to an idea, from the moment I become attached to who I think I am, I can definitely expect to take a beating. To finish the job of ruining our lives, we can get involved in this formidable set of reactions: the more I suffer, the more likely I am to seize up and curl up into a ball. A hellish vicious cycle! Fortunately practice provides a way out for us.

How can we learn to drop this vicious tendency to cut ourselves off from the world, from God, and from other people? How do you cure egocentrism? To begin with, I can stop waking up in the morning as a greedy consumer and become a little more attentive to others.

Dropping this logic of "me, me, me first" is no small deal. Nonetheless, we have thousands of opportunities to stop feeding the voracity of ego. As I cut the steak on my plate, without falling into an unhealthy state of guilt, I can glimpse the principles that dictate the way I live: Why should I think that my pleasure is worth massacring an animal?

The exercise is simple: Detect and then uproot the habit of putting oneself in the center. Above all, never exploit another person but truly love him or her. One day a monk told me very straightforwardly: "Really being enlightened is putting others before oneself, no longer regarding oneself as privileged in relation to other sentient beings."

That's no small job!

The Diseases of Ego

CHRISTOPHE *Ego* is not part of the present-day vocabulary of psychology. We speak instead of self-esteem, which defines the entirety of the ways one looks at oneself, judges oneself, sees oneself, treats oneself. As for me, I would be comfortable describing the ego as the whole set of attachments one has to oneself, to one's own image, and I would like to talk about its pathologies and all their consequences. Numerous studies tell us that self-esteem is profoundly influenced by all our social relations. Many researchers basically consider that the value one ascribes to oneself is very strongly, if not almost exclusively, constituted by the feeling a person has of being esteemed by others. In other words, the way others see us conditions the quality of the way we think we see ourselves but which really reflects the way we see ourselves through the eyes of others.

There are two major pathologies related to self-esteem, both of which bring a great deal of suffering. First, there is the excessive attachment to self that we see in narcissistic people. This has an immediate and consubstantial consequence: the more one is attached to oneself, the more one wants to be admired and the more one thinks one is superior to others and is entitled to superior rights. This is where the characteristic behavior of narcissists comes from. They think they are entitled to drive faster than other people because they think they drive better, to get in front of everybody in a line because they think their time is more precious than that of others, to put their own interests before those of other people, and so forth.

But there is also a form of self-obsession, excessive attachment to the self, that is found in people who lack self-esteem. We're talking here about negative attachment. Fundamentally, these people have the same obsession concerning how they are seen and judged by other people as narcissists do. But instead of looking for admiration and submissive behavior from others, they are highly sensitive to judgment and criticism, because they are afraid of being rejected, afraid that people don't love them enough.

Work on self-esteem began in the 1960s. Fifty years later, we've made a lot of progress. We've understood that the objective, the ideal approach to working on self-esteem, is forgetting the self. When we look at people whose self-esteem seems to be functioning properly, we see that their egos are not all bloated. They don't demand any more than necessary that others think about them. They engage in activities and relationships without continuously questioning themselves about themselves. American psychologists speak about a "quiet ego," an ego that is free from the obsession of "What are people going to think of me? Am I measuring up?"

> The ideal approach to working on self-esteem is forgetting the self.

How does one attain this objective? If you tell a person with complexes, who imagines he is somehow deficient, to think about something besides himself, he is more or less incapable of doing it. However, once he is cured, he is capable of being aware of this. I remember a patient who said to me in this regard, "When I'm with people who I find impressive and I'm not in top form, I want to become like a little mouse and disappear so that nobody notices me." Then I thought of the work we had done together in therapy, and I said, "You don't have to make yourself small. You're not that big!" In other words, don't worry, people are not that focused on you;, it's not you they're concerned with or judging all the time. Unless you stand on the table and

41

start screaming, you have your place with others without becoming an object of obsession for them.

There's an enormous number of studies on this subject. One of them that had the biggest influence on me showed that, paradoxically, it is beneficial for an individual's self-esteem to cultivate a sense of belonging, of fraternity with others. Not only does that not lower one's self-esteem but it also reassures and calms it. Conversely, the study showed that the desire to dominate created insecurity; it was threatening and exhausting. This points to a mistake made by many patients who don't have good levels of self-esteem. They think that to be accepted by others they must be admired by them. If their complex relates to a lack of culture, for example, they try to appear erudite. In earlier generations of therapy for self-esteem, what used to be done was to pump up the patients, to encourage them to see themselves positively. And many timid patients with complexes got the impression that in order not to be dominated anymore they had to become dominant. Today we emphasize horizontal relationships and not vertical ones. We put aside these dominance issues because they're very costly emotionally. We know, for example, that narcissistic subjects who have obsessions concerned with dominance, recognition, and submission in relation to other people are extremely insecure people with very high levels of stress, anxiety, and tension. The same thing goes the other way around for people who have low self-esteem.

I'll conclude with two points. Ego is a necessary evil, like a rented car. We need it to get through life, just as we need a means of transport to get from one place to another—unless one is a hermit or a contemplative who never leaves his monastery and thus may find that dropping the ego altogether is simpler. On life's roads, some vehicles pollute more than others. There are big SUVs that use a lot of gas, cars that want to be looked at and be allowed to pass others by, and—on the other extreme—unobtrusive bikes that don't pollute at all or make any noise. It seems to me we can't get rid of the ego, just toss it out the window, but we can make sure for the sake of others that it doesn't produce too much pollution, and that it's not too costly for ourselves in terms of energy, care, and upkeep.

The second point: we can't hope to get rid of the ego by despising it. In the case of patients who suffer from low self-esteem, the solution is not to continue to look down on oneself. Often such people are obsessed with themselves and irritated by others at the same time. We come back to the crucial difference between detachment and nonattachment. The idea is not to try obsessively to detach oneself from ego. Rather, our efforts should lead us in the direction of nonattachment to the ego.

Genuine Self-Confidence

MATTHIEU   I have often had occasion to speak about the dismantling of ego in Buddhist practice. Very often people are uncomfortable with this process. They ask, "Isn't it necessary to have a strong ego in order to function well in life?" Or again, "Don't many people suffer from psychological problems because their egos are fragmented or weak?"

From the point of view of Buddhism, we prefer to talk about inner strength rather than a strong ego. This strength goes hand in hand with liberating oneself from the tight grip of ego, which is the primary source of everything that poisons the mind.

The studies you're talking about have shown that compassion, generosity, kindness, and indulgence toward ourselves permit us to have healthy self-esteem. On the other hand, all the methods employed, particularly in North America, to reinforce self-esteem in artificial manners lead to narcissism. According to psychologist Jean Twenge, this is true to such a degree that over the last twenty years in the United States there has been an epidemic of narcissism. When asked, 90 percent of students thought they were among the top 10 percent of most talented people. Ninety percent of drivers—including even some who had recently caused accidents—were sure that they were better drivers than others. You don't have to be a great mathematician to realize that everybody cannot be above average!

In the United States, parents and teachers tell children from morning till night, "You're special!" The children get sucked into this game. They wear T-shirts or put up stickers that say "I'm special!" One out of ten garments for girls have the word *princess* on them somewhere.

I received a musical birthday card from America that said, "We want to tell you you're really special." Summarizing a significant number of studies, psychologist Roy Baumeister concluded that all the effort and money that schools, parents, and therapists have put into promoting self-esteem have produced only minimal effects. "After all these years," he concluded, "I'm sorry to say that my recommendation is the following: forget self-esteem and concentrate on self-control and self-discipline."[1]

Obviously we don't want to fall into the opposite extreme, as you have clearly shown in your writings, Christophe. Wholesome and healthy self-esteem is essential to thrive in life, given that a neurotic level of self-depreciation can bring about serious psychological problems and a great deal of suffering.

In sum, the self-confidence of a narcissistic person is highly fragile because it is based on a swollen ego that is out of touch with reality. When Narcissus sees that there is nothing exceptional about him, that he is not more beautiful, more intelligent, more charming, or more talented than the average, he takes a hard fall that brings anger or depression. Thus it is not by clinging to the fabricated identity of the ego that one can acquire stable confidence. True confidence is born from freeing oneself from the traps and yoke of ego.

The I, the Person, and the Ego

MATTHIEU We take our "I" to be a unique entity, autonomous, and lasting. It is no doubt useful for functioning in life, but does the concept we have of it really correspond to reality? When I see a photograph of myself as a child, I say, "This little guy riding a bike is me." Since that time, I have gone through all kinds of experiences and my body has aged, but I still think, "It's me." In this phenomenon several mental mechanisms are present simultaneously: the perception of an *I*, that of a *person*, and that of an *ego*.

The I lives in the present. It's the I that thinks, when I wake up in the morning, "I exist," then "I'm cold," or "I'm hungry." It corresponds to the experience of our current state.

The notion of the person reflects our history. It is a continuum that covers the whole of our existence, which includes physical, mental, and social aspects. Its continuity over time allows us to connect the mental representations of ourselves that pertain to the past with those that relate to the future.

And then there's the ego. Spontaneously we presume that it constitutes the very core of our being. We conceive of it as an indivisible and permanent whole that characterizes us from cradle to grave. The ego is the proprietor of "my body," "my mind," and "my name." Even though the mind is a dynamic flux by nature, in constant transformation, we can't help but imagine a distinct entity similar to a boat floating down a river.

Once the perceptions of "I" and "person" crystallize into the much stronger sense of identity called the ego, we want to protect and satisfy this ego. We manifest aversion toward anything that threatens it, and attraction for anything that pleases and comforts it. These two reactions give rise to a multitude of conflicting emotions—anger, desire, envy, jealousy, and the like.

One only has to examine this ego a little to realize to what degree it is no more than a mystification whose author is our own mind. Let's try, for example, to locate it. When I say, "You hit me," I'm not saying, "You hit my body, but that's not serious because that's not me." Thus I do associate my ego with my body. My mind, on the other hand, cannot be hit. But when I say, "You hurt my feelings," I associate my ego with my feelings, with my mind. Moreover, when I say "my feelings," "my mind," "my name," "my body," the ego appears to be the proprietor of all of that. It is not clear how an entity endowed with a definite existence could, like Harlequin, assume all these mutually incompatible identities. So the ego can only be a concept, a mental label applied to a dynamic process. It certainly is useful to us, since it makes it possible for us to connect a whole set of changing situations; to integrate our emotions, our thoughts, the perception of our environment, and such, into a coherent whole. But it is ultimately the product of a continuous mental activity that keeps an imaginary entity alive in our mind.

ALEXANDRE   What would you say to a Zen master who applies "shock therapy" and who wouldn't hesitate, if needed, to deliver a hard smack to a disciple who is stuck in attachments?

MATTHIEU   If I was a good Zen disciple, I'd say, "What hit me, the hand of the master or the intention that guided it?" Or again, "What hurt me, was it my cheek or my feelings?" That reminds me of a friend from Hong Kong who had come to our monastery, Shechen in Nepal, to receive teachings. There were more than a thousand people sitting on the floor, pressed close together, inside the temple. At one point the person sitting behind this woman, my friend, hit her on the back to get her to move forward a little. She kept being annoyed by this incident for a good hour or so. She said to herself, "I came from far away to receive Buddhist teachings on patience and compassion, and here some boor treats me that way even though he also came here to get those same teachings." But after a while she couldn't keep herself from bursting out laughing. "I had just realized," she told the abbot of the monastery, "that my body had felt the blow for a few seconds, but my ego had suffered from it for an hour."

To come back to our examination of the ego, we often conclude that our ego is our consciousness. However, this consciousness is also an ungraspable flux: the past is dead, the future hasn't been born yet, and the present has no duration. How could the ego exist suspended between something that doesn't exist any longer and something that doesn't exist yet? As for the present moment, it's impossible to put your finger on it. The ego can't survive very long if it dwells in the transparency of the present moment, free from all discursive thought. It needs to feed itself on ruminations concerning the past and anticipations of the future.

If, then, the ego is only an illusion, freeing ourselves from it does not amount to eradicating the core of our being, but just to opening our eyes. And since our attachment to our ego is the source of suffering, it is extremely helpful to unmask this imposture.

There's no reason to fear that getting rid of the ego will turn us into vegetables—just the opposite happens. The psychologist Paul Ekman said to me one day, "I've noticed that the people who seem to me to have exceptional human qualities, who give an impression of kindness, candor, and joie de vivre—like the Dalai Lama or Desmond Tutu—have a barely perceptible ego. Others instinctively seek out their company, which they find particularly enriching. These people inspire others by not making any big deal of their status, of their fame, of their ego. Such an absence of egocentrism is staggering."

Forgetting the Self—the Silence of Ego

ALEXANDRE   We hear the words *ego* and *me* all the time without really knowing what they refer to. To tell the truth, I would have great difficulty defining them. As I see it, the ego is a bundle of illusions composed of desires, fears, emotions, and representations to which we become attached, to our very great pain. We must distinguish this illusory "I," this facade, from the basic ground of our being, our innerness, which is beyond all reification. Nevertheless, the sense of ego hangs on in my mind in some kind of indeterminate way. That being the case, how can I free myself of it? Thanks to Christophe, I am beginning to refine my understanding of it. I have long regarded the extolling of self-esteem with a certain suspicion. I feared that it tended to produce a kind of cult of personality. But as Christophe has shown, without a well-structured personality, without a healthy confidence in oneself, we fall prey to many bondages.

On this point I am also fond of recalling the fine analysis of Jean-Jacques Rousseau in his *Discourse on the Origin and Basis of Inequality among Men*. He distinguishes self-love, which leads every individual to take care of himself, to avoid dangers, from vanity, which is a primarily social passion. We know all the disastrous consequences: the insanity of worrying about what people will say, hunger for the spotlight, the desire to dominate, the lust for power. Fundamentally, vanity arises from comparison. It's as though we create an idea of ourselves to which we become attached, with the result of maximal suffering. Basically this has nothing to do with self-love, which is a primitive tendency, a kind of self-preservation instinct that encourages us to take care of our lives and, in many cases, to improve ourselves. Unfortunately, however, quite often this energy goes into a tailspin and turns into selfishness. Rousseau's distinction provides me with an effective key for not sinking into the idolatry of "me, me" while at the same time also not straying into a pitiful state of self-contempt.

The great Indian sage Ramana Maharshi also provides us with a clear path. He can help us free ourselves from this "me" that jumps around excitedly in every direction and allows us instead to come back to the fundamental ground of all grounds, where joy and peace already reside. Practically speaking, I can imitate him by asking myself, "Who am I?" If one doesn't let it turn into an obsession, it is very liberating to question oneself: "Am I my body, my thoughts, my car? Am I my religious convictions, my political ideas?"

It is also liberating to interpret disturbing emotions as signals of possible ego attachment. Why the devil do I cling to an idea even though it makes me suffer? And why would I rather die sometimes than recognize my faults? On a more subtle level, another fishy thing is a kind of narcissism in reverse that lurks in the realm of spiritual practice: "I'm going to show you I don't have ego. You'll see!" In confronting this danger, there's something much better we can do than to take a dim view of ourselves. Rather than do that, let's take Spinoza's suggestion: "Don't mock, don't cry, don't hate—but understand."

Tracking the ego mechanisms that drive us, detecting our enslavements, is a joyous challenge more than a duty. Why not start off one's day by taking stock, getting a kind of inner weather report: "Hey, today my little ego is seriously agitated. I'm not in good shape. I'm very vulnerable. I'd be ready to crawl to get somebody's approval."

I also like the exercise I suggest to my children when they're a little upset. We sit silently for a few minutes and contemplate what's going on in our minds. Buddhists sometimes compare the mind of ego to an overexcited monkey leaping continuously, without stopping, from branch to branch. The practice here is just to simply and calmly watch it carrying on like a madman, without trying to change anything at all. And then why not talk to it very peacefully: "Little monkey, little sweet one." What characterizes the discursive mind of ego is perpetual dissatisfaction. It always falls prey to the disturbing emotions.

When we feel joy, the ego is eclipsed. There's no need to prove anything anymore. That's why heaping reproach on ourselves is useless. On the contrary, it tends to aggravate the little ego. Thus the road to freedom does not pass through mortifying the self but through giving the self, through joy and sharing. And little exercises repeated every day can lead us there.

Ascesis can begin by giving priority to "we" rather than "I." By the way, I learned that in Korean, people do not say "my house" but rather "our house." Experiencing ourselves as separate from others, isolated, ends up making us feel worse. If we wake up in the morning with the sole objective to keep our little me from getting injured, we'll find obstacles everywhere. Why not drop the mistaken perspective brought on by ego?

The other day my daughter was playing in the park. Suddenly I heard cries of pain. When I saw that it wasn't my child crying out, I said to myself, "Whew, it's not her." It was bizarre—there were twenty little kids and only one of them really interested me. How many sentient beings live on the earth? What errant reasoning that is and what a lack of love that I am concerned only with myself, even including those close to me, when there are millions of other individuals living on "our" planet! But sooner or later life takes on the task of reminding me that I'm not the center of the world.

MATTHIEU You speak of changing from "I" to "we." In writing books, it's very hard for me to say, "I think that . . ." People often say to me, "Your writing isn't personal enough." But my only objective is to share the ideas that are dear to me, to be a spokesman for the wisdom of my spiritual masters, and to provide information on the scientific studies that illuminate the subjects that concern us. I've tried "we," but I got rapped on the knuckles by friends who told me that in English, it sounds like the royal "we." They remarked, "Who do you think you are, the queen of England?" Nonetheless, it seems that "we" is good for our health. A researcher analyzing speech and writing observed that people who most often used "I," "me," and "mine" were more likely to suffer from heart attacks.

CHRISTOPHE   On top of that, studies on the speech of patients show that when people make progress in therapy, they tend to use "we" much more than "I."

ALEXANDRE   It's not necessarily a good idea to subject the ego to a drastic diet. Rather, we should use skilful means to get rid of it gently, and not get involved in exhausting campaigns based on will-power. As to the question of happiness, it seems to me that the ego is chock-full of preconceived ideas. Let's go so far as to take the time to ask ourselves what makes us completely happy. If your idea is making millions or becoming a star, chances are you will be unhappy for life.

How can we find real joy, the kind that our trials and difficulties can't touch? Master Dogen shows the direct path when he tells us that giving leads to detachment. Very simply, I can ask myself, "What can I do here and now for my fellow human?" From doing this I draw a strength that helps me climb back up the slope on which I'm sliding down almost irresistibly toward a painful egotism. No longer being content with a kind of totally abstract bulk generosity—that's the challenge. Sometimes it's easier to show infinite patience toward whoever comes along than to refrain from telling one's spouse to go to hell after the pettiest dispute.

Something that's a real setback for ego is self-irony. There's nothing that does the job better than a sense of humor that comes along and dislodges me every time I get stuck in a label, a concept. A hundred times a day I remember this quote from Meister Eckhart: "Observe yourself and look for yourself, and the moment you find yourself, let yourself go, there's nothing better you can do." In joy, ego leaves us in peace; it's on its best behavior. I don't remember who said that health is the silence of the organs, but I think unconditional joy is the silence of the ego.

> In joy, ego leaves us in peace; it's on its best behavior. I don't remember who said that health is the silence of the organs, but I think unconditional joy is the silence of the ego.

CHRISTOPHE   It was the French surgeon René Leriche who said in 1936, "Health is life lived in the silence of the organs."

ALEXANDRE   When ego is eclipsed, peace comes, like a miracle. But almost always our mental FM broadcasts its background noise: "Get there fast, do this, do that, that's not okay, I have to have this, I must have that . . ."

Practicing meditation is trying to lessen the impact of these thoughts at last. Ego is not there to make us happy. It may have a function, but its vocation is certainly not to lead us to peace. Let's learn to disobey it moment after moment, to cease taking its orders as gospel. And why not? Let's laugh at the way we continually criticize, judge, and condemn everybody. What wipes all that stuff out is generosity that expects nothing in return. So let's not hesitate to ask ourselves, "Concretely, what can I do today to do somebody some good?"

MATTHIEU   If the silence of the organs is physical health, then the silence of the ego is mental health! The ego is always asking two questions: "Why me?" and "Why not me?" Why did so-and-so say that ridiculous thing to me? Why did this trouble have to fall in my lap? Why am I not as handsome or as lucky as that guy there?

Every human being wants to find happiness and avoid suffering, but the best decision you can make is not to entrust this happiness to ego. Someone who only thinks about himself is not doing anything practical toward attaining happiness. Moreover, his constant failures provoke a frustration and rage that he turns both against himself and against the outside world.

A healthy ego is a transparent ego, the ego of someone who has within himself a vast space of inner peace into which he can welcome others because he is not obsessed with his own situation. By making your ego less heavy and definite, you can spare yourself a lot of problems. You become less sensitive to criticism and praise. You tidy up your thought process and turn off the mental FM that drones on all day long: "Me, me, me, what's going to happen to me?" You also begin to see better what's going on around you and to perceive the beauty of beings and things. I remember Father Ceyrac, who died at the age of nearly a hundred after having taken care of tens of thousands of poor children over fifty years in the south of India. One day he said to me with a big smile, "I come out of the subway. The people are so beautiful. But they don't know it!"

CHRISTOPHE Working on the way one reacts to compliments and criticisms is a very good exercise for patients who are suffering from a sense of inferiority. They are neurotic. They doubt themselves. They often get exploited, beaten down, manipulated by others. Sometimes, on the other hand, they become aggressive because they are uncomfortable in their skin. We show them ways to accept compliments without rejecting their favorable content but also without revelling in it, without necessarily feeling built up by it. The same thing goes for criticism. Criticisms are not necessarily true, but they always give us some information! When somebody criticizes me (if there are grounds for it), they're sending me a message, either about me (I'm having some faults of mine shown to me, and I should be happy about that) or about how that person sees me, and I should be happy about learning that too! So in both cases—a suitable reminder or a piece of new information—these are helpful messages.

We teach our patients to be open to compliments and criticisms but also to somewhat distrust them. It is extremely dangerous to have a good image of yourself only if you receive compliments or expressions of admiration, and a bad image of yourself if you are subject to criticisms and lack of recognition. This is an addiction to other peoples' views of you, an addiction just like to sugar, tobacco, or drugs. We need to kick the habit. Of course, we have a need for compliments and criticisms, to remind us of our faults or sometimes to encourage us, but we must be careful not to let it reach the point of dependency.

Shower of Gratitude

CHRISTOPHE There is a very precious notion in what Alexandre was saying: the more we feel cut off from the world, the more anxious we are to save our skin. I remember working on gratitude with patients who were suffering from problems of self-esteem. We asked them to think regularly about what they owed others at times when they were feeling happy or had experienced some success or other. The idea was for them to ask themselves, after they had taken pleasure in what had happened to them, "In this happiness I am currently feeling, or in this success I was able to achieve, what is it I owe others?" The paradoxical result was, the more they learned to function in this gratitude mode, the more self-confidence they felt. Because, fundamentally, gratitude freed them from the kind of false self-confidence you've talked about, Matthieu, which consisted of only believing in their own strengths and abilities. They were acquiring a kind of confidence that is much more intelligent and much broader. This is a kind of confidence that is rooted in all the sources of help, love, and affection around them, which they weren't necessarily heeding before and which they only called upon when they were in trouble. But we should really do the opposite. We should think of those sources around us when we are in positive states in which we have succeeded at something, attained our objectives. Instead of weakening ourselves, as narcissists might think, we are strengthened when we say to ourselves, "You owe others a part—whether big or small doesn't matter—of what you are experiencing." It increases our sense of connection and solidarity with others. This connection is much closer and more intense than we think.

One of the most beautiful definitions of gratitude I know of is that of the philosopher André Comte-Sponville, who wrote, "Gratitude takes pleasure in what it owes, whereas vanity would prefer to forget about it." I am happy to owe something to others because, fundamentally, it's wonderful that others have given me this "something." I should not let this offend me or make me feel inferior or insecure. This doesn't mean that I was incapable of achieving something on my own. Or even if that's the case, from the moment others were able to help me, that no longer matters. Let's not forget it: cultivating an awareness of what we owe others in getting to feel stronger is a detour worth taking.

MATTHIEU   Just a word about gratitude. Greg Norris, who studies the life cycle of commonly used objects at Harvard, explained to me one day that when I hold a piece of paper in my hand, at least thirty-five countries have worked together to make this possible. For example, a woodcutter cut a tree in a Norwegian forest, a Danish trucker transported this tree to a French factory, and so on. Then for the paper pulp we have to add the starch extracted from potatoes coming from the Czech Republic; and the pulp was colored or bleached with chemicals made in Germany, and so forth. On top of this, each person who contributed to this chain has parents, grandparents, children, . . . all of whom perhaps influenced him or her in his or her choice of occupation. In brief, you could read, as though in watermark all over this piece of paper, the inscription, "Others, others, others . . ."

Seeing this interdependence of all beings and all things should continually fill us with gratitude. Like the environmentalists who assess the ecological footprint of a product, we could assess the footprint of gratitude connected with those who have made it possible for us to be together here today. Little by little we would learn that our gratitude should embrace the entire planet.

CHRISTOPHE   One day a patient to whom I had taught these exercises began talking to me about the "shower of gratitude" that he took every evening in taking stock of his day! As he fell asleep he contemplated all the good things—big or little—that he had experienced and what he owed—wholly or in part—to others. And he said to me, "If you really think about it, this thing of yours really goes pretty far!" And it's true—it's incredible! If I suddenly pause and become aware of everything I owe others at this moment, I get the impression that half the human race is in this room! It's exactly what you were saying, Matthieu: gratitude toward the people who made the tea we're drinking, toward those who made the cup, toward the people from the utility company who are getting electricity to us, toward you who organized bringing the three of us together to create this book, toward the friends who are helping us out here and preparing the meals . . . It isn't long before instead of being a shower, it's a veritable Niagara pouring down on us! There's nothing in what we are experiencing here that is not due to other people—nothing! The light, the heat, the food, our clothes, the fact that we can speak to each other—we owe all that to our parents, our professors, our friends, and to tens and hundreds of unknown people. It's breathtaking, mind-blowing, and wonderful.

MATTHIEU In gift shops you often see these bowls or cups that have first names on them. You look for the one marked Paul, Virginia, Matthieu, or some other first name you have in mind. What should be marked on those bowls, but also on most objects we use, is "the others, the others, the others." That's what we should remember when we use any object at all. People moan about traffic jams, crowds in the subway, without thinking for a moment about the incredible cooperation implied in the existence and functioning of a big city.

CHRISTOPHE The gratitude exercise is very comforting. And in this "comfort" there is something that does us good and something that makes us stronger. Gratitude makes us stronger and makes us aware of external resources that are bigger than our inner resources alone.

MATTHIEU In fact we should put Narcissus all alone and naked in a forest in the wilderness and tell him, "Okay now, since you're the best, get along all by yourself."

Our Advice for Working with Ego

Three Pieces of Advice that Arose ALEXANDRE

- Practice gratitude as a spiritual exercise and, in turn, enter into this immense chain of solidarity by performing some very definite and concrete actions that help the greatest number of people.

• Be attentive to yourself. In order to liquidate ego, or at least to make it a little bit quieter, begin by really being attentive to yourself and finding out what really brings you joy. If you don't, your ego will flare up instantly when frustration, bitterness, and resentment lurk in your heart. From this point on, learn to rejoice and to be good to yourself.

• "Who am I?" Let's follow in the footsteps of Ramana Maharshi. When anxiety comes to you, you should immediately ask, "Who is afraid?" And when you pass through trouble zones, progressively discern that there is an aspect of your being that even in the midst of chaos is beyond suffering.

Three Reflections   MATTHIEU

• Stop putting labels of "me" and "mine" on yourself and on things. You will be more in harmony with reality and your mind will be vaster.

• Free yourself from the whims of ego. Be less preoccupied with the need to protect yourself. You will be more available for others.

• Be compassionate. It's the best way to achieve your own happiness.

Advice for People Struggling with Problems of the Ego CHRISTOPHE

- Be your own friend, have a relationship of friendship with yourself; but don't chase after admiration or promote your own image. It's really a matter of friendship—wanting the best for a friend is being able to be compassionate with him or her but also gently demanding.

- Create little mantras of self-compassion: "Do your best, and never hurt yourself."

- Lighten up. Say to yourself, "My ego is a little bike, not a big SUV!"

- Take a "shower of gratitude" every night. This will remove ego's useless cobwebs, bring joy to your heart, and reveal to you all your inner and outer strengths.

Learning to Live
with Our Emotions

CHRISTOPHE   The realm of emotions is a tremendously interesting one because it is fundamental for understanding the psychology and suffering of human beings. When I was little, one of the ideals of my parents in raising me was that I should be a reasonable little boy. In this expectation there was the idea that emotions shouldn't be allowed to occupy too big a place. Here we find the opposition, traditional in the West, between reason and emotion. Reason is given priority and emotions are curbed. Moreover, this fit in well with the way my family worked—there was very little expression of emotion. As though by chance, I became a psychiatrist who specializes in emotional problems.

The Afflictive Emotions

CHRISTOPHE   In the West, emotions have long been regarded with fear and mistrust. The Greeks were wary of emotions that disturbed the social order, notably hubris, excessive pride, and self-confidence. Sadness also seemed to them to be a problematic emotion because it disengaged an individual from his role as citizen. Everything changed in the nineteenth century with Darwin, who showed that emotions are initially adaptive biological phenomena found in their embryonic state in the simplest of animal species and become ever more elaborate as the brains of organisms become more complex. He naturalized emotions. Nowadays we are fortunate enough to live in a time when emotions are studied in a scientific manner.

In my profession, people come for counseling often because of painful emotions that have gotten out of control. These are mainly the fearful emotions that characterize anxiety syndromes, but also emotions of sadness or excessive shame, which stray at their high point into depression. Paradoxically, very hot-tempered, angry people rarely come for counseling. In my opinion, our society is too tolerant toward anger. Until recently, people rarely sought counseling for a deficit of pleasant emotions; the main demand was to get rid of the pain linked with "negative" emotions. But since the advent of positive psychology, we professionals have learned that after having pacified the excess of negative emotions in our patients, we should be sure patients understand that they are capable of opening to, arousing, and cultivating what are called "positive" emotions. But in that regard, there is a great debate going on today about this positive-negative terminology, which leads to a value judgment: people tend to think that the positive emotions are purely advantageous and the negative emotions are purely disruptive. This is obviously too simplistic. An effort is being made to use the terms *pleasant emotion* and *unpleasant emotion* instead.

Psychology has become very skilled in understanding the unpleasant emotions and in analyzing their relationship with painful thoughts. There is a saying in cognitive psychology that the stronger an emotion is, the stronger cognition will be. In other words, when I am haunted by an emotion of anxiety or sadness, the emotion is like a fire under the pot of my thoughts, and the stronger the emotion is, the more negative thoughts there will be, and the more I will be stuck in them. For example, if I am too upset, thoughts such as "These people are idiots and are doing their best to thwart me" will be amplified and will seem completely self-evident to me. If I'm too restless, the slightest worry will be transformed in my thoughts into a catastrophe—and so on. Conversely, if emotional intensity is less, the grip of thoughts will be weaker. That's how antidepressants and anti-anxiety drugs work; they don't directly change the nature of our thoughts but rather lower the intensity of emotional activity. We have also seen, through therapies that employ mindfulness meditation, that attention is an extremely powerful means of regulating emotion. By helping us to distance ourselves more from our emotions, it modifies the impact they have on our view of the world and on our cognition.

ALEXANDRE If emotions weren't constantly torturing us, we might not even talk about them. But they gnaw on us day after day and poison our lives. When they have us in their grip, our entire relationship with reality teeters. Under the sway of anger or panic, I can more or less say goodbye to whatever lucidity I have left. One of the great challenges of the spiritual life is immediately accepting that I can lose control. The other day while I was at the dentist, I noted a small red spot, and my discursive mind took care of the rest: the worst catastrophic scenarios occurred to me one after the other, and I visualized myself dying from AIDS, abandoned by everyone. Out of nothing I manufactured a monstrous bugaboo.

The mind creates fear; it fabricates it out of thin air. It comes along and more or less drops a cloak of illusions over the world, which we must throw off at once. To begin with, maybe the best thing is not to dramatize and to realize that one of the nasty traits of ego is alarming us for no reason, revving on an empty tank. Practicing meditation means gradually recognizing how big a resonance a small misinterpreted detail can take on. So we must see the tremendous difference between the almost physical fear that arises when a rifle goes off ten centimeters from my ears and this little red spot, perfectly insignificant, that went on to generate terrible anxiety for months.

But what chance does reason have against the fables fabricated by the discursive mind? The worst thing is, I believe in them. In this regard, I remember a woman who feared more than anything else being struck by lightning. One day, over the phone, she heard thunder rumbling in the distance. She was so panic-stricken she wanted to hang up right away. Foolishly I told her that at the very most there was a one-in-a-million chance that lightning might strike her house. Without missing a beat, she answered me, "Exactly. That's why I am so scared!" Christophe, as you've shown me time and again, it's uncertainty that the anxiety-ridden person is afraid of more than anything else. One chance in a million is already too much for somebody who is in need of 100 percent certainty in order to relax and enjoy life.

Knowing the workings of the discursive mind, seeing how it maneuvers to dupe us, is no small deal. When I'm paralyzed by anxiety, I'm sometimes surprised that I find the joys and the quiet times of everyday life insipid. It's as though I missed the adrenaline that rushes through me when I am in crisis mode, which is quite dramatic. The blows of fate are crushing, exhausting, but at least in the moment of struggling with them I know why I get up in the morning. In *The Gay Science*, Nietzsche writes, "In pain I hear the captain's command: 'Pull in the sails!' The hardy seafarer 'Man' must have learned to adjust the sails in a thousand ways; otherwise he would have gone under too quickly and the ocean would have swallowed him too soon." But later, when the ordinary flow of life and the routine have taken over again, there's a feeling of something missing. We become habituated, even addicted, to adversity. It's as though we had to be carrying a load of disaster to feel alive. Our relationship to the emotions can, to say the least, be ambiguous. The fact that they make us suffer by their excess, the fact that they make us lose our bearings, brings with it a persistent misunderstanding: many people think they have to be shivering and shaking in order to be alive, and that the effect of meditation is to cut them off from their emotions.

What drew me into philosophy was that it seemed to promise the famous ataraxia, that is, freedom from disturbances of the mind. Today I see perfectly well that I probably have no chance whatever of rooting out the thousand and one worries that agitate my mind. However, thanks to meditation, a kind of miracle occurs day after day. Sometimes I reach the point of laughing at my anxieties, of no longer being afraid of my fears.

One exercise that helps me a lot is seeing that the consciousness that experiences the fear, anxiety, or grief is never touched by them. There exists in all men and women a part that remains inviolate. No trauma can trouble it. We might compare consciousness to a big soup. It has everything in it: chickpeas, lettuce, carrots that cheer us up, and onions that make us cry. In times of unhappiness, ego only chews the onions without tasting the rest. Thinking of our consciousness as being like a big soup allows us to let emotions pass without letting ourselves be reduced to, for example, anger or pain, since they are only ingredients among many others.

What can be exhausting is the perpetual back-and-forth, the inner yo-yo that swings us back and forth from joy to happiness in a quarter of a second. It's difficult to get completely into joy without sensing that it's going to end. And in sadness we believe that we are going to be stuck with this rotten feeling forever, and that makes us sink com-

> There is a big misunderstanding that prevents us from tasting unconditional joy. We wrongly believe that that will only be possible the day that we are healed from all our wounds. But in fact this joy without rhyme or reason is possible right now, even in the midst of torment. We can attain it now, immediately.

pletely to the bottom. Nonfixation is the greatest tool. It allows us to get away from both grasping and rejecting, and begin again to welcome whatever comes along. First, I have to accept these enormous inner ups and downs; I must realize that I can wake up happy but that just one email can cast me into the depths. It's as though I have handed external circumstances a remote control that has the power of zapping me with any emotion.

The good news is that we can avoid these ups and downs, settling deep down into the fundamental ground of all grounds where there is unconditional joy. The first step is to quietly observe this incessant zapping without getting too upset about it. There is a big misunderstanding that prevents us from tasting unconditional joy. We wrongly believe that that will only be possible the day that we are healed from all our wounds. But in fact this joy without rhyme or reason is possible right now, even in the midst of torment. We can attain it now, immediately. If we wait for life to be perfect to experience it, we might find ourselves waiting for a long, long time.

Ecclesiastes comes to my aid by teaching that it is in chaos, beyond hope, that I *should* discover peace. I am glad to hear this biblical scripture hammer home its famous refrain: "Vanity of vanities, all is vanity." Reading that cures me of a lot of illusions and rids me of the temptation to believe that I am the master of the course of my life. Sooner or later everything will break down. Everything is impermanent.

I find a kind of liberation in seeing that everything is fragile. Finally I can happily give up on stability, solidity, and learn to swim in impermanence. If I keep trying at all costs to find a terra firma where I can stay forever, I will inevitably be disappointed. The Buddha's first noble truth reminds us that all is suffering and impermanence. I'm neither a Tibetologist nor a Sanskritist, but Yongey Mingyur Rinpoche, in his book *Joyful Wisdom*, formulates the diagnosis of the Buddha by saying "everything screeches." Common experience demonstrates also that no matter what we do, even if we are in the purest inner states, there is always something that's off, almost like a piece of machinery that's off and screeches. As Bernard Campan puts it, "The whole point is to let it screech joyfully." Practicing meditation is not withdrawing from the world but learning to live with it, being at peace in the midst of its squeaks and screeches.

When Modern Psychology and Buddhism Come Together

MATTHIEU Continuing with our general overview, the word *emotion* etymologically evokes the idea of that which creates motion. It's quite a vast subject, because what doesn't set the mind in motion? Depending on their point of view and what their aim is, specialists speak of positive and negative emotions—or pleasant and unpleasant emotions, as you were saying, Christophe—and give different meanings to these terms. They approach them from different angles: scientific, therapeutic, personal, spiritual, and many others.

In understanding emotions in a more down-to-earth way, in their basic relationship with well-being and "ill-being," it seems to me a few prefatory remarks are necessary. All mental activity is associated with emotions that can be roughly characterized as pleasant, unpleasant, or neutral. Most affective states, such as love and hate, are also accompanied by inner dialogue and reasoning. On the neurological level, each area of the brain is associated with particular aspects of emotion and particular aspects of cognition. In other words, the neuronal circuits that carry emotions are intimately connected with those that carry cognition. Emotions practically never manifest independently of other aspects of our experience. That means that the distinction between emotional and cognitive is far from being as clear-cut as it might appear at first glance.

From the Buddhist point of view, which is essentially therapeutic because its aim is to heal suffering and bring well-being, the most practical way of distinguishing the different mental states, in particular the emotions, is to examine their consequences. If an emotion increases our inner peace and well-being and at the same time encourages us to help others, we say that it is positive. If it troubles our mind and drives us to harm others, we say that it is negative. Thus the only criterion worth looking at is the well-being or suffering that results from a particular emotion. In that respect Buddhism is different from psychological approaches that differentiate emotions according to whether they encourage approaching—such as curiosity or attraction—or retreating—such as fear and aversion.

The distinction between pleasant and unpleasant emotions seems to me to be problematic from the point of view of the pursuit of long-lasting happiness, since it perpetuates the confusion between happiness and pleasure. Pleasure is engendered by pleasant stimuli of a sensorial, aesthetic, or intellectual order. It is unstable and can rapidly transform into indifference or even displeasure or disgust. Listening to sublime music can bring immense pleasure, but hearing it in a repetitive loop for twenty-four hours nonstop could become torture. Moreover, the individual quest for pleasure can easily conflict with the well-being of others. On the other hand, true happiness in the Buddhist sense is an inner state that is not subject to circumstances. Instead of transforming into its opposite after a certain time, it becomes more and more stable because it brings about a sense of fullness that becomes a dominant trait of our temperament over the course of months or years. It is essentially a way of being and a profound inner equilibrium linked to an accurate understanding of the workings of the mind.

CHRISTOPHE   What is the Tibetan word for *emotion*?

MATTHIEU   The Buddhist terms in this area do not always coincide with the ones we use in the West, because they don't reflect the same point of view. There's really no word to designate the positive emotions. We speak of beneficial thoughts or mental states, such as love and compassion. There are even other mental states such as mental calm or insight that we wouldn't call emotions here.

As for the word often translated as "negative emotions," it also has a broader sense. It designates not only anger, jealousy, etc., but also ignorance or mental confusion, which are sources of negative emotions, as well as forgetfulness, carelessness, and dullness. So the Tibetan word *nyomong*, usually translated as "negative emotions," actually refers to mental afflictions at large, and it evokes an idea of torment and confusion. These afflictive mental states are connected with a false view of reality that leads to mental dysfunction. It is enough to observe the moment in which greed, anger, hate, or jealousy takes hold of us to note that these emotions create profound malaise in us and drain us of energy. The words and deeds brought on by these mental states are also harmful to others most of the time. Mental afflictions also create a cleavage between ourselves and others. They prompt us to idealize what we like and demonize what we dislike. They make us believe that beauty and ugliness are inherent in beings and things, which creates a growing separation between what they are in reality and the way they appear to us. That's the reason, as Christophe was saying, that the more negative emotions one has, the more one imposes mental fabrications on reality.

Positive psychology, the cognitive therapies, and Buddhism converge at this point. During a meeting with the Dalai Lama, Aaron Beck, the founder of cognitive therapy, explained that when we are very angry, 80 percent of our perceptions are superimposed on reality. If people were attractive or repellent in themselves, we would all be attracted or repelled by the same people, which is not the case. The obviousness of this escapes us once we are taken over by desire or anger, because we pass through a "refractory period," as Paul Ekman puts it, that prevents us from realizing that the person we hate at this moment also has other qualities, or that the person we're madly attracted to also has defects.

The negative emotions also have another characteristic that is often pointed out by the Dalai Lama: they have no need to be cultivated in order to develop. You can have enormous fits of anger without needing even one second of training. As another of my masters, Jigme Khyentse Rinpoche, says, "We don't have to train our mind to achieve frustration. We don't need a booster for anger or an amplifier for pride and vanity." By contrast, even if we are naturally patient or compassionate, it takes a certain effort to become more so.

I will add that an apparently positive emotion can in fact be negative, and vice versa. Desire can sometimes translate as a noble intention, such as relieving the suffering of others or protecting the environment, but the desire for wealth or pleasure is very likely, sooner or later, to become a source of pain for oneself and others. Anger can translate as malice, but also just as indignation—a feeling of revulsion with regard to a massacre, for example. That anger is an expression of compassion and arouses a strong desire to help others.

CHRISTOPHE   When I discovered, on both a personal and professional level, the extreme variety of emotions, and in particular that of positive emotions, it changed my life! For a long time, like every good psychiatrist, I was under the impression that there was a tremendous number of negative emotions, but that on the other side, ultimately there were only two major positive emotions—joy and love. And then I understood that this was a gigantic error. Scientific studies have revealed an infinity of positive emotions: confidence, serenity, tenderness, admiration, kindness, and so on. Studies have also been done on exaltation, the emotion we feel when we are face-to-face with something so immense that it makes us feel very small, as before Mount Everest, the Grand Canyon, or anything that is totally extraordinary. There is also enthusiasm, a form of favorable reaction toward things that life or other people suggest to us, an opening to something joyfully and excitingly new, which is very important for groups. I find this "positive psychology" trend admirable. It teaches us to discover the infinite wealth of pleasant states of being and to make use of them in treating patients. I am working now to promote the study and use of these pleasant emotions in therapy because they possess considerable force and potency, and they can be cultivated.

The Role of Emotions

MATTHIEU   Specialists in evolution explain that emotions are useful for survival and for the regulation of life's main activities—reproduction, protection of loved ones, relationships between individuals, dealing with predators, and so forth. Jealousy is certainly a source of torment, but it can also be seen as the expression of an instinct that contributes to the cohesion of a couple and the survival of their offspring. Anger can be destructive, but from the point of view of evolution, it's something that allows us to get rid of whatever might harm us or hinder the realization of our plans.

Many psychologists agree with Aristotle, for whom an emotion is appropriate when it is adapted to a situation and expressed with an intensity proportional to circumstances. In the face of injustice, indignant anger can be appropriate, whereas an explosion of destructive rage is not. After the loss of a loved one, sadness is appropriate, whereas despair and depression are disproportionate and conflict with one's long-term well-being. Recently I felt tremendous sadness on the occasion of the earthquake that took place in Nepal, where I live most of the time. But this moment having passed, I concluded that rather than falling into a state of despondency at the thought that everything that had been built had to be rebuilt, it would be better if I mobilized my energy to help the victims, which we did, since Karuna-Shechen helped over 200,000 people in 620 villages.

That which is favorable to our survival from the point of view of evolution, however, does not necessarily contribute to our well-being as individuals. We cannot say that jealousy, anger, or envy are conducive to inner peace. Unbridled sexual desire might be excellent for the propagation of genes, but it is a source of distress due to the fact that it continually recurs and never attains permanent satisfaction. On the other hand, it is not a sure thing that compassion or enlightenment are useful for reproduction. The accomplished meditator who lives the life of a hermit in solitude in the mountains doesn't do much for the propagation of genes.

CHRISTOPHE Even though they're isolated, these hermits that you talk about contribute in their way to the well-being of everybody by not adding to the violence and materialism of the world and by serving as examples.

It's true that the emotions are part of our genetic heritage as human beings and are hardwired into our brains. Then they are reinforced by our education and our cultural milieu. All emotions are useful to us—anger, sadness, fear, anxiety, shame. All have very definite functions. They serve us well to the extent that they do not reach excessively high levels of intensity or last too long, and we do not lose track of their purpose.

From the evolutionist point of view, negatively or unpleasantly toned emotions are often associated with dangerous situations, perhaps life-threatening ones. Anger allows us to intimidate others (and thus to avoid costly physical battles); fear causes us to avoid potential dangers (and encourages caution in the best cases or flight in the worst); sadness causes us to slow down and reflect, and so forth. Positive emotions, on the other hand, are associated with situations of seeking resources (food, rest, or pleasant exchanges such as games or sexual relations). But what is pleasant never takes priority over what is dangerous; in nature, one has to deal with danger before seeking pleasant situations. This is why the negative emotions enjoy a kind of potential supremacy over the positive ones—in their clarity, intensity, force of their eruption, and ability to seize our attention. But without the positive emotions, we could not hold out in the long run. After the danger has passed, positive emotions revive our openness and renew our ability to relate with others, find resources, create solutions. They are our fuel for going forward. Negative emotions are a bit like the loudmouths in a family. They react faster, shout louder, and create the hubbub at the family table. But without the positive emotions, nobody would show up for the meal because it would be nothing but hell on wheels! Descartes puts it as follows in the conclusion of his treatise *The Passions of the Soul*. After having described the passions, he says in effect, now that we know them all, let's no longer be afraid of them because they are all good by nature. The key is simply to avoid their inappropriate or excessive use.

> After the danger has passed, positive emotions revive our openness and renew our ability to relate with others, find resources, create solutions. They are our fuel for going forward.

ALEXANDRE To attain liberation from the disturbing emotions, we first have to stop treating them as enemies, adversaries to be defeated. Instead we have to regard them as messengers, even as alarm signals. Then we have to try to make good use of them. What I find sad is the kind of self-affirmation that unconsciously turns into pride: "I am the way I am. I'm irritable. I'm like that; that's my nature." Self-contempt may well be a calamity, but shutting ourselves up in excessive pride is no less of a disaster. There is a great temptation to turn the poison into the antidote. But the wise man, like the child, has no need for self-confirmation—he is fully what he is, and that's that.

No longer fearing the negative emotions is a great step forward. The fears that gnaw on us today perhaps saved our lives in childhood. To this day, I still have to fight against two very tenacious hindrances: hyperanxiety and impatience. But retrospectively I can see that both of these have a function: saving my life by getting me beyond resignation, despondency, and the thousand and one obstacles I had to overcome. But now, today, it's fine; I can continue on my path without these burdensome crutches. There are instruments of survival that serve for a time and that then we must abandon in order to move on. The Greek philosophers, the skeptics in this case, have a beautiful image for this: they speak of purgative medicaments, that is, remedies that are eliminated along with the malady they cured. Excuse me for being crude, but the best example is a laxative that also leaves the body together with the problems it solves!

CHRISTOPHE It's true, the negative emotions clearly do hurt us and cost us a lot, but sometimes the positive emotions are also problematic. Joy, for example, speeds up our hearts, pumps us full of energy, but especially in children it can turn into agitation. Nonetheless, it gives us so much in return that, in the end, we are the winners—both in terms of endorphins and in existential satisfaction. In fact it's like children, who fill us with a terrible energy but give us a great deal of happiness in the long run. I'm especially thinking of moments of excess, when it gets out of control, of joy that gets us excited—at a certain point, it becomes too much, we go too far. We fail to heed the signals of fatigue from our bodies because we are in a state of euphoria. This is the problem with the pathological joy we find in bipolar illness. It pushes us to excesses, beyond caution, and, in the end, into human and financial debacles (relational conflicts and pathological spending).

MATTHIEU So it is essential to think clearly about the effect of our mental states on the quality of our living experience, short term and long term. Seen from a certain angle, it might seem normal to be constantly seeking what gives us pleasure, except that this rarely leads to happiness. On the other hand, we could cultivate an inner satisfaction that is not necessarily connected with pleasant sensations and thus might seem less attractive, but in the end it brings us a deep and long-lasting fulfillment.

The Importance of States of Mind

CHRISTOPHE Going further in our examination of the emotions, we can look at them from the point of view of two axes: the axis of valence (more pleasant or unpleasant) and the axis of intensity.

Along the second axis we find the explosive emotions, more or less out of control as they arise in us, such as anger or fear; and then the emotional states of lesser intensity, which we might call moods or states of mind. These states seem to be becoming more and more important in the eyes of researchers because they represent the biggest part of our emotional feelings. The strong emotions are so demanding in terms of physical and psychological energy that we can't afford to fall prey to them very many times in a day—that would end up wearing us out or even killing us. When you ask somebody when they last were extremely angry, extremely sad, extremely upset, extremely shameful, or perhaps extremely happy, they often have a hard time thinking of recent examples. By contrast, it is very likely that since this morning we have all already experienced several moderate emotional states, with a little sadness, a little malaise, or a little good humor or joy.

It's important to notice these unassuming states to see how very influential they are. They are a kind of compost that encourages the development of much more powerful emotions and even entire systems of thought, entire ways of seeing the world. Being continually in the grips of emotions such as resentment or irritation in relation to others plays a role in the view of the world I will have and on the way I will behave socially. That's why we encourage our patients to pay attention to these subtle, background emotions, particularly during phases when they are warding off relapses and learning the art of well-being, of inner balance.

How can we become aware of these emotional states? Here contemplative and meditative approaches are very helpful. But other ways of working on ourselves are also helpful—keeping a journal or doing cognitive therapy, which encourages us to gain insight into the links between the situations we go through, the emotions we feel, the thoughts that come up in relation to them, and the behaviors that are the consequence of this entire causal chain.

MATTHIEU In Buddhism we speak of the almost imperceptible thoughts that manifest continually in the background of our field of awareness, like water that sometimes is found running beneath the grass of a meadow. These thoughts can provoke various moods in us. If they are negative, they may trigger a sudden emotional explosion—a fit of anger, for example. If they are naturally positive or the result of training in compassion, for example, their frequent appearance will have long-term influence on our mental terrain, to the point where if any person enters our field of attention, the first feeling that will arise will be compassion.

How can we become aware of the emotional states that often manifest in us without our knowing it? If we let them develop and grow they become unmanageable, and we have no choice but to wait until they calm down. But if we examine the effects they have had on us, we realize that in the course of the storms they unleashed in us, our perceptions of other people and of the situations did not correspond to reality.

As a result of having this experience again and again, one becomes gradually capable of seeing these emotions coming from further off. One can then apply the appropriate antidote as a preventative, always bearing in mind that it is easier to extinguish a spark than a forest fire.

By refining our understanding of how to master our minds yet further, we reach the point where we can deal with our emotions the moment they arise. When this process becomes so habitual that the emotions that used to disturb us dissolve as they appear, our minds are no longer troubled by those emotions. They can no longer turn into words and deeds that harm us and others. This method requires training, because we are not in the habit of treating our thoughts this way.

Is It Possible to Liberate Ourselves from Negative Emotions?

MATTHIEU   If it is possible to get out from under the yoke of destructive emotions, it is because they are alien to the nature of the mind. According to Buddhism, the fundamental aspect of consciousness, the pure faculty of knowing, the quality of mind that is called "luminous," is an unconditioned space where emotions manifest like clouds in the sky, transitorily, under the influence of circumstances that are also transitory. When they are negative, we use various methods to liberate ourselves from them. When they are positive, we train ourselves to develop them.

Contemplatives know this. No matter how much they search the depths of pure awareness, they find neither hate nor greed nor jealousy nor pride nor any other mental poison. This means that negative emotions can only occur adventitiously, as the texts say, under the effect of circumstances and habits. And, significantly, this means that it is possible to liberate ourselves from them. The sun might be hidden by clouds, but that doesn't mean that it stops shining.

To come back to a question Alexandre was asking: Isn't it hopeless to try to defeat our negative emotions? Wouldn't it be easier to just let them wear themselves out? Experience shows that if we get in the habit of just giving them free rein, they will behave like infections that we didn't treat in time. They will become stronger and take root in our minds. We will fall under their power again as soon as their emotional charges reach the critical threshold. And this threshold will keep getting lower and lower. We will keep getting angry faster, and keep getting worried faster, and so on. That doesn't mean that we should repress our emotions. This would be a short-term solution that would be very unlikely to lead to inner peace. Because there are two possibilities: Either the negative emotions are inherent in our minds, in which case trying to get rid of them would amount to fighting against a part of ourselves and could only fail. Or else their presence in our minds is due to transitory causes and conditions, and in that case it is possible to liberate ourselves from them.

The important thing, to begin with, is to acquire a certain amount of skill in recognizing the negative emotions, and then in neutralizing them with the help of the most appropriate antidote. Buddhism teaches a great number of methods for accomplishing that, of which none in itself is superior to the others. Which one is chosen depends on the circumstances and the abilities of each person. Some are direct and obvious, such as training in compassion to combat malice. It is impossible to wish somebody well and wish them ill at the same time.

Some are more subtle, such as being mindful of the emotions without identifying with them. We have already spoken about that. The awareness of anxiety is not anxious; it is simply aware. I am far from being a good meditator, but I have often tried to apply this method. When I'm on my way to the airport in the middle of bad traffic, for example, I sometimes get worried thinking about the chain of events that would occur if I missed my plane—I would miss the connecting flight, then miss the conference I was going to attend at the destination, even though it had been planned for months. If I try to relax into awareness of this state as if I were calmly contemplating a rushing torrent flowing in front of me, at the beginning the anxiety might seem to dig in stubbornly. But if I continue to look at it with the eye of awareness, it loses its force, and at the same time the space of awareness becomes vaster and vaster. A point comes at which the anxiety is no more than a pale reflection of what it was at the beginning, and in the end it disappears.

> The awareness of anxiety is not anxious; it is simply aware.

There are many other methods suitable to the needs and aptitudes of the individual. For example, I can try to see what the emotion that is bothering me is in itself. Hate is not a madman attacking me with a weapon or a rock tumbling down the mountainside that is going to crush me or a burning fire. It may seem powerful, but nevertheless it is only a mental fabrication. And if my mind fabricated it, it can also liberate me from it. Why let it gain such mastery over me? Especially since there is nothing to grasp onto there; it's nothing but air. In Buddhist terms, we say that this emotion is *empty*, which means devoid of independent existence of its own. Recognition of this truth is liberating in itself. That doesn't mean that now we should fall into nihilism. Rather, we pass from an enslaved state into a free one. In the meditation texts, the free mind is sometimes compared to water, and the mind fettered by mental constructs to ice. All that is necessary is to heat the ice so that it becomes water. My master Dilgo Khyentse Rinpoche used to say, "Ice is only solidified water and water is only melted ice. It's the same with our perceptions of the world. Becoming attached to the reality of things through attraction and repulsion amounts to blocking the free functioning of the mind. Melt the ice of concepts, and you will have the flowing water of inner freedom."

CHRISTOPHE The behavioral and cognitive approaches are fairly close to what you describe. For us, the emotions are always a *cause*, whether it's an external cause (an event we are happy with or one that attacks us) or a cause connected with biological states (such as fatigue or lack of sleep). It could also be a cause connected with mental representations; when we represent a situation to ourselves mentally, we might feel shame with regard to what we are doing, or fear, sadness, guilt, anger, etc. In our view, emotions are a preverbal mode of response to situations: they often appear even before our thoughts reach our minds. For example, in anger or fear, our bodies tense up and react even before we begin to mentalize what is annoying or scaring us. In the evolution of the species, the emotions always precede the appearance of spoken language. In this way they hold a sort of primacy over our ability to conceptualize, even though in human beings they are inseparable from thoughts, like a playing card or a coin where it is impossible to separate the two sides. Emotions appear to our minds simultaneously through corporeal feelings and through thoughts or modifications of our view of the world. That is the first point at which they can deceive us. We can be under the impression that it is the world as it is that is causing a problem, whereas actually it is our view of the world in the grip of emotion that is causing it. And then, in a third phase, we find the consequences of the emotions. All emotions entail what are called programs of tendency toward action. Anger pushes us toward aggressive or violent action, sadness toward withdrawal, fear toward flight, shame toward concealment or hiding, and so forth.

So what should I do when I am suffering? What should I do when I am in the grip of negative, destructive, painful emotions? A first piece of advice of the utmost importance: don't wait for the last moment. The patient, regular daily work of identification and regulation is always more effective than emergency intervention at the moment the fire breaks out.

MATTHIEU That's why we often compare the starting point of negative emotions to a spark that is easy to put out and emotional states that have been allowed to run wild to forest fires that are difficult to get under control.

CHRISTOPHE It is definitely much easier to work with our minor irritations, our petty sadness, our little anxieties, our minor shames, than with major flare-ups of the same emotions. With this in mind, I strongly encourage self-observation; that is, I advise keeping a journal in which a person can establish what the connections are between life events, the emotional impact they have on us, and then the thoughts and behaviors they engender. Putting words to our emotions, analyzing their process of development, their causalities, their repercussions—all that is much more complicated than it might appear. It seems to us in our heads that it is clear, but when we get to writing it down, we see that it takes real effort to understand ourselves! Laying things out rationally this way is a first requirement. It is part of a healthy lifestyle of inner balance.

The second type of work is experiential in nature. Every time an emotion occurs, take the time to explore it mindfully. When I say "mindfully," I am of course referring to the meditative approach called *mindfulness*. Simply put, without trying to change the emotion or control it or make it go away or soften it in any way, just accept it, observe what it is made of, what bodily states constitute it, what kind of thoughts it brings up. That's exactly what our patients to whom we teach mindfulness meditation do. Going through this process, it is clear why all the studies indicate that regular mindfulness practice leads to better regulation of our emotions.

We use exercises designed to "exhaust" certain emotions. We'll put patients in situations where they will feel an emotion at an extremely intense and uncomfortable level—for example, we get them to sing in the subway with everybody looking at them; or we get them to remain standing in a group of other patients who are seated. If the patient were in a real situation in real life, he would try to stop this emotion by using flight strategies. He would leave the room, the subway car.

Or if flight was impossible, he would try to think about something else or lower his eyes to lessen the intensity of his connection to the situation. There we would encourage him not to lower his eyes, to remain in the situation, to accept the emotion. In behavioral therapy, this is called *exposure*. Basically it involves disobeying the emotion: "In spite of your presence, fear, I'm going to stay here in this situation, breathing freely and letting my thoughts go by." When these experiences are repeated, the patient sees that the emotion gradually diminishes and that he is beginning to free himself from the power of these excesses of toxic emotion.

The more I feel in life, in the course of my day, positive emotions such as affection, admiration, compassion, happiness, well-being, joy, upliftedness, the less space there will be for the arising, expansion, and flaring up of painful, destructive, and negative emotions.

Then there is a third type of strategy that I use more and more now that I am working with positive psychology and that seems to resemble the work with antidotes that Matthieu frequently talks about. The idea is as follows: the more I feel in life, in the course of my day, positive emotions such as affection, admiration, compassion, happiness, well-being, joy, upliftedness, the less space there will be for the arising, expansion, and flaring up of painful, destructive, and negative emotions.

Is There Such a Thing as Addiction to Painful Emotions?

ALEXANDRE   There is something in the human soul that both fascinates and frightens me. It is the capacity we have to hurt ourselves. What is the use of guilt and brooding if not to spoil our lives? A friend of mine who's a worrier told me that he felt a sense of emptiness, out-and-out withdrawal, when his fears gave him a bit of a respite. Where does this cruel addiction come from? In the Epistle to the Romans, St. Paul provides a very disconcerting description: "For I do not do the good I want to do, but the evil I do not want to do—this I keep on doing." In this regard, the Greek philosophers spoke of acrasy, intemperance, the famous weakness of the will. No logical argument seems to have the strength to overcome certain habits. Very stupidly, I adore cashew nuts. Eating them gives me mouth sores, but I eat them anyhow. A thousand and one inner conflicts turn our inner life into a battlefield. Here too, the first step is to observe these struggles tranquilly without trying to solve the problem immediately. My weakness of will plays lots of tricks on me, which I often laugh about. For medical reasons, I had to lose weight, so I consulted a personal trainer, who strongly advised me to take up sport. He added, however, that the main thing was what happened in the kitchen and that I had to change my eating habits. The door had barely closed behind him when I rushed to the refrigerator and engaged in an eating orgy. Since I surely was going to screw up anyhow, I might as well go all the way! Why this nearly instant self-sabotage? In trying to be happy I find the same destructive forces. It's as though my mind has an autoimmune disease that causes it to attack its own integrity.

MATTHIEU   The fact that the discursive mind insists on perpetuating that which makes it suffer is one of the aspects of ignorance. Our problem is addiction to the causes of suffering. How does this addiction develop? In the beginning, pleasant sensations incite us to seek out what produced them again and again. But since it is in the nature of pleasant sensations to become duller the more we experience them, they gradually become neutral and even end up being unpleasant. But we still keep desiring them. The neurosciences have demonstrated that the neuronal networks in the brain associated with pleasure are not the same ones associated with desire, or wanting. The result of this is that through repetition we can reinforce the network connected with desire to the point of continuing to want something that has ceased to be pleasant and even makes us suffer. This is, roughly speaking, the definition of addiction. Even if we don't want to suffer, we can't keep from falling back into situations that cause us to suffer.

Eckhart Tolle explains this phenomenon of sometimes seeking out what hurts us in a picturesque way: When the ego fails in its narcissistic enterprises to continue to exist, it falls back on a plan B and builds itself a "pain-body," an alternative strategy for reinforcing its identity, this time in the mode of victim. In this way the ego can survive by feeding itself on complaints and recriminations. Even if no one else wants to listen to us, we endlessly recount our sad stories as we perpetuate our self-pity. We fully invest in this pain-body. According to Tolle, "the pain-body is the addiction to unhappiness." It feeds on negative thoughts and inner melodramas, but has trouble digesting positive thoughts. It stays alive by constantly chewing on the past and anxiously anticipating the future. It cannot survive in the pure air of the present moment, which is free of mental fabrications.

CHRISTOPHE   Why do we come to the point of causing ourselves to suffer? This is a question that concerns many people. Myself, I'm capable of doing things that I know will cause me pain, such as overworking, for example. However, I'm not sure we *like* to suffer. Some time ago, some of our psychiatric colleagues tended to treat women who had been beaten as masochists. They got two things mixed up. When a woman said, "I love him even though he beats me," that is not the same thing as saying, "I love him because he beats me." It's a little bit the same problem with regard to the violence one inflicts on oneself. It's not necessarily masochism. Often one might also do it because one doesn't know what else to do, like a dog who scratches itself so frenetically that it creates wounds but whose itching sensation is too strong to do otherwise.

MATTHIEU   Nagarjuna, the great Buddhist philosopher of the second century, wrote that it's good to scratch when you itch, but happiness is greater still when the itch is gone! He concluded from this that although it's good to satisfy desires, it is infinitely better to be free of them.

CHRISTOPHE   Sometimes we do absurd or painful things out of boredom. A recent study shows that when students are placed in a room for ten or fifteen minutes and they are given the choice of either doing nothing or administering small electric shocks to themselves, a significant number of them (two-thirds of the males and a third of the females) choose to give themselves electric shocks! It might be more reasonable to theorize that the younger generation, hooked on screens and music, has lost the habit of inaction or introspection, rather than jump to the conclusion that they are driven by masochism!

The same goes for food. Most of the time we don't eat because we're hungry but rather because we feel like eating, because we are attracted by food or it's mealtime. We confuse one pleasure with another. Am I really hungry, or do I just feel like sitting down to the table with my friends? Or do I want to eat just because the food smells good? There's a gap in awareness, a moment of absentmindedness. Typically it's a matter of inflicting suffering on ourselves or sometimes making a mistake that we know we're making, but at the moment of doing it we're not being attentive enough to what we really need. It's true that being vigilant and strict with ourselves can be painful or tiring, but being that way a little bit, a little bit more often, we can significantly reduce the suffering connected with these behaviors. It's a classic problem in addiction: taking drugs clearly ends up causing one pain. But nobody wants to suffer: in the beginning we're seeking pleasure; in the end we're just trying not to suffer from the state of withdrawal.

MATTHIEU Freeing oneself from addiction is a big challenge for three reasons. First, it's not enough to advise someone suffering from addiction to visualize the object of his addiction as something repellent. Quite often people hooked on something are already disgusted with it, but they can't help still wanting the thing that disgusts them. Second, freeing oneself from addiction takes an enormous effort of will. One of the effects of addiction is to weaken the activity of the areas of the brain that are connected with willpower. Third, to kick an addiction one has to train oneself to gain control over the impulsive desire connected with this addiction. But addiction inhibits the activity of the hippocampus, a region of the brain that normally makes it possible to translate training, of whatever kind, into functional and structural modifications of the brain. (This is what is called neuroplasticity.) These three obstacles make it particularly difficult to heal oneself of an addiction.

ALEXANDRE The path of happiness requires a detailed process of unlearning. In Christian mysticism, as in the Zen tradition, we are encouraged to die to ourselves, to leave everything behind—our convictions, habits, desires, illusions. First we have to liberate ourselves, then we have to strip naked. By the way, in Japanese, the term that means "achieve salvation" also means "to get undressed." So why not begin immediately with this inner clearing out? The fact that Buddhism insists on the right means of livelihood tells me that it is impossible to attain happiness if I lead an uncontrolled, stress-ridden, egotistical life. How can I reach peace if from morning till night I only obey my ego? To free oneself little by little from a lifestyle that is hostile to peace of mind, it may perhaps be necessary to go back to this Aristotelian insight: "It is by smithing that one becomes a smith." That means that practicing virtue is what makes us virtuous. For this, a conversion is required: If I wait until I'm confident before I perform confident deeds, there's a good chance of postponing progress forever. We have to do just the opposite—we have to dare to take concrete action right now.

Fortunately we're not alone on this ground. Sometimes all we need is to immerse ourselves in the way of life of those who have preceded us on the path. Who better to give us a fresh push to root out the toxins of discursive mind one after the other? On the other hand, in the company of bad-mouthing and malicious people, our virtue withers. If we spend our days planting bad seeds, we shouldn't be surprised if we find thistles and thorns all over the place.

Meditating is learning to defuse the bombs that rain down in our minds and to let float away the scenarios in which we imagine ourselves to be super-tough guys. When the discursive mind serves up as though on a platter the worst stuff there is in us, just simply observe; don't do anything. When the storms of the mind are raging, abstaining from reacting sometimes takes almost superhuman courage. What helps is knowing that the ugly weather shaking my ego might be a ten on the emotional Richter scale, but it still won't kill me. Indefatigably, always, one has to let the emotion pass, not feed it, let it exhaust itself by itself. This long ascesis, repeated a thousand times a day, consists in letting yourself float among the waves until you see that they don't last.

The Desert Fathers remind us that the bigger deal we make of ourselves, the more we suffer. The challenge consists precisely in taking on this paradox: take good care of yourself, respect your own rhythm, but at the same time liberate yourself from that little ego that keeps driving you nuts. Uprooting the negative emotions is more like a marathon than a sprint, hence the danger of becoming exhausted before the race is over. Because of that it is urgent for us not to delay in eliminating what is weighing us down. Among the burdensome emotions, denial and outrage never seem to quit. A Zen nun gave me a masterful lesson one day. This young woman of forty was suffering from an incurable cancer. She told me that for a long time she had considered the disease an enemy. For months she roused herself to do battle with this adversary, until the day when, thanks to meditation, she began to view the cancer as a friend, a messenger, a liberator. It isn't necessary to receive a blow as heavy as this to get started on a radical change of view. Our little troubles provide us with enough opportunities to move forward on this. Meditating, trying to understand, making progress—all that is fine; but never without infinite patience with regard to our weaknesses. Sometimes we really need a short truce in the battle to be able to drop our weapons.

MATTHIEU The Tibetan word we translate as "renunciation" is actually associated with the determination to liberate ourselves, not with depriving ourselves of what is truly good in life. At a certain point, we no longer tolerate our addiction to the causes of suffering. When a bird escapes from its cage, we can't say that it renounced its cage—it liberated itself from it. Whether the cage is made of iron or gold makes no difference.

The Myth of Emotional Apathy

MATTHIEU   Some people think that liberating ourselves from the emotions results in an inner void that turns us into zombies. They are getting freedom of the mind mixed up with a mental void. The goal is not to make thoughts and emotions disappear but to prevent them from proliferating and enslaving us. Masters and students who attained great inner freedom did not turn into vegetables. On the contrary, they manifest more good qualities than other people. The Dalai Lama, in my opinion, is a perfect example of courage, joy, compassion, and openness to others. He has simply emancipated himself from the mental states that usually distort the mind. By eliminating hate, resentment, greed, and other disturbing emotions from our mental space, we make room for altruistic love, joy, and inner peace.

> The goal is not to make thoughts and emotions disappear but to prevent them from proliferating and enslaving us.

CHRISTOPHE   Several studies show that when experienced meditators are exposed to situations designed to arouse emotion—photos of disfigured children or unpleasant scenes—their minds are not at all dulled by emotion. What is observed is simply a diffusion of the emotional impact in their brains that is different from the comparable event in the brains of nonmeditators. Notably there is less activation of certain areas of the prefrontal cortex that are associated with, among other things, processes described as self-referential (focusing on oneself, thinking of oneself). Roughly speaking, the emotional activation is there (meditation does not desensitize you), sensitivity is not modified, but the nature of the cerebral activation is not the same (meditation permits greater detachment).

MATTHIEU   Very revealing studies have been carried out involving both practitioners and nonpractitioners of meditation that allow us to see, using MRIs, which areas of the cerebral neuronal networks are activated. In this case, the idea was to identify which parts of the brain become active when a practitioner engages in a meditation with attention focused on altruistic love, open presence, and so on. Each type of meditation has a different "signature" in the brain. The brain gradually changes, functionally and structurally, as one trains. The person also changes of course, that being the object of the exercise. So in one of these studies, for example, a group of experienced meditators and then a group of beginners had the sound of a woman screaming with fright played for them. It was observed that the seasoned practitioners heard the cries without manifesting reactions of avoidance or distress. However, at the same time a whole range of positive emotions, such as empathy, solicitude, compassion, was observed. In the case of the control group, which listened to the same cries, people tried to carry out a kind of mental anesthesia. The practitioners reacted similarly when subjected to pain. They perceived its intensity as much as, if not more than, the untrained subjects, but they manifested less apprehension when the intensity of the pain was increased and quickly regained their composure when the pain stopped.

How to Cultivate Benevolence

MATTHIEU   In Buddhism there is a fundamental notion that is also found in positive psychology: the absence of negative mental states does not necessarily entail the presence of positive mental states. In other words, joy is not just the absence of sadness, benevolence is not the mere absence of malevolence, and so on. Simply remediating the negative states results in a neutral state but not in the positive states that bring a sense of fulfillment.

CHRISTOPHE   Complementing what you're saying in the framework of therapy, when you cure people of depression, the idea is not to leave them in a neutral state but in a state where they can experience the positive emotions once again. These emotions will be presented to them by their life circumstances and by other people, but if they have not been taught to receive them better or to engender them themselves, that's not enough.

MATTHIEU In positive psychology they say that the absence of a pathological state is not necessarily an optimal state, it's just a "normal" one, whereas an optimal state has to be specifically cultivated. In other words, the normal state only makes it possible to function normally, but to live in an optimal fashion or to fully actualize one's potential, one has to cultivate other values such as benevolence and compassion, and liberate one's mind from the grip of disturbing thoughts.

CHRISTOPHE I believe that love, compassion, gentleness, and intelligence are contagious. Every time you perform an act of tenderness, affection, or love, every time you uncloud somebody's mind by giving them a piece of good advice, you alter the future of mankind a tiny bit in the right direction. And every time you say something stupid or do something nasty, and every time those things are repeated, it's a setback to the progress of humanity. So each person cultivating the greatest possible number of positive feelings and deeds is vital for everybody.

MATTHIEU To cultivate compassion you have to begin by realizing that, fundamentally, everyone wants to avoid suffering and aspires to be happy. Realizing this is of particular importance for those who have a negative image of themselves, who have suffered a great deal and believe that they are not made for happiness. What those people have to learn first is to be tolerant and compassionate toward themselves.

Once you have recognized your own aspiration to happiness, it is important to realize that this aspiration is common to all beings. Then you will feel closer to them; you will be sensitized to the value of their aspirations and be concerned for their destinies.

The point is, you have to train in compassion. In the beginning it is easier to do it by thinking of someone who is dear to you. You let yourself be pervaded by love and unconditional compassion toward that person, and you remain in that state for a moment or two. Next you extend that compassion to beings you know less well. They also want to be happy. Then you go even further. You include in your compassion even people who have wronged you or are harming the world. You don't wish for them to succeed in their harmful actions but rather for them to be liberated from their hatred, greed, cruelty, or indifference, and for them to learn to be concerned for the welfare of others. You view them the same way a doctor views his sickest patients. And, finally, you embrace the totality of all beings in a feeling of boundless love.

Happiness and Joy

CHRISTOPHE   Being pretty much a quiet introvert, for a long time I was distrustful of joy because I was afraid it could go too far, that it was very close in that respect to excitement and euphoria. Happiness, on the other hand, seemed like a positive emotion that was just as pleasant as joy but with two advantages over it: in general, it does not arouse agitation, and it is discreet. Being more inward than joy, it was less likely to offend others. Since then, I have reviewed this classification in my mind and I recognize that joy, through its contagious quality, its spontaneous, almost animal quality, has a great deal to offer others. When the people we love are joyous, we are ready and willing to be contaminated.

ALEXANDRE   If I insist on joy, it's because it seems much simpler, more accessible to me than happiness. It seems to me that the imperative to "be happy at all costs" leaves many people by the wayside. Being more humble, joy also seems to me to be closer to our weaknesses, to our limitations. I can get to it even if I am suffering from chronic pain or passing through a period of mourning. There is nothing that needs to be crushed in order to heed its call. Even someone working hard from morning till night can have this experience. Why equate joy with exuberance, superficiality, when above all it is saying yes? It is a profound and authentic yes to reality just as it comes. Luckily, we have Spinoza to remind us that joy is the passage of man from a lesser to a greater perfection. Every time life gains some ground, every time I make some progress, joy swells my heart. One step further and truly it will be the ego that bursts. In *The Eighth Day*, Christian Bobin refers to "an elementary joy of the universe that is darkened whenever one pretends to be someone or know something."[1]

MATTHIEU   I have the feeling that we are fundamentally in agreement but that we are attributing slightly different meanings to the words *joy* and *happiness*. Buddhism describes a profound happiness, *sukha* in Sanskrit, that pervades and underlies all our experiences, whether they are joys or sorrows, and that at the same time is a state of wisdom that has been freed of all the mental afflictions and, consequently, perceives the true nature of things. It is intimately bound with understanding the way the mind works. Joy, *ananda* in Sanskrit, is a kind of radiance of sukha. It fills the present moment with bliss. When it becomes more and more frequent, it forms a continuum that we might call joie de vivre.

Some psychologists say that it is impossible to be happy in prison, because the happiness that one might feel in such conditions is, in their view, unjustifiable. But we have the case of an American friend of mine, Fleet Maull, who was sentenced to many years of prison for a drug offense. He lived for a long time in an overcrowded room with no windows, where there was noise at all times. It was in these extremely painful circumstances that he began to meditate several hours a day. In the beginning he found it very difficult, quite understandably, but he persevered. After eight years he became absolutely convinced of the effectiveness of spiritual practice, of the transformative power of compassion and of nonreality of the ego.

One day he was called to the bedside of another prisoner who was dying and was his friend, and for five days he kept him company through the dying process. Following this event, more and more often he felt a sense of freedom and immense joy. His inner confidence had led him to experience something indestructible, independent of circumstances, even though his situation was barely tolerable. I think that in this case it was sukha, which is a lasting way of perceiving the world rather than a transitory joy.

ALEXANDRE I am literally wonderstruck by people who have persevered in joy despite the blows of fate. Poverty, injustice, and disease don't have the last word. This mystery, this hope, is worth all the learned discourses in the world. Knowing true joy is discovering in everything an opportunity to liberate oneself, to grow, and maybe even to rejoice. This inner accessibility, this humble and infinitely profound giving of the self, lies far beyond mere feeling. It is not a naive "hooray" but a genuine, serene yea-saying, a yes addressed to what is. I like the fact that St. Paul makes joy a fruit of the Spirit—the fact that it is something that remains accessible to the poorest and most deprived makes me happy and consoles me profoundly. We shouldn't make an honors list of the best emotions—that would mean still being attached to them. We have to make our journey without baggage.

MATTHIEU Each person expresses himself through the words that make sense for him. But it seems to me that the joy Alexandre is speaking of corresponds to what others have described as an inner freedom that allows them to deal with adversity.

CHRISTOPHE I am simply uncomfortable with the hierarchization "joy is better than happiness" or "happiness is better than joy." All the positive emotions—joy, happiness, etc.—occur when one feels harmoniously connected with the world, whereas the negative emotions are always a mark of a rupture in the connection between the world and us, whether we're talking about anger, sadness, or fear. My profound conviction is that for ordinary beings like us, with the exception of a few sages, joy, happiness, and love are perforce unstable states that are not given to us to experience in a lasting way. It's an illusion to try to preserve them in a can. We have to accept once and for all that we are just part-timers when it comes to happiness, joy, and love, and this is absolutely normal. That is why we have to make an effort to make them reappear regularly in our lives. We need both joy and happiness. When I'm happy, it seems to me that I'm reconciled with my past and my future, whereas joy anchors me firmly in the present and gives me the full measure of grace of being a living being in this instant.

ALEXANDRE   The notion of impermanence heals us from a lot of our pain. And the idea of being a part-timer in relation to happiness provides deep solace. Giving up clinging to anything is what makes it possible for us to progressively extract ourselves from conflicts and unhappiness. For someone in daily pain, it is encouraging to see that neither weakness nor fatigue nor sickness nor disability nor—in a word—the imperfection of the world puts joy out of reach for us. The appropriate exercise is to tirelessly dare nonfixation. Everything is ephemeral, even unhappiness. The words of Spinoza say the essential and serve me as a motto: "Do good and remain joyful."

MATTHIEU   Canned happiness is the illusion that it is possible to indefinitely prolong a kind of perpetual euphoria, as Pascal Bruckner puts it, based on circumstances; whereas, in actual fact, by nature happiness can only be ephemeral and fragile. Perhaps it could be said that joy is more related to the quality of the present moment, and happiness, in the sense of sukha, has a lasting mode of existence that corresponds in a certain way to our state of inner freedom. It is a state, as Georges Bernanos writes, that "nothing can change, like the vast reserve of calm waters beneath a storm."

Our Advice for the Good Use of the Emotions

Advice for Profound Development   MATTHIEU

- Sharpen your attention in order to become aware of negative emotions the very moment they arise. It is easier to put out a spark than a forest fire.

- Get to know the emotions better. Train in distinguishing those that contribute to your well-being and the well-being of others from those that destroy it.

- Once the harmful consequences of negative emotions appear clearly, familiarize yourself with their antidotes, the positive emotions.

- Cultivate the positive emotions until you become one with them.

Dealing with Emotions   CHRISTOPHE

- Love all of them. All the emotions are signals of our needs. The positive emotions tell us that our needs are satisfied or on the way to being so. The negative emotions tell us that they are not satisfied. Listen to, and reflect on, what is happening with your basic needs in order to act.

- Cultivate the pleasant emotions. Take care to nourish them in a way that is beyond the automatic mechanisms of your habits. Studies have shown that experiencing two to three times more pleasant feelings than unpleasant ones is an optimal balance, and a realistic one (you can't always be in a good mood).

- Don't get discouraged. It is one of the great tasks in your life to work on your emotional balance. And you will regularly have relapses; you will once again fall prey to absurd fits of anger, inappropriate fears, and exaggerated sadness. You have to take into account from the very beginning that the journey will be punctuated with these lapses. That's why I detest sayings such as "A leopard cannot change its spots" that tell us we can never change. We are in a training period, an apprenticeship, therefore we have to accept these relapses. There are no shortcuts on this journey. But you always get to your destination if you keep walking.

Let It Pass, Practice, Clear Out Your Mind ALEXANDRE

- Let it pass. Zen encourages us not to consider emotion as an enemy. Thus spiritual practice consists in not getting on the train of negative emotions but watching its cars pass by. "Hey, here's anger." "Hey, here's fear." Daring nonfixation allows us to get through storms without carnage. It's no big deal if anger, fear, or sadness pay me a visit. Provided that they never set up housekeeping in my heart. So a thousand times a day, let it pass.

- Practice. Learning to swim, to float, and to calmly watch the waves go by takes time—lots of time. Peace comes inch by inch. That is why it is necessary to devote yourself to practice daily.

- Clear out the temple of your mind. For a long time I thought that happiness came from victory. Today I think instead that it's a matter of clearing ourselves out. Rather than accumulating skills or knowledge, we must get free of all the things that weigh us down: habits, reflexes, fears, cravings . . . The nugget of happiness, of true joy, lies beneath tons of mud. So let's throw out all that useless stuff and turn the obstacles of life into skillful means for getting through to that joy.

4

The Art of Listening

The Characteristics of True Listening

CHRISTOPHE   Listening is a process similar to humility, in which one puts others before oneself. Highly narcissistic people listen badly, and at times when we are anxious, euphoric, or caught up in too many self-centered preoccupations, we are not capable of quality listening. Even though we can sometimes pretend we're listening!

There are three basic mechanisms in listening: respect for the other's speech, letting go, and the ability to allow oneself to be touched. Respecting the other's speech is above all not judging what the other is saying while we're listening. We automatically tend to judge what we hear: we appreciate it, don't appreciate it, agree, disagree; we find it accurate or stupid. It is difficult to keep these judgments from reaching our minds, but when we notice them, we can acknowledge them and detach from them, and then do our best to return to true listening.

> In true listening, you don't prepare your response— you just listen and let go.

The second movement in listening is letting go. My patients have taught me this. Highly timid and highly anxious people are so afraid of not being up to the level of the people they're talking to that they listen badly, because they are already preparing how they're going to respond. In true listening, you don't prepare your response—you just listen and let go. You might sometimes have the feeling that this approach is a bit risky, but your answer will be more profound and appropriate if you have totally abandoned the idea of preparing it.

This letting go is also the condition for sincere and authentic listening in which you are ready to let yourself be touched, be moved, be without judgment, be without control, be without desire to dominate. Ultimately you let yourself be there with no intention at all.

My introverted temperament has always resulted in, without any effort or merit on my part, my preferring listening to talking. Even so, I have seen how, over time and through working on it, I have been able to improve my ability to listen, notably through the practice of meditation. Meditation has taught me how to be there without preparing my responses, how to totally let go, and how to render myself totally permeable and open toward what others are saying.

In the profession of caregiver, this is not all that common. Studies show that on average, doctors interrupt their patients after twenty or thirty seconds.[1] They tend to look for symptoms, quickly find out the answers to their questions, and then dominate the exchange. Several of my colleagues—old, very experienced general practitioners—have told me that almost all the mistakes made in caring for patients result from listening errors. Doctors don't let their patients talk enough, they don't ask them enough questions, they are too quick to push the exchange to where they think it should go. They think that giving care is providing diagnoses, then prescribing and advising. They think it's about providing medicine and advice more than it's about listening. This is a little bit like the profession of parenting. You want to give your children advice, educate them, console them, fix their problems, and you tend not to let them talk at times when it would be precious for them to do so.

As for listening in couples, there is an exercise in couples therapy for when it is very difficult to have one of the two speaking without the other interrupting, looking up at the ceiling, or fidgeting in his or her chair. You tell them, "You're going to talk about the way you see the situation, and your partner is going to go sit on the other side of the room, turn his or her back, and just listen. I don't want to hear a word from him or her. He or she is simply going to listen attentively for five or ten minutes, and then we'll reverse the roles." For the same reason, I sometimes encourage my patients to write to their partner when they have difficulty talking to each other. First, in writing you frequently go straight to the essential; you are less subject to impulse and therefore also less subject to aggression and resentment. But also here the partner is going to be obliged to read patiently without interrupting or trying to justify him- or herself. Reading is like listening without the possibility of immediate response. It slightly increases the chances that ·the messages of the other will be received.

MATTHIEU   Listening is a gift one gives to the other party. To listen well, it is not only necessary to be patient with the other, but it is also necessary to be concerned for the speaker. In the case of the Dalai Lama, the quality that most strikes people who meet him, aside from the compassion he shows for all, is the way he listens. He is totally and immediately present to the person to whom he is speaking, in private or in public, even if they are just a passerby at the airport.

Because of lack of consideration for the other, we often imagine that we know what our interlocutor is trying to say and that we have already understood the ins and outs of the problem. Condescendingly, we sometimes make a premature, incomplete response that is often inappropriate. Even if we come up with some sound advice, we still keep the other person from communicating. It is very frustrating to not be able to finish your thought.

Many people complain about not being listened to. It seems to them that the other person is not interested in them. Political debates furnish frequent examples of this kind of indifference. The protagonists start interrupting each other immediately, and then when that still doesn't satisfy them, they all end up speaking at the same time, as though it's a sign of weakness to let the other person talk, an unacceptable concession.

It's better to let the other person talk and take the time to point out calmly if he or she has made some errors. The first step in listening should be to show that one is sincerely interested in offering undivided attention.

Some people are pretty much incapable of listening to others. I remember a Bhutanese official whom I often had to deal with. When I asked him a question, he never waited for the end of my sentence and replied in advance, "No, no, no!" That led to some pretty funny exchanges, such as, "Do you think we can leave tomorrow?"

"No, no, no! Be ready at nine o'clock."

I myself tend to reply a little too fast, anticipating what people are going to say, and even if it turns out that I've guessed right, it's not a good way to talk to someone. I often regret it, and I must correct it!

CHRISTOPHE We all do what you are describing—when we are upset, in a hurry, or sometimes when we're tired. People come to see us, they start talking. We imagine in advance how their sentences are going to end, what they want to tell us, and we give them answers that might be relevant, but without really ever having listened to them. In that way, we've only done half our work. When the other person speaks, he doesn't only want to get answers but also wants to feel your presence, some solidarity, some affection.

What Exactly Does Listening Without Judging Mean?

MATTHIEU The important thing is not to judge the other as a person. That doesn't keep us from judging what he says or does from the point of view of the well-being or suffering that might flow from it, or from understanding the reasons that have led him to cause harm to himself or others, if that is the case.

One can judge others in two ways: absolute or relative. Judging absolutely is decreeing that someone is fundamentally bad, that they have no empathy at all, that they will never stop complaining because that's how they are and there's no reason for that to change. This type of judgment that presumes character traits are carved in stone once and for all is contradicted by the experience of meditation and by the discoveries of the last twenty years in the fields of neuroplasticity (our brain changes from being exposed to new situations or as the result of physical or mental training) and epigenetics (even our genes can be modified). Studies in these areas have proven that it is possible to change the manner in which we manage our thoughts, emotions, moods, and, finally, even our character traits.

Relative judgment, on the other hand, only applies to the current, temporary situation of the person we are judging. Even if someone manifests unpleasant character traits and behaviors, we can take into account the role of their personal evolution and their environment. We don't judge the person himself but rather his state of mind at the moment and the factors that have influenced his conduct. If somebody hits you with a stick, you don't get mad at the stick; you know that behind the stick there is an individual. Let's take that reasoning further. This individual is manipulated by hate, which, in turn, has its source in ignorance. So it is really hate that we should consider as the enemy, not the person. By looking at it this way we don't escape the problem posed by the person's behavior, but we leave the door open to compassion for that person who is the victim of hate and ignorance.

CHRISTOPHE I have the feeling that there are situations in which the moment of judgment, the moment of diagnosis, and the moment of giving advice should definitely be separated from the moment of listening. It seems to me that in dealing with patients I don't necessarily agree with as human beings, being in a state of listening, as far away as possible from judging, can have a very significant impact on them. If I'm judging them when I'm listening to them, even slightly, they feel it. And frequently I notice that the simple fact of being listened to with kindness helps people see the absurdity of some of their points of view. When the person has finished talking, I ask them for further clarification: "So if I understand you correctly, you behave like that?" And I have the impression that when I manage to defer anything having to do with judgment, not only do I listen better but also the work of transformation begins right there. At a certain point, of course I will have to revise my ideas, and, moreover, sometimes I take the time to do that, which I didn't used to do. For example, I say to the patient, "Give me a few minutes now, before I answer you, to reflect on what you just told me."

MATTHIEU   I understand your point of view, but what I was talking about had more to do with the diagnosis a doctor would arrive at on the basis of compassion, by being attentive to all the systems and evaluating the potential for suffering that is present, without making a moral judgment. The compassion that underlies this approach has the sole purpose of putting an end to any form of suffering. That said, it is without doubt very comforting for patients to be able to say to themselves, "Here's someone who is listening to me and trying sincerely to understand me."

CHRISTOPHE   Yes, I see that my patients fully understand that. But earlier on I didn't dare do that because it seemed to me that, as a technician, I had to have ready-made solutions at hand. It seems to me I do better work when I succeed in separating listening and analysis, even if I do it artificially, even if maybe implicitly judgment is always there. Moreover, that's what we say to patients about mindfulness practice: You can't keep yourself from judging, but you can be aware of the presence of the judgments. And to the best of your ability, tirelessly open your attention to your presence, to your listening, to your breath. Judgment is there, thoughts are there, but don't reduce yourself to just this judgment, to just these thoughts.

The Face of Listening

CHRISTOPHE   Twenty years ago I worked a lot with patients suffering from anxiety and social phobias. Such patients are very ill at ease during verbal exchanges and quickly detect, sometimes mistakenly, expressions of judgment or rejection on the face of their interlocutor. I remember well the difficulty some of my patients were having talking to me. My way of listening was disturbing for them. "When you listen to me, you frown and I get the feeling you don't agree with me," they would say. And, truly, I was so immersed in empathy that their story was painful for me, and I had a pained expression on my face. Since then I have understood that even the expression on my face has to reflect benevolence. I have made progress. I listen to them with compassion, smiling gently, and try to carry over onto my face something that has the quality of compassion and not mere empathy.

MATTHIEU This misunderstanding reminds me of a story told to me by Aaron Beck, the founder of cognitive therapy, when he was still a psychoanalyst. He was listening, in silence, to a patient doing free association. After a while he noticed that she seemed upset. When he asked her what was troubling her, she exploded, "I've been talking to you for an hour now, and I have the impression that you're paying no attention at all to what I'm saying!" Aaron Beck asked her, "But why didn't you say so?" The patient replied, "I thought it wouldn't fit the rules of free association." At that moment Aaron Beck realized that something was wrong with the system of psychoanalysis. What was bothering his patient as he was listening to her was not that her brother had stolen her raspberry tart when she was five years old, but the thought, of course unfounded, that her analyst was not listening to her. He concluded from that that the most important thing was to teach patients how to manage their emotions in the present moment, how to become aware of the distortions of reality they indulge in, and to begin freeing themselves from what is troubling them right here and now. That's one of the reasons he decided to give up psychoanalysis and found a school of therapy, called *cognitive behavioral therapy*, which since that time has proven its effectiveness.

What you say reminds me of Paul Ekman, who distinguishes two types of emotional resonance: convergent and divergent. In convergent resonance, I suffer when you suffer; I feel anger when I see you being angry. If, for example, your wife comes home very upset because her boss behaved badly with her, indignantly you exclaim, "What a boor! How could he have treated you that way!" In divergent resonance, instead of feeling the same emotion as your wife, you step back and while retaining your concern you say, "I'm really sorry that you have to deal with such a jerk. What can I do for you? Would you like a cup of tea, or would you rather take a walk?" In both cases, the other person appreciates your concern with their feelings.

Parasites on Listening

ALEXANDRE   Basically we come equipped with two ears but no manual to tell us how to use them. In my turn, I too will risk suggesting a few implements that we can slip into our listening toolbox. Listening is what you say, Christophe, letting go; and not judging the other absolutely, as you say, Matthieu. Nothing is worse here than the boxer's approach—trying to deliver a knockout blow to your opponent. Epicurus was right to point out, "In trying to learn together through discussion, he who loses wins more since he is the one who has increased his knowledge." To put it simply, I can immediately stop systematically anticipating my interlocutor's responses and especially put an end to the nasty tendency to put words in his mouth.

Learning to listen also entails identifying the parasites that are creating static on the line. Heidegger's notion of *ambiguity* certainly helps to see the problems. Too often I don't fully listen to the other, and I refer everything back to myself, to my history, to my mental categories. This is a vicious impulse that drives us to toss off phrases such as "That reminds me of my mother-in-law," "You remind me of my cousin," "I went through the same thing as a kid." I keep

> Listening means stopping, daring not to have a ready-made response, ceasing to enshroud the other in endless labels.

coming back to *my* opinions without letting the other person really exist. Listening means stopping, daring not to have a ready-made response, ceasing to enshroud the other in endless labels. The notion of ambiguity also vaccinates me against the risk of turning suffering into something banal.

MATTHIEU   Why particularly the word *ambiguity*?

ALEXANDRE   Because in overlaying the history of my interlocutor with my history, I deny him the right to be different. I deny that there might be more than one interpretation of the real. I bring everything back to me. I create a sort of forced equivalence between the other and me. I shut him up in my scenarios.

It takes real ascesis to get out of that. Fortunately we can rely on the masters in this regard. Socrates, for example, gives us a wake-up call to keep us from shutting ourselves up in cookie-cutter definitions. So many misunderstandings and mistakes cut us off from the other. So learning to identify all the prejudgments we are burdened with is a matter of the utmost urgency.

We also have to wipe out condescension. My teachers often hit me with an "I understand" that often didn't sound too authentic. I had the impression they were looking down from the top of a cliff on a child drowning far below. This regard from on high, far from consoling me, accentuated my solitude. Yes, these phrases such as "I know you as well as I know myself" or "I understand where you're coming from" really have to be employed with the greatest caution. Not shutting up the other in our mental templates, being always able to marvel at the uniqueness of every person is a major step toward freedom.

Listening is above all remaining silent and daring not to be too closely guided by our inner radio, our Conceptual Mind FM Radio, which comments on everything. From morning till night, it judges, analyzes, compares. The more importance I give that, the less available I am to another person. The exercise here is to become aware of the thousand and one thoughts that come between me and the other. Even if we can't turn off our radio, it's already enough if we can become aware of the interference it creates. Let's recognize that at times we are so overwhelmed by these radio waves that the other hardly exists at all. How can we listen to a parent who has lost a child when we are totally paralyzed by the idea that such a thing might also happen to us?

Fatigue, discouragement, haste . . . So many factors affect the quality of our listening. Without actually being present, I am merely in the same location as my interlocutor. That is why it is necessary to listen to the interlocutor's body, mind, and psychological state in order to remain present.

Words can kill or cure. I remember one day scolding my son Augustin for some minor issue about his homework. His words were

> I try to relate to the words that hurt me as mere sounds, inoffensive in themselves. Why give them so much power? Why confer on them the power to destroy joy? Letting these sounds, this wind, just pass—that is the challenge.

a lesson to me: "Papa, when you were yelling at me, I pretended your words were caresses." Since then, in the face of mockery, criticism, or bad news, I try to relate to the words that hurt me as mere sounds, inoffensive in themselves. Why give them so much power? Why confer on them the power to destroy joy? Letting these sounds, this wind, just pass—that is the challenge.

MATTHIEU Dilgo Khyentse Rinpoche used to say that if we give too much credence to all the words we hear, our minds come to resemble grass that is blown back and forth by the wind in the high mountains. He also gave the advice not to be overcome by vanity when receiving compliments. It's better to think that the praise is like words heard in dreams, or that it is not for us but for qualities that others think they see in us. On the other hand, if we receive justified criticism, it is best to be humble and take that opportunity to recognize our own faults.

ALEXANDRE Lending an attentive, compassionate ear also means identifying the parasites: fatigue, stress, projections, fear, and anger. Basically it's a matter of making ourselves inwardly available. Often I miss the point when somebody tells me of his suffering. Helpless, I serve up some platitudes in order not to just say nothing. So why should we not simply admit, "I'm with you with all my heart, *but* I'm dead tired and I don't know what to say." At the hospital when my dad was about to die, I also sensed the danger of just filling the void, hiding embarrassment under a flood of empty words. It's an awkwardness that comes from an inability to endure silence.

CHRISTOPHE Sometimes when we go to the hospital to see someone who is dying or fighting illness, a little commonplace talk can be comforting. People might think that palliative care workers spend the time talking about life and death, but most of the time the conversation is on ordinary subjects. You watch television with the patients, talk about the weather, who's coming to visit, or the menu. It's not easy for everybody to get into serious and solemn subjects in these situations. I have a lot of admiration for people who have the courage to pay regular visits to patients in palliative care. No matter what they talk about, their presence is already an extraordinary gift.

MATTHIEU It's fallen to me a few times to stay with a dying person, and it always seemed to me that the best way to be with them was just to be present, in silence, to look at them with affection, take their hand—without being intrusive. You have to be totally available, with compassion but without an agenda.

> You have to be totally available, with compassion but without an agenda.

ALEXANDRE "Totally available but without an agenda"—what an example of the art of living! Silence is something you learn. And it takes a heap of courage not to jump on the least pretext for breaking it. In the beginning, when I was talking with my spiritual father on the phone, I was struck by his long silences. I always thought we had been disconnected. So I got nervous: "Are you still there?" And tirelessly he would reply, "Yes, I'm listening." Every time this happened I discovered a new possibility for another quality of being, for an immense inner availability. Praying is plunging into silence totally, being mute and listening. Meister Eckhart initiated me into this contemplative life. Before him, my prayer consisted of a long series of requests; I was filling the void. Now I'm beginning to abandon the requests, or rather I enlarge them to include humanity and all suffering beings. Prayer comes from being available every moment, from the wakefulness in which you learn to say yes to whatever comes, without rejecting anything, without ever clinging.

I remember the good priest who told me, "In the silence, let God worry about God. Just become pure listening." At the beginning of his Rule, St. Benedict says, "Listen, O my son, to the invitation of the master, and lend the ear of your heart." Concretely, at any moment I can descend into the depths of my being to discover silence and peace beneath the din and racket of conceptual mind.

Daring to Be Silent

ALEXANDRE   Here's what is perhaps an eminently revolutionary act: daring to live a contemplative life. Sometimes it amounts to flat-out rebellion. On the path, there's no lack of obstacles. For a few years now I've committed myself to my spiritual father to meditate an hour a day. And for me, to put it bluntly, this is a matter of life and death. If I hadn't taken this time to dare to slow down and live a bit less mechanically, I would have gone down the drain a long time ago. When I'm laboring under a lot of obligations, I'm always hoping to find some little corner where I can get some work done—in a taxi, at a bus stop, anywhere. But where can you go to get away from the noise? One might say that silence is frightening, that it suggests the void, death; that it awakens ghosts, betokens a deficit. But immersing yourself in it is entering into a healing fullness. Praying, meditating, means abandoning roles and labels and living from silence to silence. But the trial you have to go through to get there can be severe. For agitation to disperse and calm to dawn, you have to pass through a lot of desert.

In the meditation hall on a very stormy day, I felt that calm was still there in the basic ground of my being. Outside, lightning and thunder were raging and great sheets of water were pouring down. Suddenly I became aware that I was listening to the rain in a dry place. I truly perceived that nothing, absolutely nothing, can damage our minds. Since then, when anger or fear reappear, I keep that memory with me, the taste of that experience. I can listen to the rain from a dry place, let fears and bad moods quietly pass.

MATTHIEU   My dear mother often says, "Silence is the language of the future." From my retreat place in Nepal, I see the Himalayan range extending before me for two hundred kilometers. The silence is so perfect I can hear the farmers from more than a kilometer away, and sometimes the deafening noise of a storm front coming toward me and getting stronger as it approaches. The external silence opens the doors of inner silence. That way it is easier to experience the freshness of the present moment, which takes us closer to the ultimate nature of things.

I remember an autumn morning when I was sitting alone on the shore of the great Lake Manasarovar, at forty-six hundred meters of altitude, near Mount Kailash. The sky was an intense blue and its luminosity was nearly blinding. The silence was perfect. Suddenly I distinctly heard cries that I recognized as those of mandarin ducks. I scanned the surroundings without being able to locate them. Then I finally saw them, floating peacefully two hundred meters from the shore. Their cries were carried over the surface of the lake, and I had heard them as though they were coming from right next to me. I thought of an episode in the life of the great yogi Shabkar, who one day was on the shores of this same lake, at the end of the eighteenth century, and who later wrote: "One day as I was resting on the lakeshore, I experienced a freedom devoid of any object of concentration, a clear, vast, and open state."[2]

In meditation, in the moment between when past thoughts have ceased and before the next thoughts have arisen, there is an inner silence, an absence of mental gossip, the freshness of the present moment. Ideally one could allow one's mind to rest in this state of inner clarity and simplicity. With great mastery in meditation, one can remain in this silence in the middle of traffic jams or in the crush of the crowded subway. If this isn't possible, it is important to seek out conditions that are conducive to meditation.

ALEXANDRE   Resting in this vast peace is dying the great death from which one is reborn more alive, born anew. For a long time I thought only the saints and sages were in a position to do this. But this ascesis is perhaps simpler than it appears. A hundred times a day I can

Silence, like the nature of our being, cannot be tainted. One can yell at it, hurl the worst insults at it, but nothing can trouble it. In the same way in the ground of all grounds, the basic ground of being, there is a part that remains always inviolable, which no blow of fate can damage. Any of us, as wounded as we may be, can relocate, can sink down into this joy.

do the exercise of dying to my little ego, of setting aside the world of ideas somewhat. Silence, like the nature of our being, cannot be tainted. One can yell at it, hurl the worst insults at it, but nothing can trouble it. In the same way in the ground of all grounds, the basic ground of being, there is a part that remains always inviolable, which no blow of fate can damage. Any of us, as wounded as we may be, can relocate, can sink down into this joy.

MATTHIEU The nature of the mind, which is also called *Buddha-nature*, is the silence of the mental afflictions, the silence of delusion. It's like the space that clouds can hide from view but which remains unchanged. Or like gold, which can be entirely covered with mud but never soiled. The nature of the mind is fundamentally pure and inalterable. Ignorance can veil it temporarily, but it cannot spoil it.

ALEXANDRE I like the image of gold that is inalterable, or of the sky. How can we establish ourselves in that when everything is going wrong? First, where can we find the audacity to put ourselves on a word diet? When I arrived in South Korea, I very soon got wised up. I was able to meet my spiritual father, and I was burning with the desire to confess all my troubles to him. He replied to me, "Alexandre, talking tires you out. Keep silent. Don't break your silence unless it's something vital." And here I had just dragged myself nearly ten thousand kilometers to get there. But I took the lesson: what I keep trying to export from outside is something that is to be found in the heart of silence. Pouring out one's heart does not liberate. The true consolation is to be found elsewhere. And precisely to this point, the mystics teach us that to accomplish the will of God is to descend into peace, to cease to be the toy of the exhausting coming and going of emotions. They tell us that silence heals. Go forward on the path of yes and stop all commentary—that could be the essence of practice.

The Zen tradition speaks of three forms of silence: the immobility of the body; the eclipse of mental activity, that is, stopping or at least making a temporary truce with Mental FM; and, finally, the silence of the heart, immutable peace. Every day there are a thousand opportunities for us to take little cures and plunge into it: in an elevator, in bed, on a train.

Praying, meditating, is progressively renouncing our continuous talking and thinking. In short, daily practice reveals what pollutes the silence, what prevents us from having access to real joy, from going forward fresh, free, and full of love. Going fully into the silence also means discovering a part of ourselves that eludes all wounds and remains intact despite agitation and the blows of fate.

Of course, being silent, daring to be quiet and do nothing, opens one to the return visit of ghosts, obsessions, fears, dark ideas—everything we repress and keep down, which can continue to spoil beneath the clamor

> Going fully into the silence also means discovering a part of ourselves that eludes all wounds and remains intact despite agitation and the blows of fate.

of our daily routines. Basically what we have to do is fall completely in love with silence, having already created space for it. A retreat can quickly turn into torture if we are doing it for duty's sake, under constraint. One day my cell phone rang while I was sitting. My master warned me, "Alexandre, if that phone rings one more time, you'll have to leave." That was a wrench for me. Being cut off from this gadget was tantamount to an amputation for me. When I put my phone in airplane mode, I know it's terrible, but I felt an extreme sense of loneliness, almost a sense of being abandoned. The father spotted my distress and said, "Alexandre, another kind of connection with others is possible, a more inward one, a deeper one." In truth, seeing my enslavement liberated me at once. With one step, we can drop our dependencies and rejoice in our existence and love its deficiencies. Nonetheless, as for me, as soon as the retreat was over I immediately got on my cell phone again.

On the path, we should never deviate from the essential, from the peace that abounds in our hearts. Going on a word diet also means savoring the joy of communicating with others beyond the gossip level. Speaking is a sacred act. Basically I have to keep learning to listen, to keep silent, and to keep away from excesses and exaggerations when I do speak.

From the time I arrived in Seoul, I wanted to confess all my errors to my master. But I had to start from a new place. I had to dare to let go of the past. I remember writing down all my difficulties, my failures, my sins. The exercise was liberating, but I was quavering in my boots at the thought of what the father's judgment would be. His response came, very laconic: "I read it all." Like a high-pressure hose, these four words blasted away the leaden layers of guilt that I had been carrying around with me for years. I saw in them a call to freedom, a sign of infinite love. There were no major pronouncements, no reproaches, zero condemnation. Zen opens the way, a radical one, to stripping away everything. The Gospels also teach us to go the whole way with this, to get rid of hypocrisy and idle talk. "But let your 'Yes' be 'Yes,' and your 'No,' 'No.' For whatever is more than these is from the evil one." Not that we have to do away with all nuances. We simply have to grow in truth, far from overemphasis, bad-mouthing, and mockery.

Moreover, true love protects us from embellishment; it says goodbye to roles. For a long time I stupidly judged love by the number of I-love-yous I collected. A foolish and vain arithmetic. Today I descend into the ground of all grounds to liberate myself from all idolatry, and love with no reason, without fuss. The Gospels lead me to the way of Zen. With infinite patience, one has to let oneself be enriched by the silence. Then you see that everything arises from that and everything returns to it, moment by moment.

CHRISTOPHE   I adore silent retreats! And interestingly, they reveal exactly the same mechanism that fasting does. You see that stopping talking, like stopping eating, is not difficult, even though maybe for extroverted big talkers there might be some trouble at the beginning. But the main thing is, you see much better what talking means. You see your relationship to talking, to useless talking, to automatic talking, inaccurate talking, hasty talking. When you come out of silent retreats you have acquired the taste for true speech. It's the same as when after fasting, you'd rather eat real food than junk food. You've gotten the taste for speech that doesn't happen unless there's really something to say, not just idle talk, talking to fill space, drivel.

I recall getting out of a silent retreat I'd done with Jon Kabat-Zinn. We had spent forty-eight hours without talking, and Jon had set up the breaking of the silence in a very touching way. Instead of saying, "Okay, now you can start talking again," he recommended that we turn to the person next to us, whether we knew that person or not, put our mouth quite close to his ear, and for five minutes tell him in a soft voice what had happened for us during the forty-eight hours of silence. The person on the receiving end had to become pure listening, without comments or facial expressions. It was a powerful experience—even for me. I'm not a big talker, and speech has sometimes failed me, and I had the feeling of being listened to in an extraordinary way. When it was my turn to listen to the other person, it was just as amazing to say to myself, "You don't have to say anything, show anything, respond in any way." It seemed to me I was in a state of listening that was stronger and purer than the one I am in with patients, to whom I visibly show compassion or encouragement. It was stripping totally naked what listening could be. It was presence without speech, without a face, with your consciousness totally turned toward the other, devoted to her or him.

Being There, Present

MATTHIEU   With regard to the quality of presence, I always go back to the example of my spiritual masters. When I arrived in

Darjeeling on June 2, 1967 (that's one of the few dates I remember precisely), I didn't speak Tibetan and could just gibber a little English. At the beginning, I just sat there in the presence of the person who was going to be my principal master, Kangyur Rinpoche. At the end of two weeks, his elder son arrived and I was able to ask him a few questions. Up to that point it was only nonverbal communication. I spent hours seated in silence before this master, who lived very simply in a small hut with two small rooms with his wife and two of his children. Every time I try to describe the quality of his presence, words fail me, as if I were trying to define the undefinable. I can say, for example, that there was a sense with him of constant availability and of boundless kindness, that sometimes he sparkled with joy and at other times he was impressively serious. But in saying those things I'm aware that I still have not touched on the essential.

This kind of presence can sometimes be felt by a whole crowd. At the time of the celebration of the fiftieth anniversary of the Rights of Man in Paris in 1999, Amnesty International had organized a rock concert at Bercy with Peter Gabriel and other musicians, and they asked the Dalai Lama if he would be willing to make a surprise appearance, which he gladly agreed to. As he was waiting in the wings, he took the hand of an electrician as though he had been his friend forever. And then came the announcement: "And now for the surprise guest of the evening, the fourteenth Dalai Lama of Tibet!" When he came out onto the floodlit stage between two rock songs, fifteen thousand young people rose to their feet like a single person and gave him a mighty ovation, the loudest of the night according to the applause meter.

He walked to the front of the stage and said, "Listen, I don't know anything about your music, but I see in your eyes the light in you, your youth, your enthusiasm." Then he said a few words about human rights. A shushing went through the crowd creating a hush so he could be heard better. And then when the Dalai Lama finished speaking, everybody was on their feet and there was tremendous applause. I admit that the emotion brought tears to my eyes. None of these young people had come to see the Dalai Lama, but nonetheless an extraordinary contact was immediately created between him and them. I suppose that they immediately felt the authenticity of who he was and what he was saying. This phenomenon cannot be brought about artificially, even with a lot of help from communication experts. There has to be real togetherness, authentic presence, true speech.

CHRISTOPHE I had an amazing experience over six months working as part of a service for welcoming autistic children into boarding schools. At the time, they were pretty much left to themselves; the teachers and psychologists spent most of their time at professional conferences. I was a young intern at the time, just out of university, and as much as I detested the professional conferences, that's how much I loved spending time with the children. Some of them were severely autistic and they needed a lot of attention. I don't know if what I did was very therapeutic, but I gave them some presence. There was no therapeutic or pedagogical objective, or any other kind. My goal was just to sit down with them. First I sat quietly about ten meters away from them, then nine, and so forth, until I was close enough to participate in their rituals. And at that point, suddenly, they took my hand, put it to their face, or they touched my face slowly. It was a simple communication, but extremely intense. And through presence there was a very strong communication, the only one, moreover, that they were capable of tolerating.

Regarding presence to oneself, I advanced a great deal in this thanks to meditation. Before meditating, my self-knowledge was a little intellectual, erratic, episodic—not a real presence to myself. In meditative practices you work a great deal on presence to yourself, presence to your body, your thoughts, your emotions, to the whole of your being. And the more this presence to yourself can be of good quality, the more it becomes a factor for personal progress and a factor that provides greater capacity for helping others. Patricia Dobkin, a colleague of mine from Quebec, did some studies based on evaluation of patients, which showed that caregivers who practice meditation had an increased quality of presence, which resulted in improvement to all their technical skills.[3]

Our Advice about Listening

Advice on Listening   ALEXANDRE

- Do silence cures. Take time during the day for some silence cures in order to let what is troubling you deep in your heart pass through. Let whatever goes through your mind arise, manifest, and disappear. Dismiss fixed ideas, which without doubt make us quite unhappy. Dare to take these little retreats to leave agitation behind and descend more into your depths.

- Identify parasites on listening. When you're speaking with someone, spot what is acting as a parasite on a true encounter: speed, fatigue, prejudices, misunderstandings, the risks of ambiguity. The ascesis here is to truly lend your ear—completely.

- Keep yourself available for others. In concrete terms, pick up the phone and call a person who is alone or going through hard times. Listen to him, support him without necessarily hitting him with advice; just give him the chance to be perfectly what he is.

Advice for Good Listening   CHRISTOPHE

- You get much further listening than by talking. The proverb says, "You have two ears and one mouth, which means you should listen twice as much as you talk." Speech transforms us because it forces us to clarify our ideas. But listening is more powerful because it opens us to universes other than our own.

- Always remember that listening is giving—not only giving answers but also presence. Listen first, and reply afterward, and don't forget that these are two different things. The time of listening that goes first gives our replies authenticity, weight, and increased effectiveness.

- It is necessary to partly empty yourself in order to listen well. Empty yourself of your fears—the fear of not knowing what to say, the fear of not having answers to give. Empty yourself of your certainties. Empty yourself of your weariness. But we have limits where listening is concerned: there are moments when you just need to be alone in order to renew your resources!

Advice for Listening with Compassion and Humility MATTHIEU

- Consider listening as a gift without reserve to the being who is in front of you. Even if that person is full of ill will, listen to him with compassion, without smugness, but with a profound desire to find a remedy for the causes of his suffering.

- Don't get ahead of what he is saying, thinking you have already gotten the point.

- Avoid any condescension in your attitude. The same way as water is collected at the lowest point it flows to, it is in a position of humility that you receive from the other that which will permit you to help him.

The Body

Burden or Idol?

ALEXANDRE To embark "properly" on a spiritual path, you cannot forget the body, unless you want to run right into a wall. We are not machines, after all, or disembodied souls. Needs, impulses, desires, pains, pleasures, joys, and sorrows—we have to build our lives around all that. How do we avoid screwing up our health? How do we avoid stress, dependencies, and exhaustion so as to dare an art of living that restores to the body its true vocation—as an instrument of peace, a vehicle of enlightenment? If we are negligent with regard to the hygiene of life, sooner or later we will crash and burn. The body can alternately be a burden, an obstacle, an idol, or a responsibility. How do we dare to attain a sane balance in the midst of our passions and conflicts? And above all, how do we love our bodies? In order to enter upon the practice of ascesis, we must fully inhabit it and celebrate our life in that place.

Inhabiting the Body

ALEXANDRE Having contempt for the body, being disgusted with it, looking down on it, leads nowhere. And angelism is something to avoid like the plague. Blaise Pascal was right a thousand times when he pointed out that "man is neither angel nor beast; and the misfortune is that he who would act the angel acts the beast." In my view, to deny our needs, to pretend to have already solved the problem of our impulses and contradictions, is to consign ourselves to inevitable failure. Embracing a spiritual path certainly does not mean fleeing the body—quite to the contrary. It means trying to incarnate wisdom, getting it to take root in everyday life.

How can we progress toward peace if we are worn out, exhausted, if we aren't taking proper care of ourselves? And what should we say about the risk of walling ourselves off in our ego mind? If we cut ourselves off from the body, from its rhythms, and neglect the *laws* of our physical nature, we run a great risk of destroying ourselves. One day a friend of mine, the psychiatrist Christophe Massin, gave me a precious tool: "Watch out for overexertion and avoid it as much as possible." Since then, whenever I'm going full speed ahead, as soon as I run out of steam, his words calm me down immediately. Finally I dare to slow down a bit. There's a whole art in learning to rest. I'm not sure that those who have had to struggle their whole lives know how to grant themselves respite, even a brief one.

> Embracing a spiritual path certainly does not mean fleeing the body—quite to the contrary. It means trying to incarnate wisdom, getting it to take root in everyday life.

Using our pleasures well is also not something we can take for granted. Sometimes when I go back home, my eyes pause on the little red lights that indicate whorehouses. In Seoul there are lots of them. How sad it is to see this phenomenon becoming a common commodity! I lament seeing sexuality, this gift of life, so often degenerating and becoming the occasion of depressing alienation. It's a safe bet that a totally pacified human being would no longer live the flesh as a torment. In the meantime, without straying into an attitude of repression, I think a useful thing would be to come up with a lifestyle that takes into account our impulses and desires. What makes this more complicated is that in sexuality there are psychological aspects, biological aspects, and emotional hang-ups.

CHRISTOPHE   The body, as you pointed out, is often ignored or mistreated, as if we had an eternal body. We imagine this just the same way as, for a long time, we used to imagine that nature would remain proof against our pollutions and indefinitely repair our negligent behavior toward it. There are times when we mistreat our bodies as we mistreat nature—through negligence, through lack of awareness of its needs, it limits—its fragility. I had a striking experience during a trip to India in the region of Benares. We had come across some *sadhus* who were painstakingly washing themselves. The guide explained to me that they belonged to a religious group that considered the body to be a temple that must be honored. I really like the idea of respecting one's body like a temple, making it the subject of sacred rituals. This is not particularly an obsession with self or hypochondria. Rather, it is deference toward an entity patiently developed by nature that has been placed in our care for a few years.

It is also important to bring up the subject of sexuality when talking about the body. You were saying that sexuality was subject to psychological and biological influences, but I think there are also very strong sociological influences. It's astounding to see how contemporary society has turned sex into a commercial product. There is commerce in porno films, in purely sexual encounters that are purely for kicks with no commitments or obligations. Sexuality has been desacralized, despiritualized, and "de-relationship-ized." This is indirectly a way of not respecting the body, which is not just a utensil, a vehicle to be dominated for the satisfaction of our pleasures.

ALEXANDRE   On the path of accepting the body, my relationship with Joachim freed me from a tremendous weight. For a long time, death terrified me. Just seeing a hearse was enough to plunge me into a terrible state of malaise. But my life healed me a little by giving me a friend who was an undertaker. For hours at a time I would listen to him talk about his work. Little by little, almost in spite of myself, a great confidence arose in me. Then I took it to the next level by accompanying him for a few days on the job. His gentleness and his faith in life delivered me from my torments. In the cold room, I watched him taking care of men and women, mamas and papas, with infinite tenderness. In the beginning I was surprised that he didn't wear gloves when working with the bodies. His words converted me: "An hour ago this woman was in the arms of her husband, her son, or her grandchildren. Why would I wear gloves?" Joachim revealed to me, there where I least expected it, the goodness of life. Suddenly I was looking at a toothless mouth and thinking about the tender words it had spoken. In the midst of the coffins I understood what a miracle the body is. I left the morgue with an unexpected hope in my heart. I finally recognized that the body was not a burden but rather the instrument of enlightenment, and that from then on my task would be to celebrate life in it.

It's always the same call that is heard: there's no time to lose; you must practice. Joachim told me the story of a waitress who died from a heart attack as she was carrying a plate to a customer. The precariousness of life never ceases to amaze me. It alternatively terrifies me and fills me with wonder. I imagine that young woman getting up in the morning and going to work. At no time did it occur to her that she was going to die that day. Life is fragile. Every moment is a gift that we should appreciate fully.

The Body Made Me a Doctor

CHRISTOPHE As a doctor, I obviously have a special relationship with the body, which is at the heart of our profession. The first year of medical studies was very theoretical. We learned biochemistry and anatomy, but we were not in contact with the "real" body. I really entered the profession of medicine when I walked into the dissection hall in the second year. On a zinc table lay a cadaver that had been preserved in formaldehyde. It made a strong impression to look at this face and to work on this body that had been a person. We were four students to a cadaver. After the competition of the first year, this moment was a pitiless screening process. A certain number of us fainted on the spot and left to study law—including the student who had been first in our class! This is a great paradox, but nothing makes you think more about life than a cadaver. I think I became a doctor in those moments—without really understanding it—of being with, manipulating, and dissecting cadavers. It went beyond learning techniques. All kinds of thoughts about life and death proliferated in my mind.

Another thing marked me strongly. I was part of the last generation of students for whom dogs were sacrificed in the course of physiological instruction to demonstrate to us the mechanisms of arterial pressure or digestion. They were collected by the dog pound and designated for this sad end as guinea pigs. One day, a dog who had been insufficiently anesthetized partially regained consciousness and began to howl with pain. We were outraged and began to protest. We were among the first to come to the conclusion that these experiments had to end, that courses were enough. I still remember the face of the physiology instructor, amazed that we could not tolerate the dog's cries. I think that for him—and it was drawing toward the end of his career—this sound had been a part of his daily experience for so many years that he just didn't hear it anymore.

In medicine, the encounter with the body is often violent. I remember the first sick person who fell to my charge when I was an intern in my third year. I remember the department where I was working, the bright autumn sun, the room, the man's face. He was a man of thirty-five, a smoker whose leg had just been amputated as a result of Buerger's disease, a serious form of peripheral vascular disease connected with tobacco. I discovered that in our society there is a strong tendency to hide this kind of reality. In traditional societies, even children see more sick bodies and cadavers. We little Westerners have been very protected.

At the time when I started medicine, organicism was dominant, that is, the body was considered a sum of organs vaguely in interaction with each other. The principle of "specializations" (cardiology, dermatology, nephrology, etc.) reflects perfectly this medicine of isolated organs rather than a medicine of whole people. This approach made great progress possible, but it also has its limits. Today we are in the process of rethinking the body in terms of being a subtle entity, complicated and intelligent, in which all the organs influence each other and dialogue with each other. The organs possess a capacity for self-reparation and sometimes self-healing that we must respect. I return to the comparison between the body and nature since, at this point, we view nature as an intelligent whole that we must observe and respect rather than dominate and mistreat. It is a whole with parts in intimate interaction. When you act on one element of it, the rest is strongly affected.

Analogously, when I began in psychiatry there was no interest at all in the body. Patients were considered purely as minds that you could have lie down on your couch. Psychoanalysis, which was dominant at the time, was an intellectual discipline based on the concept, the word. Later on, working on my own on emotions, about which we had been told pretty much nothing in our university studies, I discovered that they were the connecting factors between mind and body, rooted simultaneously in both. Nowadays everybody working in the field of psychology has finally understood that the body is not just a utensil or a sum of organs that needs to be reduced to silence so it doesn't disturb us. Rather, it is the entryway to our mind, a complex, intelligent entity that we need to care for through various means, such as meditation, diet, physical exercise, and so on.

In this treatment of the body, a balance has to be found between denial and contempt, on the one hand, and obsession with the body, on the other. In this regard also, like many young Westerners, I had relative contempt for my body. I remember fracturing my shinbone while skiing. I had so much work to do that I walked on my fracture for a week, convincing myself that it was only a sprain. But I was in so much pain that I finally went to have it x-rayed in the department right next to the one I was working in. My colleague looked at the x-rays for a long time, admiring the magnificent fracture, then he turned to me suspiciously and asked me what I had been doing walking on it for a week. "What is your area of specialization?" he asked me. I told him I was a psychiatrist, and I saw an expression on his face that was both perplexity and relief. "Oh, you're a psychiatrist. I understand." Today, with the help of age and experience, I try to be more attentive and respectful toward my body.

The natural movement of the death of the body occurs after another natural movement: aging. Personally I'm not touched by the chronological thresholds—being thirty, forty, fifty—but rather by the stages of the life of my body: when I began to lose my hair, when my beard hair started turning white, when I couldn't play rugby anymore, when I felt my first lasting joint pain. This aging of the body teaches me detachment, that is, all these little limitations force me to accept getting older and prepare me to accept leaving my body one day. Resigning ourselves to age normally can help us have less fear of death. It seems to me that aging is made for that, to make it so that at the end, you don't regret leaving the body.

The Body in Buddhism

MATTHIEU   In Buddhism the body is described differently in accordance with different levels of teaching and spiritual practices. This variety corresponds to that of the abilities and mental dispositions of various individuals in the same way as the variety of a pharmacopeia corresponds to various diseases.

In Theravada Buddhism, the body is mainly perceived as an object of attachment, since it is through the intermediary of the body that we become attached to the pleasant sensations registered by the senses. These attachments quickly turn into craving, grasping, and then into dependency. In order to counter the tendency to treat our bodies like idols and spend our time dressing and preening, and in order not to perceive others' bodies as mere objects of desire, the Small Vehicle teaches different meditations. One of them consists in imagining opening a body up and looking at what is beneath that nice skin and attractive face. That is a bit like the dissection sessions that Christophe was talking about, even though the goal is different. One imagines the organs, the veins, the blood, the bone, the flesh, and so forth; and one removes them mentally one after the other and mentally places them in a pile in front of oneself. The objective, of course, is to conclude that there is nothing in this pile of flesh that's worth one's infatuation. To become aware of the ephemeral nature of the body, one also visualizes it as the skeleton it will soon become.

In the Great Vehicle, or Mahayana, that of the bodhisattvas, we consider the human body as highly precious because it permits us to attain enlightenment. Of course, it is not really precious unless we take advantage of the benefit it offers. In this context it is compared to a ship that makes it possible for us to cross the ocean of existences conditioned by suffering. Without making an idol of the body, we respect it and care for it as we might a boat. It would be absurd to have contempt for it, to not maintain it, or to subject it to austerities.

Finally, in the Adamantine Vehicle, or Vajrayana, we identify the body with a deity of wisdom who symbolizes the qualities of enlightenment: wisdom, compassion, altruistic activity, and so on. Like the Indian sadhus you mentioned, Christophe, the Vajrayana also sometimes views the body as a mandala that is the seat of a great many deities representing these spiritual qualities. The idea here is not to construct a superego but rather the contrary. The deity of wisdom with whom we identify has no more substance than a rainbow. Identifying with him or her is no more than a skillful means whose goal is to reduce our habitual attachment to an ego and to a coarse physical form, and to permit the Buddha-nature that exists in us to manifest.

Regarding sexuality, it is the normal expression of a biological desire like hunger and thirst. It awakens in us very intense emotions because it involves all the senses at once. In those people who have not attained a certain degree of inner freedom, it brings about—like other very powerful sensorial experiences—strong attachments that bind the mind even more to the cycle of suffering. For those who have gained mastery of their minds and realized perfect inner freedom, these sensations are experienced in the simplicity of the present moment, in the bliss of a mind free of all attachment and all expectation. They then become means of spiritual progress.

In the end, it is the mind that is the master of the body and of speech. Even if desire is embedded in our physical constitution, it cannot express itself without a mental representation. That might be voluntary or involuntary; it might form slowly or appear suddenly, but it always precedes desire, because the object of desire is first reflected in our thoughts. The understanding of this process that can come about through mind training permits us to manage the manifestations of desire in a liberating way.

From the point of view of Buddhism, the body does indeed have an influence on the mind, but it is as a depository of energies, conceptual patterns, and tendencies of which the initial origin is the mind. Such tendencies, according to Buddhism, may sometimes go back to much, much earlier births. They are thus the equivalent on the level of consciousness of heredity on the physical plane. In spiritual practice, we may secondarily put passing emphasis on the body through the use of particular physical exercises, but the ultimate goal of these is to transform the mind.

The Body and Meditation

MATTHIEU All the practices connected with body and speech are thus only secondary means to freeing the mind from conflicting emotions and ignorance. With regard to speech, for example, the Sanskrit word *mantra* means "that which protects the mind." It protects it from errant thoughts and mental states that perpetuate mental confusion and suffering. Regarding the body, it is doubtless true that posture, for example, has an influence on our mental states. If we meditate in a position that is too relaxed, we are highly likely to doze off. Conversely, a posture that is too tense is conducive to mental agitation. We must find the right balance. If it is difficult for us to sit cross-legged, we can meditate in a chair or on a high cushion, or even lying down, as Alexandre often does because of his pains. We should avoid letting the body lean to the left or the right, forward or backward. The texts say that in a body that is properly straight, the channels of subtle energy are also straight, and that is favorable for clarity of the mind.

ALEXANDRE In his magnificent book *The Wise Heart*, Jack Kornfield tells the story of a practitioner suffering from an incurable illness. When the doctors gave him up for lost, he went to see his master, Taungpulu Sayadaw, sure that the time had come for him to prepare himself to die. The lesson here is luminous. Far, far away from resignation and despondency, the holy man advised him to do everything possible to heal himself. Because even if an illness increases its ravages, still we have to advance on the path. And with infinite kindness, the master comforted him, "Don't die yet." Not yet! He was alive, and this life, even though it is fragile and transitory, all the way to the end gives us a chance, as miniscule as it might be, to progress toward enlightenment. I like this invitation to live all the way to the end. The body is neither a burden nor an impediment. In the *Phaedo*, Plato compares flesh to a prison, a tomb. I don't want to turn it into an idol, but I prefer to see the body as a vehicle for making the journey to joy, love, enlightenment, and union with God.

CHRISTOPHE Pursuing the subject of the importance of the body, when we consider the dietary question, the following is very striking: the problems seem to arise in the body, they reach their high point in the body, and the solutions are also in the body. For example, trying to regulate eating disorders such as anorexia or bulimia just by reflecting about them won't work. The power of the mind is not sufficient; rehabilitation has to happen in the body. And often we see that patients who are the subject of the disorders do not know their bodies well. They don't make the distinction between real hunger and the mere urge to eat—because it's time or because they see other people eating, for example. Meditative practices, like other ways of practicing observation, are not only the first steps to improvement, but often necessary steps for any kind of work on impulsive behavior.

Working in the opposite direction, embodiment of our intentions gives them an incredible power, as I discovered through various meditative practices. The examples that touch me the most are the meditations on altruistic love and the meditations centered on compassion, where you take the time to associate your breathing with intentions of altruistic love. You feel the way these feelings can become physically instilled in us, in all the parts of our bodies. Little by little you enter into a state of comprehension, of clarity, of pacification, of inner strength, connected with intentions of altruistic love. Most of us would never get there without the support of the body. It's the body that makes the difference between mere reflection and meditation.

The Body-Mind Connection

ALEXANDRE The experience of being disabled, which is ingrained for all time in the core of my flesh, provides me with no end of challenges. The doctors really bum me out when they proclaim, without even examining me, that my physical pain comes from stress. This kind of hasty and rather reductionist judgment comes fairly close to abuse. Nevertheless, that doesn't keep me from recognizing the enormous importance of our psychological state for the way we relate to pain. If I feel at peace and in good surroundings, it seems to me that my physical suffering is a bit less bitter. You have to work on two levels: taking care of the body and pacifying the mind. It's terrible to say to somebody suffering from chronic pain, "You're not the only one" or "That's not what you're going to die from." That's a little bit like a man who has ten thorns stuck in his foot and then he gets a splinter—is there anyone who would dare tell him that if it weren't for the splinter he'd be okay? It's really important to be careful not to add the drop of water that will make the vase overflow. You have to know the limits of the person you're dealing with to be sure you're not about to push him too far.

If we neglect the body, sooner or later we'll have a nasty bill to pay. For me a bad toothache or serious fatigue is enough to show me the fragility of my patience, of my love. That is why it is important, for the sake of others, to listen to and respect one's natural rhythm.

As for your exercise, Matthieu, I'm not sure if, when desire reaches its apex, imagining the guts and bones of the girl I'm attracted to would suffice to calm the beast.

MATTHIEU That's not something that can be done in a few seconds. You have to familiarize yourself with this exercise until you reach the point where, spontaneously, you wonder how it's possible to be attached to this or that body. You can also pursue your examination down to the level of atoms and say to yourself that in the end it's impossible to become attached to infinitesimal particles. But this is only one method among others. It is considered more effective and more profound to train, for example, in managing the emotions as they arise in the manner already described.

As for the relationship of body to mind, thirty years ago the scientific community considered it a totally harebrained idea that mental events could have a major influence on the body. Meditation was seen as an exotic practice that appealed to hippies who had lost their grip on reality. Things have changed a lot since then. Thanks to the efforts of Jon Kabat-Zinn, mindfulness-based stress reduction (MBSR) is now used in hundreds of hospitals throughout the world. On the level of research, twenty years ago you could only find about ten articles a year on the effects of meditation, whereas nowadays four hundred to five hundred studies are published every year on this subject in serious scientific journals.

In the process of studying the effects of mental states on the body, we have come to a better understanding of the placebo effect, a concept that had to be restored to respectability. Quite often people think that they've been trapped or tricked: "You feel better? Ha ha! Do you know there was nothing in the pills you took?" In reality, the placebo effect, which gives 15 to 40 percent positive results depending on which conditions are treated, shows the effect of the mind on the body. It should no longer have a pejorative connotation attributed to it. When we say to someone who is feeling better after having ingested some harmless pills that it's a placebo effect, the person is often upset and treats us as though we are a batty scientist. But what is more noble than the effects of the mind on the body? It is not necessary to take little pills devoid of active substances to demonstrate its importance. Why not work directly with our minds in order to improve the effect the mind has on our bodies? That seems to me more direct and more intelligent, even if people get a kick out of being given a mixture of Himalayan gentians and ruby powder. Meditation is the most noble of the placebos.

In addition, the works of Paul Ekman show that the body-mind relationship functions in both directions. This great specialist on emotions and facial expressions has discovered that around fifty facial muscles are involved in the different facial expressions associated with joy, surprise, fear, etc. Generally when one feels a particular emotion, a very definite group of muscles is activated. But it also works in the other direction. Paul asked a group of subjects to activate progressively a certain number of muscles in their faces—to lift their eyebrows, widen their eyes, turn down the corners of their mouths, and so on—without telling them what emotion each corresponded to. Then he asked them what they felt. The fascinating thing is that they almost always felt the feeling normally associated with the muscles that were used. The mere act of adopting a certain facial expression is thus capable of triggering a specific mental state.

I'd also like to mention the concept of *embodied mind* proposed by the neuroscientist Francisco Varela, who, among other achievements, was the cofounder of the Mind and Life Institute, which I'm also part of. He explains that the consciousness fully manifests when it is associated with a body that is integrated into a physical and social environment. A brain that remained confined to a jar would be incapable of conceiving of the world.

CHRISTOPHE These stories about placebos are always amazing. You are perfectly right, Matthieu, to point out the tendency to associate the placebo effect with a trap or an error, when in fact it just simply shows the powers of the mind! When our mind puts itself at the service of our body, when it listens to our body, that can have considerable effects. And the studies are countless. With regard to body-mind retroactions, heaps of studies on the smile, for example, show that when you smile—on the condition that you don't at that moment have a reason to cry, on the condition that your life

> When our mind puts itself at the service of our body, when it listens to our body, that can have considerable effects.

is "normal" at that moment—you slightly improve your mood.[1] For the reasons that Paul Ekman demonstrated, there is a total harmony between our bodies and our minds, which works in both directions. A happy brain will bring about a happy face, but a smiling face also in its turn facilitates positive emotions. We also have the same kinds of studies on posture. When you do questionnaires on self-esteem or satisfaction with life, according to whether you have the people sit slouched or straight, you get slightly different results. Respecting the body does the mind good.

Our Advice for Working with Your Body

The Two Messages I Want to Pass Along   CHRISTOPHE

- Let's respect our body the way we respect nature. It doesn't belong to us, not exclusively, anymore than nature does. We are tenants of the earth just as we are tenants of our body. Our body will be taken back from us as nature will survive us when we are no longer there. I like this passage from Nietzsche: "To the despisers of the body will I speak my word. I wish them neither to learn afresh, nor teach anew, but only to bid farewell to their own bodies—and thus be dumb."[2]

- Let us love and accept aging; let us see it as a help for not being attached to our body, as a means to prepare us for leaving it, without regret, quite gently, like something that has been temporarily lent to us and will be recycled for future generations.

Care for Your Body Without Idolatry ALEXANDRE

- Follow St. Francis de Sales, who tells us, "Care for your body so that it will be pleasing to your soul," and consider your body as a child that has been entrusted to you.

- We should see our body as like a house that has been lent to us. We are the fortunate tenants, and we should take care to maintain it every day. I can devote a few minutes during the day to cleaning the nooks and crannies of the house and to listening to the signals that warn me of wear and tear, such as fatigue, stress, exhaustion—in short whatever conflicts with joy.

Using the Body Well MATTHIEU

- When the body is well, respect it without being excessively attached to it. Use it as a support for making progress toward understanding and inner freedom, or as an instrument that allows you to flourish and contribute to the well-being of others.

- When the body is unwell, instead of sinking into despair, use this unwellness as an opportunity to transform yourself and to grow by transcending the obstacle of illness.

6

The Origins of Suffering

CHRISTOPHE   As human beings, we are all experts on suffering. Whether it is our own suffering or that of the people close to us, we all know it intimately. So since doctors seem to be the ones people go to, to seek relief from or an end to suffering, I'm going to step up and be the first to speak on this subject.

The Cartography of Suffering

CHRISTOPHE   To explain suffering to my patients and show them how we're going to work with it, I attempt to establish a distinction—reductive but instructive—between pain and suffering.

Pain is the biological, organic, or existential part of suffering. A cavity in a tooth causes biological changes that bring about a nagging sensation. Sometimes pain also finds its way into the body through an event that takes place—the loss of a child, a friend, or a dear one. Finally, pain is a reality when it injures us. Suffering refers to the impact of pain on the mind, on our way of seeing the world. Take the example of tinnitus. This humming or whistling in the ear is a relatively minimal form of pain (there are, without doubt, afflictions that are much worse), but it can bring major suffering because the impact of this minor perturbation tends to produce obsession. It occupies the mind and sometimes requires psychological help. I can't make my patients' pain go away with words alone—sometimes it takes drugs; sometimes time, as for bereavement—but I can help them understand their suffering and lessen it through methods such as psychotherapy or meditation.

The second way of understanding suffering consists in defining its opposite. The opposite of suffering might be enjoyment, but when you are suffering you don't want to enjoy, you just want to not suffer anymore. The opposite of suffering is therefore peace, tranquility, serenity, the possibility of forgetting oneself and taking advantage of life.

This brings us to the third point. What characterizes suffering is that it cuts us off from the world. Simone Weil speaks very accurately of the "degree of pain at which you lose the world."[1] Pain isolates us and, fundamentally, the opposite of suffering is rejoining the world, taking up a harmonious and untroubled connection with it again.

ALEXANDRE   I took up philosophy a bit in the same way one takes monastic orders, precisely in order to try to find a remedy for suffering. I wanted at any cost to destroy pain and save my skin. When I was very young, I was in the company of people who, in the midst of the worst trials, maintained an immense joie de vivre. I wanted to discover that joy too, to do whatever it took to attain it. That was the enigma of my life!

It is important to distinguish the pain that comes with the human condition, from which it is difficult to escape, if not completely impossible (sickness, death, earthquakes, the loss of a dear one), from the torments of the soul. To the inevitable blows of fate, a whole jumble of emotions comes and adds itself on—denial, frustration, discontent, and so on. The good news is that this jumble of emotional pain is not irremediable. Thus the real question becomes, How do we cross this ocean of suffering without sinking in it and without bringing aboard ship all the useless cares and worries that eat us up and leave us drained of blood? In this regard, my disability is like a powerful revealer, showing me how much the pain is accentuated, exaggerated, even created out of whole cloth by the discursive mind. If I stick to the facts, if I keep both feet on the ground without going along with my fears and projections, I will suffer significantly less. In making my way through a crowd, when I don't pause over the looks I get, the stares that come to remind me that

I'm not completely like the others, I remain in a state of profound joy. But as soon as I begin to take all those eyes staring at me seriously, I'm screwed. In that regard, my little four-year-old daughter is a healer for me, since she has not yet laid a whole set of labels on her infirm papa.

I like Buddhism's diagnosis here, as well as that of the Christian mystics: the reason we are struggling in a state of unhappiness is ultimately because we are exiled, and a thick layer of illusion, desires, and fear is veiling our true nature, the fundamental ground of our being, the ground of all grounds. Like Buddhism, positive psychology also delivers a properly revolutionary message: Our emotional pain is far from being decreed by fate. This state of unhappiness can be alleviated, even fully avoided. Once we have this diagnosis, we can joyfully begin on an art of life and an ascesis that will cause that which encumbers and weighs on our lives to progressively wither away. I also find in reading Meister Eckhart or the writings of Angelus Silesius a bold invitation to rid ourselves of the little ego that tyrannizes us, to empty the temple of the mind so that joy can finally shine there. I like the notion of ascesis because it does away with all sense of resignation and makes it possible for every practitioner to move forward, to make progress. It authorizes immense hope by describing a very concrete way to arrive at the goal.

> The exercise here is to move forward on the path, to convert, to familiarize yourself with wisdom. How could one not view this with joy, the joy of a prisoner escaping prison, who is becoming free?

Ancient philosophy evokes the image of the gymnast, the soldier; in short, a person who trains daily to perfect his skill. *Askein* means in Greek "to exercise, train." This is the source of ascesis, which is often misinterpreted to mean "renunciation" or "privation." The exercise here is to move forward on the path, to convert, to familiarize yourself with wisdom. How could one not view this with joy, the joy of a prisoner escaping prison, who is becoming free? Everything then becomes an opportunity for progress, for deliverance.

To put this very concretely, I can use whatever comes along as an opportunity to lighten my load, to liberate myself. For example, mockery, my fear of "what will they say about me," really ruined my life by taking me far away from being able to say a joyous yes toward reality just as it presents itself. And that is why nonfixation is such a potent cure. As soon as I reduce myself to a mental representation, to an image of myself that I create, I suffer. The way to do away with this unwholesome mechanism is never to identify with anything at all. In the midst of the insults, every time I take myself too seriously, a thousand times a day, I come back to this exercise that strips us naked and extricates us from roles, wounds, and expectations.

Any person who practices ascesis runs the risk sooner or later of falling into voluntarism, which is the belief that everything depends on us, that will and reason are what rule the life of masters. During a brief stint working in palliative care, I discovered a flagrant injustice: will alone is not enough. Certain patients had built up a fabulous state of mind, exerted a great deal of energy—but their illness won out anyway. Others were luckier. The challenge is this: keep a positive view of spiritual exercises, of their considerable effects on our state of mind, on our health, and even on our immune system, but still bear in mind that not everything depends on us.

It's abusive to trivialize somebody's suffering and condemn them for not being able to stop it. I had to laugh the other day at the dentist's office. He admonished me: "Whatever you do, don't move. If you do, it'll ruin everything!" That's sort of like yelling at a child, "Go to sleep, goddammit!" With my infirmity, the more I try to control my movements, the more my body rebels, tenses up and does what it wants. What more urgent invitation could there be, once more, to dare to let go? So in this damn dentist's chair the other day, I countermanded the doctor's orders and told myself, "You can move as much as you want. Don't control anything. Don't even try to relax." And the miracle happened. I remained absolutely still. All the same, it's bad medicine to be rude and crude with a person who is suffering and say things such as "Snap out of it!" or "Get a move on!" Words like that are just as counterproductive as they are inhuman.

For somebody who's stuck with his physical suffering or some inner unhappiness all day long, an art of life is indispensable to keep these problems from becoming the center of one's existence. First, I agree with Schopenhauer that having pain end is not necessarily enough to bring us to a state of happiness. Often I would give anything to get rid of some pain, and when relief finally comes, I'm not even happy about it. Ingrate that I am! As a result of keeping my eyes fixed on the future, I forget the thousand and one gifts that are there, within hand's reach. That being the case, the best exercise is the practice of gratitude, which should be done fully, from the bottom of one's heart. Look at that special smile, appreciate this dish, take a look at the sky. We should open ourselves to that which is given. Living with a wound day after day is more like a marathon than a sprint, and exhaustion is never far away. We need extreme vigilance not to become embittered.

Ascesis requires us to do whatever we can so that pain will not have the last word. Simone Weil saw the cruel machinations of suffering clearly. In her *Gravity and Grace*, she confesses with disarming honesty the brutality that would take hold of her when she was suffering from violent migraines. It reached the point where, in order to free herself of the pain, she wanted to hit someone on the forehead in the exact place where her pain had become intolerable. This shows us how pain can drive us mad, to the point of malevolence. How then can we not take out our excess of injury, our setbacks, on the first person who comes by? This philosopher's self-baring lucidity sets me free. She provides me with the help I need to avoid traps such as the desire for vengeance, the tendency to assign blame, and to spread out around me the pain I can no longer take on myself.

One day, at the height of a severe earache, my son was crying out so loud I didn't know what to do. I felt helpless and lost my composure—and I was stunned to discern in this state an element of anger against my son. Clearly I had chosen the wrong target! It's crazy how suffering can make us lose our bearings. My love for this little child was so great that, panicked and at a loss from hearing these cries of his that I could do nothing to soothe, I caught myself falling into this stupid reflex: "Stop crying. You're making me feel terrible!" A weird paradox: instead of completely and defenselessly taking this little guy in my arms and doing my best to console him, I unconsciously reproached him for causing me pain. So I have to do whatever I can to disarm these fears, these defense mechanisms. Identifying the causes of suffering and doing no further harm are eminently altruistic acts.

MATTHIEU   Starting on the simplest level, we can say that the term *suffering* includes all the mental states perceived as undesirable. Suffering can be initiated by physical pain or a state of mind such as distress, fear, or any other feeling that we would like to have go away. It could be transitory, as in the case of many headaches, or long-lasting such as despair, a feeling of meaninglessness, or profound unhappiness.

Why do we have the capacity to suffer? From the point of view of evolution, the ability to feel suffering is necessary for survival. Physical pain is a warning signal informing us that something is threatening our physical integrity. Children who have no sense of pain usually die before ten years old. Lepers, whose limbs may become desensitized, continue to walk on their stumps, which aggravates the deterioration of their bodies; others might burn themselves horribly without realizing it. Mental pain is also an inner warning signal. It warns me that there is something I must remedy in order to restore my mental balance.

Suffering manifests on several levels, which Buddhism has clearly identified. It is not limited to what seems unpleasant such as intense physical pain or tragic events that disrupt our lives. It has more subtle aspects, which are not within the realm of immediate feeling. For instance, there is "suffering connected with change," which is due to the impermanent character of that which appears to us momentarily as pleasure or happiness. If one is good-looking and in good health and everything is going well, one is unconsciously attached to the idea that this situation will last. This attachment becomes the starting point for an inevitable process of suffering, since everything is continually changing, even though we may not see this. One of my spiritual masters expressed this truth in a brutal fashion: "What you generally call happiness, we call suffering."

Buddhism also speaks of a type of suffering that is even more imperceptible than the suffering connected with change. We sometimes have the vague, intuitive feeling that nothing is ever satisfying, even when, purportedly, everything is there to make us happy. This is underlying suffering, connected to our distorted perception of reality. This inaccurate perception, in Buddhism, is one of the definitions of ignorance. If we think things will last and that, in themselves, they are desirable or undesirable, beautiful or ugly, beneficial or harmful, then we are out of sync with reality, and the consequence of that can only be discontent. To the extent that we have not dispelled the fundamental ignorance that creates this gap between our perceptions and reality, we are doomed to suffering.

According to Buddhism, suffering has at least one good quality: it brings about disenchantment with regard to artificial happiness and incites us to liberate ourselves from the profound causes of unhappiness.

Self-Inflicted Suffering

CHRISTOPHE You brought up something fundamental, Matthieu. Just as pain is a warning signal that pushes us to quickly alter our behavior or our environment—or perhaps consult a doctor—suffering informs us that we are on a path that leads away from what could provide balance or harmony. For example, resentment or anger is painful. And that's good news! Imagine painless anger or cold and celebratory hatred! Those might be problems presented by people who are really sick. The fact that envy, jealousy, hatred—the emotions we call "negative"—are also painful is a blessing because these emotions lead us away from what we ought to do for others and for ourselves. On this point Buddhism is clear, and medicine and our culture in general should take further inspiration from this understanding. We might then often say to patients, "Listen to your suffering; respect it; it has a message for you."

> Listen to your suffering; respect it; it has a message for you.

But that is difficult to accept, because when you are suffering, what you want above all is for it to stop. That is the first duty of a doctor. Once the pain has been relieved, we can open up the hood and invite the patient to look in and understand what the pain signified.

Can suffering help us to correct errors in our view of the world? Listening to you, Matthieu, I thought of a patient I like a lot. It's a woman who's getting older and who experiences a terrible fear of aging. She's beautiful, and she doesn't want to just get old. As a result, she frequently has turned to plastic surgery so she can stay physically attractive. When you see her from a distance sitting in the waiting room, she's a pretty woman who catches your eye. But up close you see that she's an older woman, even though she has to a certain degree kept her looks. Her attitude exposes her to innumerable causes of suffering. First, there's the suffering of recognizing every morning that her age can be read on her face. When she has affairs, this gets worse. How can she allow intimacy, let herself be seen without makeup the morning after or in a harsh light? What suffering! And for what gain? By trying to avoid the torments of aging, she inflicts much worse ones on herself—at least as I see it anyway.

It must be three or four years now that I've been seeing her, and I've begun to say to her gently, "You know, trying to keep looking so young is a big effort for you. It causes you a lot of trouble. Isn't there another way to be attractive, seductive, to share yourself intimately? Aren't there other things you could do with your life that would bring you as much pleasure?" This is a little direct, and not too "psychotherapeutic," but considering the way she lives and her relative solitude, I think I'm the only one who could say that to her. Since she likes me, since she feels that I don't judge her and that I have compassion for her, she listens to me politely. But it's hard for a person to change course. From the outside, I clearly see the errors of her way of looking at the world and her priorities in life, and I try indirectly, through little tricks, to get her to loosen up this fundamental illusion that causes her so much suffering. I don't get the feeling that I'm helping her in any miraculous way, but it seems to me that little by little she's evolving. For example, she's going out more and more with men who are closer to her in age. In short, there are moments when I feel that the help she needs doesn't fit completely in the framework of psychology. This woman puts me, a behavioral psychiatrist, in a somewhat tough place. In particular, there's a point where I'm afraid I might shake her up too much. If I told her, "You see, this is no longer appropriate for your age; your obsession with youth is a mental aberration," obviously that would be a catastrophe. What exercises would you propose, Matthieu, Buddhist monk?

MATTHIEU   You always have to try to remedy the immediate suffering, but if you do nothing about its deeper causes, it will unfailingly surface again. It's like taking aspirin when the pain is coming from a more serious illness. That only masks the problem. People are often deluded by the notion that if they were good-looking, rich, famous, and powerful, they would automatically be happy, whereas in fact the chances that those factors will make a person happy are no better than the chances of winning the lottery. The suffering in life is already enough to deal with; it is inevitable and unpredictable without adding to that the pointless suffering of tormenting yourself for no longer being twenty when you're eighty. You could perhaps say to this patient, "You want to be happy and suffer as little as possible, you're absolutely right. But for this to be possible, and especially for it to be lasting, you have no other choice but to look at yourself sincerely and take stock of what *really* contributes to your well-being and what actually causes you suffering."

> You always have to try to remedy the immediate suffering, but if you do nothing about its deeper causes, it will unfailingly surface again.

CHRISTOPHE   That's true, but in the end I sympathize with her. We live in a society where a high value is placed on women being young and pretty. As I see it, this patient's case has tremendous extenuating circumstances. The women over fifty that we see in the media are all Botoxed, liposuctioned; they've all had facelifts. Once that is the case, we are all subject to the tyranny of that. But she poses a real pedagogical problem for me: How can I make her understand that her age denial has become the greatest source of her suffering? I know that as long as she has not admitted and understood that, she will continue to be unhappy. Maybe therapy can't help her. Maybe a shock is necessary, a terrible upheaval in her life. Or maybe she should drop everything and enter a convent!

MATTHIEU Fortunately there are other solutions than entering a convent.

CHRISTOPHE In dealing with situations like this, I'm always uncertain. I hear you, I'm drinking in what you say, and I see perfectly well how precious all this Buddhist wisdom, all this psychology, could be for this woman. But how high a dose of it can I give her?

MATTHIEU Without talking to her about philosophy or Buddhism, you could help your patient to identify other sources of well-being, such as taking a walk in the woods or by a lake, or any other simple pleasure that might bring her inner peace or permit her to distance herself a bit from her obsession with her appearance.

CHRISTOPHE Absolutely. I regularly try to get her to taste the quality of this type of experience.

ALEXANDRE I like the idea of "extenuating circumstances" that you mentioned. The patient who refuses to get old and fears death reveals the tendency that exists to overvalue success, resplendent health, and high-level performance. And then when the machine begins to screech, the cortege of fears reappears at the gallop, and this happens all the more since we have ousted the religious traditions and made death a taboo. Yes indeed, we have extenuating circumstances, and it's no small achievement to extricate ourselves from the pounding of the media that pushes us to believe that happiness is an object of consumption. There's only one thing that is urgent and that is to practice, to embark on the path, and then don't hesitate to ask yourself what real joy is about. Without idealizing the past, we have to have a good look at what the going models of a successful life are today. If our vision of happiness is narrow, it is perhaps because it is conditioned by fashion and advertising, and because that cuts us off from the true happiness that is described in the spiritual traditions. There are so many fantasy images that pull us away from the reality that can heal us, hard though that reality may be. Paradoxically, I believe that it's contact with reality that is our salvation. The world is super hard, tragic in some sense. But as soon as you run away from it, as soon as you take refuge in illusion, you are doomed to a painful, hard landing sooner or later.

Among the causes of our unhappiness there is the need to have a suit on when we leave the house and play a role in order to be liked, in order not to disappoint. Daring to take a more contemplative approach means getting back to a deeper level, heeding our inner compass and disregarding the thousand and one influences that bring nothing but agitation. If, first thing in the morning, I find the world sad, I can immediately make an effort to see how my mind is projecting onto reality. In the tradition of St. Ignatius, a distinction is made between consolation and sadness. Before getting involved in blaming anything or anybody, I have to recognize all the thoughts that are keeping me from seeing simply. If I'm going through a period of major troubles, feeling totally down, I see pain and evil everywhere, and I'm incapable of finding the least reason to be happy. By contrast, if I'm going through a period of consolation, everything seems terrific. The exercise is to realize that the world is independent of my moods. The ascesis consists in purifying one's vision so one can appreciate the world as it is.

> The world is super hard, tragic in some sense. But as soon as you run away from it, as soon as you take refuge in illusion, you are doomed to a painful, hard landing sooner or later.

MATTHIEU In Buddhism it's said that sometimes the whole world seems to be our enemy. This is, of course, the result of our mental fabrications.

ALEXANDRE It's crazy the endless supply of illusions I maintain about myself. A Zen master was kind enough to give me a heads-up about this. He told me, "Ninety-nine percent of your thoughts are total illusion." Seeing that the overwhelming majority of my mental representations are just smoke and hot air is a tremendous help to me in extricating myself from suffering and finding peace. As soon as some anxiety comes up, to my sorrow I believe with a belief as hard as iron that it's real. But it's only an illusion, a phantom without substance. It almost becomes a game to let my mind run free and create all the thoughts it wants. If one doesn't take them too seriously, with a bit of detachment, one can amuse oneself watching them arise and then disappear. Often, in the face of a persistent obsession, I remind myself that it's nothing more than one thought among the thousands of others that have gone through my head today.

MATTHIEU Unfortunately it's really easy to identify with thoughts when you forget to observe them in the free space of awareness.

ALEXANDRE The inner search also liberates us from worrying about what others think of us and allows us to come close to pure love. What fascinates me about the spiritual masters, in addition to their infinite kindness, is that they are perfectly free from concern over what others think of them. Whereas in my case, I can be totally dominated from morning till night by the desire to please or at least not disappoint. The example of the masters strengthens my desire to devote myself wholeheartedly to practice and set aside arguments such as "I don't have the time." Taking into account the number of hours I waste on Facebook, in order to commit myself full time to ascesis I think I would have to be some kind of a saint. Nowadays it's a challenge just to escape from the television screen and the urgings of the ads. Those who have gone before us on the path must have had tremendous determination—in their eyes, nothing was more important than their spiritual lives. Ultimately I am the master of very little in this life, but devoting twenty minutes a day to meditating, praying, pulling out the roots of suffering, still remains within the realm of possibility for me. Why has the spiritual life become almost a luxury when there is really nothing more important in the world?

I am the master of very little in this life, but devoting twenty minutes a day to meditating, praying, pulling out the roots of suffering, still remains within the realm of possibility for me. Why has the spiritual life become almost a luxury when there is really nothing more important in the world?

MATTHIEU   One of my masters used to say, "Roughly speaking, you work eight hours and you sleep eight hours. So you have eight hours left. You have to spend some of them relaxing, washing, and doing other routine chores, but if you were to tell me that you don't have twenty minutes to meditate, I'd have a hard time believing you."

Analyzing Unhappiness: The Causes of Suffering

ALEXANDRE   I've always wanted to ask a psychiatrist this question: Where does the tendency to inflict pain on ourselves come from? Why do we stick so stubbornly to our guilt and brooding? Why this inner torture? Where do we get this capacity to inflict suffering on ourselves, given that life is already so hard?

CHRISTOPHE   I more often ask myself the question "how" than "why." *How* should I help people to get out of their suffering? The question *why* is unfortunately not always followed by an improvement in symptoms.

Brooding is often a wrong route that we take when we are obsessed by the why. Because there is not always an obvious or soothing answer to why. Whereas *how* incites us to action, *why* can make us go around in circles. We think we're reflecting on our problems and their solutions, but in fact we are brooding. We are like a snake biting its own tail. We don't see that dwelling and brooding on solutions to situations that don't have immediate or available solutions only increases our suffering.

We can also make ourselves suffer in order to punish ourselves for the fact that, at that moment, we feel helpless to solve our problems; so we go ahead and castigate and beat ourselves up for that.

MATTHIEU In Buddhism this also has to do with the disarray that prevails in our minds due to ignorance. We are ignorant not because we don't possess an encyclopedic knowledge of things, but because we don't make the distinction between what might create more suffering and what might liberate us from it. We could also say that ignorance is a kind of addiction of which we endlessly create the causes. It's like continuously sticking your hand in a fire although you don't want to be burned.

> We are ignorant not because we don't possess an encyclopedic knowledge of things, but because we don't make the distinction between what might create more suffering and what might liberate us from it. We could also say that ignorance is a kind of addiction of which we endlessly create the causes. It's like continuously sticking your hand in a fire although you don't want to be burned.

Recently I was walking with a friend in the early morning on a deserted beach near Los Angeles, and we saw a person approaching in the distance. When he reached us, we said hello, and then, doubtless intrigued by my monk's robes, he started a conversation. He was in his sixties. Almost immediately he said to me, "My problem is women. I think about them all the time. Have you got any advice?" I did my best to come up with a few suggestions. Pointing to the vast ocean and the cloudless sky opening above and before us, I said, "Look at this immensity, so clear, so luminous, and so simple. If you let your eye and your mind fuse with that, don't you have the feeling of being very distant from your obsession?" He looked at me with a vaguely uneasy look and exclaimed, "But there are no women in the sky!" He plainly did not want to distance himself from the causes of his torment.

If we avoid accepting the fact that we have aged, we perpetuate an illusion that is bound to crumble sooner or later, and we suffer quite uselessly. When the Buddha taught the first of the Four Noble Truths, the truth of suffering, his goal was not to plunge his hearers into a pessimistic view of life but to make them recognize their suffering. After that, like a good doctor, he explained the causes of this unhappiness. That was the second noble truth, that of the causes of suffering, that is, ignorance and the other mental afflictions. Then he showed that understanding the causes was of no use unless one undertook to free oneself from them. If doing that was impossible, we might as well, as the Dalai Lama put it, "pick up some good beer, go to the beach, and, above all, don't think about suffering." But like all things, the causes of suffering are impermanent, which means we can get rid of them. Thus the third noble truth puts the emphasis on the fact that suffering is not irremediable. It is due neither to chance nor to divine will. Rather, it arises from a fundamental error. Now, this error has no reality in itself; it is nothing but the absence of truth. It is sufficient to become aware of the truth to make the error, as profound as it is, disappear, just as it is sufficient to light a lamp to dispel the darkness in a cave, even if it has been immersed in darkness for millions of years. Since it is indeed possible to remedy the causes of suffering, the next step consists in putting the means of doing this into effect. This is the object of the fourth noble truth, which describes the path for progressing from ignorance to understanding, from slavery to freedom, from suffering to happiness.

By the way, when I was writing *Happiness: A Guide to Developing Life's Most Important Skill*, a friend told me I should be the last person in the world to write a book on this subject, since I had never experienced any major suffering. It's true, the toughest thing I've had to bear was some years in the somewhat harsh environment of a mountain hermitage, without running water, electricity, or heat. But in retrospect, those years were among the happiest ones of my life. I lived by the side of my spiritual master and devoted myself to meditation. So I didn't experience major suffering. For that I couldn't offer you a poignant and edifying example like that of Alexandre. Nonetheless, like everybody else, I do know what suffering is, and I have witnessed extreme pain and tragedy. My humble contribution to our discussion on suffering is to examine it through the knowledge of beings who have discovered its profound causes and who have liberated themselves from them. Buddha is often compared to a physician. The physician, even if he is in good health, is able to diagnose the illness that has struck his patient, conclude the most appropriate treatment for it, and apply it with care and compassion.

The Looks of Others Can Kill or Cure

ALEXANDRE The first time I ventured out of the institute in the company of a friend, we encountered a boy who shouted at my friend, "Hey, you forgot the leash!" Another time, I went out on a bike excursion accompanied by a disabled pal. As we passed by, the neighbors got alarmed and called the cops, who conducted us straight back to the institute. All this is to say that the way others look at me has been one of the great challenges of my life, and I very quickly understood that it could both kill and cure.

The force of concern for what others think can sometimes sneak up on us from unexpected angles. If we have a disability or some other injury, we might find ourselves drawn to overcompensate for it, to achieve some kind of positive recognition. We might feel we have to surpass ourselves, rise above the level of anonymity, somehow dazzle the gallery. A mechanism like this drives us into a mad quest for applause, and that leads to further suffering: dependency, the need for approval, recognition, and consolation.

How can we remain on guard, wary of this mechanism so that we can avoid falling into role-playing or trying to use others as instruments of approval? To dare to open to a genuine encounter, we have to shed our shell and all our protections. For example, at the institute I found that with a simple "How are you doing?" I could really show an interest in another person, try to understand him, lend him a compassionate ear. Today, with this expression usually being degraded to the level of a simple hello, a polite reflex, I still don't forget the significance of it, which is to approach the other, create bridges, and love. Continuing from back then, I still like to use a "How are you doing?" or "Are you happy with your life?" to establish a relationship that goes straight to the essential, beyond masks and roles.

CHRISTOPHE Telling yourself "If nobody mocks me and I succeed in not identifying with my image, I won't suffer" seems to me to be saddling yourself with a very difficult mission, Alexandre, even an impossible one! Because this suffering comes from rejection, a withdrawal of love, a lack of compassion, it is thus not subjective, it is biological. It's violent to be rejected, like a slap. If somebody slaps me, I can't say, "I'm in control. It's nothing serious. I'm not suffering." It's physical pain that you get from a slap, and I think it's physical pain you get from being excluded. We are social beings, and the refusal of love, rejection, hurts us in our bodies even before it affects our minds and shakes the image we have of ourselves.

On the other hand, the endeavor you undertake following that, your efforts not to sink into the suffering connected with being rejected, is really an extraordinary labor in the face of the selfishness, the stupidity, and the incomprehension that some people have with regard to disability. But it seems to me you can't deny the existence of this pain. Even if through your intelligence, your practice, your greatness of being, and what you are able to bring to readers, you avoid getting bogged down in the swamp of this suffering.

ALEXANDRE When you're really having a hard time, the temptation to harden yourself and shut yourself up in a shell is very great. Yes, the mockery will always get to me. I would be lying and deluding myself to pretend I'm beyond all that. Doing the spiritual thing in the manner of putting on a nice show doesn't lead anywhere, except to a lot of lies and suffering. It takes a bloody lot of courage to renounce adopting a fixed, definite response when you're faced with what hurts you, and to accept being vulnerable. One day, I don't remember what criticism I got on Facebook that made me run with my tail between my legs to my spiritual father to get some consolation. His response healed me: "If you base your identity on slander, rumors, and other people's opinions, there'll never be an end to your suffering!" But how can you decrease this alienation, this hypersensitivity to nasty comments and criticisms? The eyes of my children, and those of my wife and friends, save me and help me not take all the mockery and misunderstandings embedded in certain situations so seriously. So when in the subway I hear tittering around me, I close my eyes and bathe myself in the benign and compassionate looks of my family and other close friends, and that allows me to demolish that little pinching in the heart that, if not digested, can do so much harm in the long run.

The importance of projections never ceases to amaze me. Sometimes everything happens as though each person were living in *his* world rather than *the* world. I am often surprised after a conference to have somebody come up to me and tell me, "I loved it when you said such and such." But more than once it has been the exact opposite of what I was trying to communicate. In the beginning I would get up in arms and fight these misunderstandings. I would try to correct these distortions, until I saw that everybody understands on the basis of their experiences, their convictions, the roads they've traveled. Our job turns out to be to get out of the way somewhat, put our preconceptions aside, and let reality be what it is.

> Our job turns out to be to get out of the way somewhat, put our preconceptions aside, and let reality be what it is.

A thousand times a day I think of the words of my spiritual father. The moment I get on the subway, even though I just want peace and quiet, something always goes wrong. One nasty blow leads to another. But this is just the point. Every one of those nasty blows can become a call to practice, an occasion to decentralize and recall that I am not what others perceive me to be. If I took it one step further, I could rejoice in being made an object of ridicule.

MATTHIEU If we want to find inner peace, we cannot depend on the opinion of others and the image they have of us, whether it's right or wrong. My second master, Dilgo Khyentse Rinpoche, often used to say that any speech, pleasant or unpleasant, friendly or hostile, is like an echo. If you yell insults or compliments at a cliff, can you be hurt or flattered when the echo comes back? Some people say nice words with evil intent, and others come out with unpleasant words but with good intent. You can be praised in the morning and insulted at night. If you always get stuck on these words, you will always be troubled.

> You can be praised in the morning and insulted at night. If you always get stuck on these words, you will always be troubled.

Taking the point of view that what you hear is just echoes does not mean falling into indifference. Rather, it means no longer offering your ego as a target for flattery or sarcasm. The Dalai Lama often says, "When some people treat me like a living god, that's nonsense. And when others treat me like a wolf or a demon in monk's robes, that's also nonsense." This means that he doesn't identify with being a living god, a demon, or any other ego representation. He knows that deep within him there is an inner peace that is firmly grounded in an understanding of the nature of his mind. This peace is not sensitive to criticism or praise, which can only affect the ego. He simply does not identify with this ego.

It's obvious that identification with an imaginary ego that is supposed to be the very essence of our being is at the heart of our problems. The true nature of the mind can be compared to the sky, which is completely unaffected by any dust you might throw at it. Of course, it's easier to say this than to live it day to day, but one thing is for sure: the further you go in this direction, the less vulnerable you are to the remarks and looks of others.

> The true nature of the mind can be compared to the sky, which is completely unaffected by any dust you might throw at it.

CHRISTOPHE   Listening to you, Matthieu, I can't help thinking that on a daily basis that's practically a superhuman attitude! I imagine there can't be more than twenty people in the world who are capable of that.

ALEXANDRE   At need, I immerse myself in the attitude of Christ as portrayed in the Gospel of Matthew, which for me is far from being natural, given the extent to which my heart can harden into a logic of vengeance and reprisal. But it says there, "If anyone slaps you on the right cheek, turn to them the other cheek also." This example never ceases to inspire me. One of the hardest things in the world is to reconcile infinite gentleness with firmness. In concrete terms, how can I react to being mocked? Why should the question of what "they" think of me become one of the major concerns in my life? Why do I get hung up on this little ego and close myself up in it? Progressively I could strip away these thousand and one attachments that dupe me into believing that I'm a bundle of reactions, emotions, and opinions. Of course, a very potent mechanism wants me to identify with my body and my thoughts, especially when I'm suffering. But why not play with thwarting this instinct and smoking it out wherever it is at work extending its ravages? And never forget the words of Marcus Aurelius: "We are born for each other."

MATTHIEU   It is not as superhuman as it seems. Everything is a question of the degree of our inner development and the degree of development of our vision of things. If a person attaches great importance to his image and is continually occupied with how other people see it, he will be highly sensitive to what they say about him. But a person who, though he may not be perfect, has accustomed himself to think of the words of others like illusions, echoes, or the lines of actors in a play will understand that he has no reason to suffer from them, even if as a result of habit they momentarily affect him.

If, as in the frequent situation mentioned by Alexandre, others are insensitive or harsh with us, we might initially be saddened by it. But in a second phase we can find a certain consolation in understanding that the scornful attitude of others can in no way affect our basic being. We will thus feel compassion for those who wrong us, because they are in the grips of ignorance and stupidity. For in doing wrong to others, they mainly wrong themselves.

Reacting in this way is not a manifestation of weakness but rather of inner strength and freedom. This is not an expression of your constantly being willing to let other people walk all over you, but rather it shows you are a person who reacts with determination, dignity, and compassion, and does not let himself be thrown off balance. To answer Christophe, there may perhaps be only twenty people who have attained a degree of development sufficient to react in this way perfectly, but anybody can cultivate the same vision of the world as them and gradually integrate it into his being, until one day it becomes second nature.

CHRISTOPHE But that seems really hard to me! I try to guide my patients in that direction, and I attempt to make headway in that direction myself, but I think that enormous progress is already attained when we accept that mockery or injustice exist and that they are painful. We are social animals. When a human being is the object of malice, mockery, or physical or moral violence, it is normal for that person to suffer. That's no error in his vision of the world. If somebody breaks my toe with a hammer, it is normal for me to experience pain. So, in fact, the real work consists in preventing this pain from extending to our whole being, and then restraining the generalizations of this pain from contaminating our vision of the world, of others, and of ourselves. We must avoid thinking, "All human beings are filthy bastards" or "I'm totally pathetic." We are capable of limiting the pain caused by these attacks and preventing it from completely taking over our being and

> The real work consists in preventing this pain from extending to our whole being, and then restraining the generalizations of this pain from contaminating our vision of the world, of others, and of ourselves.

cutting us off from the world. But we can do this much better if, firstly, we have accomplished the psychological work that you both describe very well and that you both embody, and of which you cite particularly accomplished examples such as the Dalai Lama; and secondly, we feel love and compassion both toward ourselves and others.

MATTHIEU   Excuse me for insisting, but experience shows, particularly in the case of those who practice a little meditation, that even if you are far from having attained perfect mastery, it is easier than it seems to stop continuously identifying with ego. Though it may be normal to suffer from mockery and injustice just as from physical pain, it is also just as normal to look for ways to stop reacting to these behaviors or to immunize yourself to them the same way you get vaccinated for a disease. That doesn't mean that you become a dehumanized robot, or that you cease to perceive the malicious and abusive aspect of mockery and injustice. Rather, you no longer suffer from them as disproportionately as before. You gain inner freedom from them. Your mind becomes big enough to accept bad circumstances without having them shake you. A handful of salt in a glass of water makes it undrinkable, but if you throw the same handful of salt into a big lake, it doesn't change the taste of the water at all.

Can We Get Away from Unhappiness?

MATTHIEU   To free oneself from misery, it is essential to honestly seek out its causes, to understand what the deeds, words, and thoughts are that provoke it. If I think I have "everything I need to be happy" and yet I'm not, that's because I'm mistaken about what the causes of happiness and suffering are.

I think it's also necessary to make a distinction between suffering and unhappiness. Our sufferings are provoked by a great number of causes that we have no power over. Being born with a disability, getting sick, losing a dear one, being caught in a war, or being the victim of a natural catastrophe are all beyond our control. Unhappiness, however, is not fundamentally tied to external conditions. It depends on the way our mind functions. A change, even a very small one, in the way we manage our thoughts and interpret external circumstances can significantly transform the quality of our lives.

Quite often what we take to be happiness is really suffering in disguise. This mental dysfunction prevents us from identifying the causes of suffering and remedying them. Not being crushed by the obstacles that are strewn throughout our lives doesn't mean that we are no longer affected by these obstacles. Rather, it means that they can no longer get in the way of our inner peace, or at least in the way of our progress toward this peace.

> Not being crushed by the obstacles that are strewn throughout our lives doesn't mean that we are no longer affected by these obstacles. Rather, it means that they can no longer get in the way of our inner peace, or at least in the way of our progress toward this peace.

On the path, it is essential to never get discouraged. It happens to me as to everybody to encounter problems. One of our humanitarian projects falls through, someone behaves in a nasty way in a situation—I see that I was not always as nice as I should have been. For a few hours those things affect me, and I reproach myself for them. But I know they won't last because, thanks to the teachings of my masters, I have inner tools and resources that will allow me to overcome these obstacles and recover my inner equilibrium, my determination to improve myself, and my joie de vivre.

ALEXANDRE   How wonderfully hopeful to learn that mental suffering is only a dysfunction, because what could be more terrible than the total absence of horizon that would result if that weren't the case? That would be a little like we were suffering in our flesh and the pain was nearly killing us, and after a ton of analyses and x-rays the doctor arrived and told us, "There's nothing that can be done." Then to the pain would be added guilt, in the form, "I *shouldn't* be in pain." Instead of that, why not see from the beginning that misfortune, the samsara that plunges us into chronic discontent, is nothing but a kind of inner derangement?

One day I was trying to get a piece of advice from a Zen master that would liberate me on the spot. He confined himself to the following response: "Alexandre, don't forget that it's in chaos and disarray that joy is hidden, that it's at the heart of samsara that nirvana shines."

Thus it is possible to find happiness even in the midst of our wounds and psychological troubles. Who ever said that we had to be perfect in order to attain authentic joie de vivre? On the surface there could be waves forty-five feet high, whereas in the depths calm reigns. Everybody, no matter what their external circumstances, can bring about this inner relocation. The way is open to everybody: disabled people, the rich, the poor, the sick, the outcasts. This is what is truly revolutionary.

> It is possible to find happiness even in the midst of our wounds and psychological troubles.

MATTHIEU   Just as you say, there are two levels of experience, which are often compared to the tranquil depths of the ocean and the waves that stir up its surface. Even if a storm is raging above, below the ocean remains calm. A person who only sees the surface and is unaware of the peace of the mind deep down is at a loss when the waves of adversity shake him.

The Remedies for Suffering and Some Pitfalls

CHRISTOPHE   Alexandre spoke of his love for his children. We cannot hope to limit our suffering if there is no love around us. I often have patients whose solitude is their major problem. They would do much better in dealing with their woes if they were surrounded by loving people. That would enable them to avoid falling into despair, nihilism, and hostility toward the human race every time they are subject to significant suffering. Even the least crumb of affection is precious then! I believe a caregiver can give his patients love, that neighbors can give love to the people next door, that unknown people on the street can give love with smiles. Alexandre, you have sometimes been mocked, but there are also people who came along and consoled you to some degree with a kind look. All these little things don't take away the pain, but they help us not to crash and burn entirely and move in the direction of destroying our connection with the world.

MATTHIEU   Giving and receiving love decreases the influence of ego, and this has the effect of making us less vulnerable. Is it because "I" becomes "we" that there is a kind of opening, that we are less focused on the ego? When a child has a tantrum, it might hit its mother, but that's not the same as if an unknown person or a colleague at work did it. The mother, in her love of the child, receives the blows differently. The fact that love diminishes the barrier between me and another person means that the target of the blows, the ego, is much less present. And the more transparent the ego is as a target, the more arrows pass through it without affecting it. By contrast, the more the ego is perceived as real and solid, the more the arrows strike it with full force. That is the reason that love and compassion are the supreme remedies for suffering caused by ego.

As for the desire to escape from the vicious cycle of suffering, once again, the Tibetan word often translated "renunciation" means "determination to get free," to liberate oneself from the suffering into which ignorance has plunged us. It is only when this determination is present that the process of liberation can truly be set in motion.

ALEXANDRE   Here again we are not talking about voluntarism, the reign of willpower or of a rigid ego that has fully empowered itself. This determination has nothing to do with this kind of uptightness. It is more supple, more open, so it adapts perfectly to reality. It embraces the flow of life moment by moment.

MATTHIEU   It's a conscious reaction associated with a strong sense of resolve. You say to yourself, "There's no satisfaction in this. I'm through! I've sweated this long enough! I'm going to do everything in my power to liberate myself from it, no matter how much time and effort it takes."

CHRISTOPHE   Does that also apply to discouragement about oneself? All those depressed people, in despair over not being able to get their lives back under control. Is the solution for them to take a self-compassion supplement? How do you see that?

MATTHIEU   The two forms of compassion, compassion for oneself and compassion for other people, go hand in hand. Compassion for oneself allows those who hate themselves to discover that deep inside them, they would prefer to not suffer, if possible, and therefore they ought to be kinder, less scornful, and less uncompromising toward themselves. If they also train in feeling compassion for others, they will include others in their daily preoccupations and stop focusing just on themselves. Practiced together, these two forms of compassion are inseparable from the realization of the interdependence of all beings, and from the fact that one is not alone in suffering and wanting to be happy. One leaves behind egocentrism and ceases to divide the world into "my side" and "the other side."

ALEXANDRE   When we embark on a spiritual path, we must inevitably face the spiky question: Can we master our minds? Do we have power over the stream of thoughts that passes through us from morning till night? One day, in the midst of an anxiety attack, I went to see a doctor and told him about my state of generalized anxiety. When I told him I was afraid of everything, he replied, "You shouldn't be." Telling somebody suffering from anxiety that he should not be disturbed is like pissing in a violin—it doesn't help at all, quite the contrary. The temptation of voluntarism is always lurking, as if wanting to get out of it were *really* all it takes to succeed in doing it. The challenge is to discover and practice this exercise: let it pass. I dream of a doctor who encourages patients to train their minds, who transmits the concrete tools they need to help them to get through their torments.

MATTHIEU   The Tibetan word that is translated "to meditate" in fact means "to cultivate" or "to habituate oneself." In the case you mention, what is needed is to gradually acquire the ability to manage one's thoughts and emotions. With habit, one can succeed in identifying the disturbing emotions as soon as they begin to hatch. It's like training yourself to spot a pickpocket. At the end of a certain time, even if he mixes in with the crowd, you won't have trouble spotting him, and he won't be able to steal your wallet. Meditation as habituation also makes it possible to deal with mental afflictions before they take on too much force. In the beginning that might seem difficult and a bit artificial. Then, with training, the process becomes natural and you can easily put it into effect.

Acceptance Is Not Resignation

CHRISTOPHE   It's very hard to say to people who have suffered all their lives that in suffering there is light and that, as Hölderlin says, "where the danger is, also grows the saving power." When I tried speaking to my patients about acceptance, it drove them batty. They felt they had already had it up to their ears with suffering from the time they were born and they didn't want to accept any more of it. I quickly backed off. Personally I am perpetually at the beginner's level with this, always in the process of relearning to accept suffering, to accommodate it, to give it a place in my life. How can we transpose these pearls of wisdom, these experiences, or these facts supported by science that we know about into tools that are comforting, encouraging, or usable by the people who are going to read our book? We are sure those things are important, but we are not sure that our readers are going to be able to accommodate them in the situations they're in when they read these lines.

MATTHIEU   I have often noticed that we often conflate acceptance, or adaptation, with resignation. Recently, in a conversation with some academics, I explained that training the mind by means of meditation makes it possible to modify our perceptions of painful situations and helps us acquire the skills we need to face the ups and downs of life. They categorically

> We often conflate acceptance, or adaptation, with resignation.

replied that it was dangerous to recommend this kind of adaptation to suffering. For them, that amounted to telling suffering people that all they had to do was become accustomed to their conditions. It amounted to telling slaves, battered women, people rotting unjustly in prisons, and other oppressed people that the best thing for them to do is to meditate so as to become content with their fates, rather than calling for justice and an end to their oppression.

This reaction is based on a misunderstanding. Acquiring the ability to face painful circumstances with courage and serenity is to provide oneself with a precious asset that will make it possible for one to suffer less. That does not at all mean resigning oneself to it. One simply avoids adding further distress and exasperation to the pains one is suffering already. One avoids double suffering.

Of course, you can't just tell patients, "I advise you to accept your suffering, and now just go ahead and work it out." You have to tell them that you are going to make use of all possible means to put an end to their difficulties, but it would very useful, from their side, to take a different attitude toward their situations.

CHRISTOPHE   But, concretely, what have the moments in our lives been like in which we've had to console someone or to console ourselves? What have those sufferings been that we ourselves have had to confront or that those close to us have had to confront? How did we relate to those sufferings at that moment?

Laying on a lot of advice to someone who's suffering is an extremely dangerous exercise. You can irritate people, upset them, and drive them to despair by serving up wise words on how to deal with suffering, even with the best of intentions. You have to clothe your advice in lots of affection, gentleness, caution, and wait for the right moment. It also seems to me that you can't work with somebody's suffering except when you're not suffering too much yourself. In the midst of their pain, the person only has one wish: not to suffer anymore. That person will not be very receptive to didactic messages. They will only want the analgesics: drugs, affection, love, distraction. So I apply the utmost in strategy and tactics in dealing with the suffering of my patients and friends.

MATTHIEU   As a therapist, can you give us an example or two?

CHRISTOPHE   I was very touched by a recent experience during a conference about suffering at a Zen monastery. There must have been a hundred and fifty people in the hall, and a very stricken fellow stood up and told us that his son was a schizophrenic, that he suffered regularly from delirium, destroyed everything in his house, and that he was institutionalized at that moment. He didn't know what to do and was asking for advice. I was very frustrated, because in complicated and heavy cases like that, it takes hours to understand and a lifetime to try to help. But dodging and hedging in that moment by saying "It's too complicated for me to respond adequately or advise you in just a few words" also seemed nothing but a cheap evasion, a cop out.

One of the Zen masters present then said something to him that I find conceptually accurate, but very hard in human terms. He spoke to him of impermanence and acceptance, if I remember correctly. I saw by the man's face that this was no comfort to him, and I thought to myself, "What could I say that might help, in a few words and just a short time?" I stood up to speak without knowing what I was going to say, and I heard myself tell him something like, "Listen, you are incapable of helping him. It's been years that you've been trying and haven't succeeded, so accept your helplessness without giving up being present at his side, showing him that you love him even if you can't help him, and accepting this deep inside you. Because at the moment, nothing else seems possible." This is an attitude that we often adopt in medicine: First accept being incapable of helping the way you would like to. The father's wish for his son to suffer less was justified, but as long as he didn't accept that there was nothing he could do, he suffered double. He suffered from the plight of his child and inflicted a further dose of suffering on himself by not accepting his own helplessness. Next, be there for the patient as much as possible. After that, I said to the pain-stricken father, "Whatever you do, every time you are there at your son's side, every time you talk to him and try to establish a connection with him, your presence will be something important for him, to a degree that he, you, or I will never be able to measure." I had the impression that these words comforted him, and at the end of the day he came and thanked me. I don't know what happened to him. It's complicated. Sometimes you do people some good at one moment, but in the long run . . . Did these words finally open a path for him and diminish his pain in the long term?

ALEXANDRE   I could only dream of such a compassionate and on-the-dot therapist as that. Because there are two dangers: betting the farm on your will, or the opposite—abdicating and giving up. Voluntarism, believing completely in our willpower, ignores our limits. This is the famous problem treated by many philosophers of the weakness of the will and of the difficulty of changing in the down-to-earth circumstance of daily life. It's as if the heavy force of inertia were preventing us from making progress, as though there were some kind of thermostat inside us that maintains our old habits against all winds and tides, even though this status quo is painful to us. Though I know well enough that a certain behavior is harmful, I can hardly wait to go and do it anyhow. But resignation is no better—just throwing up your hands is a kind of self-abuse. Nothing is worse when we're suffering than the feeling that we're paralyzed and can't do anything about it. If I consult a doctor, I'm sure to leave his office with some solution, as minimal as it might be—some piece of advice, some tool, an exercise. Throughout our lives the possibility of making progress persists. Even on our deathbeds we can liberate ourselves, transform inwardly. The practice of meditation remains available, whatever our problems. Often when the doctor could no longer do anything, I have found in spiritual practice a way of opening up a horizon.

In order to make progress, why not imitate the Buddha, who, like a doctor, gives a diagnosis? Unhappiness initially pushes me in the direction of wisdom. If I examine the path I have traveled, I have to admit that at the beginning I did not practice meditation for altruistic reasons but because of radical discontent and an inability to live in the present moment. Paradoxically, I think I have more ability to face the blows of fate than to take on the little problems of everyday life and to appreciate happiness when it is there. It's almost tragic, but it seems to me much easier to accept my disability because I have no choice, there's no cure for it. If I glimpsed the least hope of a cure, I would knock on every door and shout my SOS in all directions. But there is something comforting, almost soothing, in telling myself that there's no use in getting worked up about it. By contrast, where I sense that it would be possible for me to improve things, immediately I begin putting out a total effort. Deciding what to try to overcome and what to accept takes tremendous judgment and discretion. And here Epictetus provided me with a precious tool, by showing that each day I have to clearly distinguish between what depends on me and what doesn't. Speaking of Epictetus, he presented himself as "a slave on the road to freedom." In my turn, I could ask myself, "What am I a slave of? What are the illnesses of my soul?" My disability placed me very early in the arena of battle, of joyous combat. But though it is important always to make progress, I found that having my regard always focused on the future, on what might come later, weakened me considerably.

Recently a friend of mine killed himself at a moment when he was getting a little better. A former drug addict, he *chose* to leave this world a few months after having freed himself from this dependency. After having struggled so much, it can be hard to then realize that the life and the routine existence we worked for do not measure up to our expectations. And what tremendous effort it took to succeed in surviving . . . In short, I take away from this that we must remain very vigilant, that our fragile spot is not always where we think it is, and that even the good times require ascesis, an art of living.

Along the way, my children give me huge support and transmit a lot of confidence to me. When I'm moving through a very crowded area of Seoul, all I have to do is look at the eyes of my little daughter to unlearn my fear. Celeste does not say to herself, "Papa is a cripple. We're going to croak right here in the middle of all these cars!" Buddhism and positive psychology authorize us to have a bit of hope: we all have the possibility of deprogramming fear, distrust, feelings of insecurity. Every day we have to renew ourselves and repeat this slow unlearning process. I haven't left off questioning myself about the tenacity of our obstacles and the difficulty of leaving behind the mental poisons once and for all.

MATTHIEU I want to come back to the example you gave, Christophe. It reminds me of public encounters where people pose similar questions to the Dalai Lama. Some of them come with the sort of suffering that has no evident solution, like that father with the schizophrenic son. They come expecting that someone who has been meditating for sixty years, who is a great moral and spiritual figure, will give them some new and specific advice. But quite often the Dalai Lama begins by replying, "I don't know." Then he remains silent, as though absorbed. You might say, "That's weird. So he's never reflected about illness, or bereavement, or disability, or euthanasia, or abortion, and about all the other problems that people ask him about?" In fact, when he says "I don't know," he means that there's no ready-made answer. After a few moments of silence, he adds, "Every human situation is different. Without knowing the specific details of your situation, how can I give you appropriate advice?" He doesn't try to get a person to believe that he has a miracle remedy for their disabled or sick child. However, there is another phrase that he often comes up with: "One thing is certain in all cases, being there with love and compassion cannot but do that person you are desperate to help some good."

In general, people underestimate the good that that kind of presence does.

CHRISTOPHE When you encourage people to give up on their desire to be effective and to move instead just to loving presence, you're trying to get them to change the way they are looking at the situation. In the end, everything the father of the young schizophrenic fellow was trying to do in his helplessness (take him to a different doctor, get him to get out of the house instead of just lying around smoking, etc.) I counseled him to continue doing, just in a spirit of love, while at the same time accepting that it would not necessarily help heal his son. The important thing is not to go about things in an uptight way, with anxiety or despair, or repeating to oneself, "If he doesn't listen to me, he's just going to get crazier." Just say to yourself, "At this moment, this is what I can do, whether it works or not." This kind of advice doesn't necessarily encourage people to do anything different from what they're doing already, but it leads them to do it in a different spirit—without being obsessed with being listened to, without looking for immediate results.

MATTHIEU We shouldn't underestimate the impact of this kind of attitude. You might think that it's just an insignificant little touch, like putting a piece of tape on a broken jug. But, fundamentally, the good or bad qualities of our lives are determined by the quality of each moment in our relationships with others in the world. If our way of relating is touched with compassion, that makes an enormous difference for the person experiencing it.

CHRISTOPHE Yes, and I think that acceptance has a liberating effect. It opens up a new horizon, that of compassion. When that father, in a state of despair, was attempting to relate to his son ("My God, this is horrible!"), compassion was there but it was obscured by his desire for things to change, his obsession with the idea that he was not doing enough, by guilt. If he were to say to himself, "Okay, he's a schizophrenic, you're his father, do what you can, be present and loving as best you can, . . ." that would allow for his compassion, which is already there, to emerge. That would ease the father's mind, and perhaps also, little by little, be more helpful to the son.

MATTHIEU Resignation is not the answer here but rather simply accepting, for the moment at least, that there's nothing you can do. This kind of acceptance, instead of closing down the horizon as resignation does, makes it possible to add something positive. The Canadian writer Rémi Tremblay just published a very touching book called *La chaise rouge devant le fleuve* (The red chair by the river), in which he talks about his son who is suffering from a drug addiction that he can't get over. The author explains how for a long time he tried to sweep his own suffering under the rug while being caught in the vicious circle of hope, expectation, and disappointment. You never want to see your children suffer, but the author learned, he tells us, to accept that suffering without either feeding it or running away from

Acceptance of a situation that cannot change or that will take time to change leaves the door open for adding the liberating dimension of love.

it, without ignoring it or letting it push him into action. Now he is more successful at remaining present, listening to his son, and he speaks of this presence as a "posture of love." Being there more for his son helps him to be calmer and more loving and thus capable of better judgment and more appropriate action.

In other words, acceptance of a situation that cannot change or that will take time to change leaves the door open for adding the liberating dimension of love.

CHRISTOPHE And more than just "adding" it. The possibility of love also has to be *liberated*. Compassion was there for sure, but it couldn't express itself because acceptance hadn't happened. Often acceptance does the trick: you stop struggling against things you're helpless to change, and suddenly all the goodness in you can finally come out.

The Practice of Acceptance in Everyday Life

ALEXANDRE Acceptance can be frightening if we look at it as an absolute requirement. Accepting our whole life in one big lump is on the level of the impossible. In this regard I borrow a highly efficacious practice from Alcoholics Anonymous. For a dependent person to say "I'm going to stop drinking forever" is a crushing thing, insurmountable. Right away, just to get past that bad moment, you pour yourself a shot. So the exercise consists in committing to stopping drinking hour by hour. I can apply this principle to the big challenges in my life. Thus instead of trying to solve all my psychological problems all at once, once and for all, I concentrate my efforts on a moment-by-moment basis. The same goes for our little problems. The person with an overeating problem can definitely go so far as to say, "This afternoon I'm not going to touch this cake."

MATTHIEU   I'm very fond of a word of advice of an English lord to his son: "Take care of the minutes and the hours will take care of themselves."

ALEXANDRE   Acceptance represents a big piece of the spiritual life. So we should prepare ourselves completely or, rather, make ourselves available for saying a joyous yes to life. Why should we always associate acceptance with effort or with resignation? Spinoza wrote in his *Ethics* that it's not renunciation that leads to beatitude but, on the contrary, beatitude that leads to detachment. The Dutch philosopher brings me to the understanding that a minimum of inner peace is a prerequisite to liberating oneself and accepting reality. So, paradoxically, ascesis is, first, treating ourselves well, finding out what really makes us happy; and it allows us to advance. Joy, not uptightness, is what leads to acceptance. The first step is to make sure I'm not accepting the thousand-and-one rejections and denials in my heart. What is needed is to say yes to everything, even my resistances—so in the end, it's accepting that I don't accept.

Nothing gets in the way of acceptance more than resignation and fatalism. The misunderstandings on this point are legion. In *Ecce Homo*, Nietzsche says that the greatness of humanity lies in the *amor fati* (literally, "the love of fate"), not wanting anything other than what is, and, even better than that, loving what happens to happen.

MATTHIEU   There's nothing more counterproductive than saying to oneself that the present *should* have been other than it is. We must accept it with clarity and fortitude, which doesn't at all prevent us from taking a constructive attitude toward the future.

ALEXANDRE   We also have to remember that alone, without a network of friends, without a family, it would be much harder to say yes to our suffering. When I'm in very bad shape, I pick up the phone and call a companion in suffering. I listen to him and try to devote my entire attention to him. This little exercise gets me away from centralizing on myself; it pulls me out of the black hole for a while. By the end of the conversation I'm always pretty much restored. On a more prosaic level, when my printer is screwed up or I miss a train, instead of blowing my top and getting lost in "Oh, if I had only . . . ," I immediately ask myself what I can do to limit the damage. Accepting is not throwing up your hands but rather, quite to the contrary, finding the way forward in what is, in what I can change. If my house burns down, what's the best thing I can do? Lose myself in anxiety, yell at the person who forgot to turn the gas off, or immediately run to get a bucket of water?

CHRISTOPHE   Alexandre, you were saying that when you're not feeling well, you call someone, not to complain, not to be comforted, but to make a connection. That right away made me think about what I do when I'm not feeling at all well. The worse I feel, the more I need to be alone. I absolutely must settle in and sink into my suffering. In this sense, meditation has been something revolutionary and a salvation for me. Taking the time to explore why I am suffering, what is happening in my body, the thoughts caused by what is happening in my body, the impulses, desires, and projections I'm being pulled toward—looking at all that in the light of mindfulness. Thus accepting suffering is, first, observing its ramifications and the power it exercises over me, and then to see what I'm going to do about it. Am I going to take a walk in the woods? Call a friend? Write? Give my attention to somebody else, as you were saying? In all these cases, I need to be alone in order to get back in touch with myself and to conduct this work of examination.

I try to transmit this attitude to my patients, along with the mindfulness practices. When we are transforming the notion of acceptance into the *practice* of acceptance, we work initially on all the little bits of suffering. We show the patient how to accept the tiny frustrations, the really minor suffering: "I wanted to go out and it was raining," "I wanted to make a good meal for my friends and I was sick." That's our obsession in behavioral psychology. When I want to teach somebody to ski, I don't start on a really hard piste on a bad-weather day. If we want to work with somebody on acceptance, we look with them at their daily life and try to find things that are easy to accept. Accepting these little things may be easy but it's also a saving grace. For example, the day you're able to accept that your little son or daughter is not understanding the explanations you're giving them for their math homework, you are able to say, "Okay, it's a normal situation. Breathe and accept that so you can see how you might deal with this problem instead of getting irritated, wanting to counteract it, wishing it were not the case, or considering it abnormal." If you're able to tell yourself that—if you're able to breathe and smile instead of getting upset—this little sidestep can open up a world of possible changes. Then, little by little, you move on to other exercises. These are real exercises in acceptance. They give us the pedagogical means to turn the notion of acceptance into experience.

ALEXANDRE   Why do we ever turn acceptance into a completely disembodied practice, a distant concept? It opens the field to unparalleled joy. The Zen tradition, as well as the great Christian mystics, provide us with a way to achieve it. Paradoxically, the way is very concrete. Instead of getting lost in theories, we carry out actions that will liberate us little by little. And at all times we say yes to what is. Here again, when the house is burning, pitch right in, grab a bucket of water, so you can get out of the situation safe and sound. Discoursing on acceptance without acting is like looking at a burning building and giving speeches while the people inside are dying.

Acceptance comes from unconditional love. It takes a whole lot of inner freedom to stop wanting to transform somebody else to the way you

> Acceptance comes from unconditional love. It takes a whole lot of inner freedom to stop wanting to transform somebody else to the way you want them to be, to dictate their behavior, shape their opinions.

want them to be, to dictate their behavior, shape their opinions. The temptation to take power over others is always there, even unconsciously. In this regard, a good marital relationship is not far from the connection that you can maintain with a spiritual father, a connection devoid of any sense of scheming or vengeance. One of the most healing experiences is to love another person and be loved without having to prove to them who we are in our basic being. For many long years I woke up with "I'm fed up with this life!" In examining the causes of my weariness, I saw that social pressure was a big part of it. The fear of disappointing others can crush us in the end. Liberating oneself, extricating oneself from this, requires replacing this needy approach to others with pure love that never asks for anything in return.

And, Matthieu, you gave me a fabulous example on the occasion of a conference we attended. When a person got stuck in a question that just kept dragging on and on, you simply said, "Although I don't in the least wish to interrupt you, I think we will stop here." It was a masterful lesson! Whereas I was painfully doing my best to keep listening, you made me understand that there is a more appropriate, freer approach. The desire not to disappoint leads us astray. It takes a lot of courage to commit a just act. Basically I had not given a thought to the thousands of people who, like me, wanted that question to end. In our society you have to be incredibly free in order to no longer be overcome by the desire to please—and yet still not fall into a state of indifference.

MATTHIEU Personally, when I'm feeling bad, it's often because some person, aside from one of my spiritual masters, has said harsh words to me, justifiably or not. In either case I have to have a moment of solitude. If the reproach was justified, even in part, this silence gives me the opportunity to look inside myself and lucidly take the measure of my imperfections and sincerely wish to rid myself of them. If the reproach was unjust, I also look inside myself, but to acknowledge what is unchanging there and inaccessible to injustice and the opinion of others, meaning the presence in my heart of my compassionate masters and the luminous nature of my mind, peaceful and unchanging.

Persevering After Suffering

MATTHIEU When people have experienced major misfortunes, it often happens that their courage fails and they sink into despair. But if they succeed in overcoming these obstacles, they may well end up feeling a sense of greater achievement. How often do we hear people say, "I came out of that tragedy or that illness a bigger person"? Suffering is never desirable per se, but once it is there, we ought to mobilize all our resources and make use of all our relationships with other people to turn that suffering into a means of self-transformation. It's a little like when you fall in the water: instead of just letting yourself sink, you use the water as a support so you can swim and get back to the shore. You use the suffering itself to find the force to face it. Once you have acquired that kind of resilience, your future confrontations with trials and troubles will never be the same.

I met my master Kangyur Rinpoche in 1967. The following year I went through several major upheavals in my personal life. I saw then that if I looked into the deepest part of myself, beyond the sense of sadness that dominated my thoughts, I found an inalterable and luminous peace in which I felt in perfect communion with my master. This experience was a major opening for me. It gave me a feeling of confidence so great that I could say to myself that no matter what obstacles I met from then on, I would always be able to return to that space of inner peace.

CHRISTOPHE That's a fundamental notion. I like to talk about the "postwar" experience, an idea that you develop in one of your books, Alex, *La construction de soi* (Building the self). When we have emerged from some suffering or gotten through an ordeal, we can prepare ourselves to face the next suffering or ordeal (because they are always there in our lives). We can remain at war. Or else we can each take the time to savor our moment of peace and look at our life from a different angle, develop a different relationship to it. This is the postwar experience that prepares us for true peace. It's not amnesty or indifference, it is just the awareness that adversity has prepared us to better appreciate nonadversity.

MATTHIEU   After having found this new inner strength, we know that from now on we will have the ability to land on our feet. We also have greater inner freedom, which makes us less vulnerable to adversity.

CHRISTOPHE   When one has overcome adversity or suffering, rather than trying to forget about it, it's interesting to do a complete review of what has taken place. For example, when I have prescribed antidepressants or tranquilizers to patients and they feel better, I always insist that we take several sessions to work over what happened. I ask them: "How are you feeling now, with the drug?" "Why isn't it like it was before?" "How do you see the world?" "What has changed, the world or you?" "What should we think about that?" Positive psychology also delivers this message: every time a person mobilizes their forces, finds the energy to confront adversity, it's a major phenomenon that we should definitely work to understand better. In our work, we don't just analyze the suffering but also the way we were able to respond to the suffering, then get beyond it. We experience the fortifying effect of that.

MATTHIEU   The idea of resilience comes to mind. It frequently comes up in relation to people—often in relation to children—who have come through severe ordeals better than some others. At the World Science Festival in New York, I participated in a discussion on resilience. I tried to put the accent on an important point: resilience is not only an ability that one acquires (or doesn't) through the force of circumstances when one is confronted by cruel and painful situations, but it can also be intentionally cultivated by training the mind, just as is the case with a certain number of other inner qualities. We can include in that the ability that I spoke about before, of finding in ourselves, at the very core of our experience, a place of peace and freedom to which we can return at any moment and in which we can rest our minds, even in the middle of difficult circumstances. In Buddhism we speak also of putting on the armor of patience, this word—*armor*—being understood in the sense of resilience or fortitude. Love and compassion are two other important aspects of this strength of mind. The more our minds are filled with compassion, the less our thoughts spin around obsessed by our own troubles. Basically resilience is the feeling of being better equipped to face new trials. This is a little like a good horseman or a motocross champion who feels that, even if the terrain suddenly becomes very uneven, he will be able to maintain his balance and get past the obstacle.

ALEXANDRE I like the idea of resilience very much. It has destroyed a bunch of preconceptions and opened up a path to healing for thousands of people. But let's not make an imperative out of it! We always have the lurking danger of classifying people. On one side there would be the superheroes, the resilient ones, those who face winds and tides and come out well. On the other side we'd have the losers. But life is not that simple. Along the way we might totally capitulate at some point, but then pick ourselves up and go forward again. Healing is never accomplished once and for all. To get through our difficulties we also need resources, a more or less conducive environment, and a bit of luck. Often trials come along that weaken us, and resilience consists precisely in making do with available means and continuing ever forward.

MATTHIEU We don't choose a stormy day to learn to swim or sail, but rather we do it in fine weather, under conditions in which we are not immediately forced by the difficulties of the task to go under. If every time we encounter a squall our ship goes down and we are incapable of facing the challenges of life, it is partly because we failed to train when things were going well.

However that may be, true fulfillment can only manifest when we have liberated ourselves from confusion and conflicting emotions, when we perceive the

> True fulfillment can only manifest when we have liberated ourselves from confusion and conflicting emotions, when we perceive the world as it is, without veils or distortions.

world as it is, without veils or distortions. And for that, we have to begin by acquiring a better knowledge of the way our minds work.

We must also free ourselves from the fixations brought on by our egocentric mode of thinking, which drives us to want the world to conform to our desires. The world is not an online sale catalog from which we can order whatever we want. Even if satisfying our whims of the moment were possible, it would not lead to profound satisfaction but rather to the arising of new desires, if not indifference and fatigue.

If you are going to overcome suffering and attain a feeling of enduring fulfillment, the pursuit of ego-oriented happiness dooms you to failure. Selfish satisfaction can only be transitory, like a castle built in winter on a frozen lake.

Relinquishment of our egocentric fixations goes hand in hand with greater opening to others and with the realization that our happiness and unhappiness depends on others. Altruistic love based on understanding the interdependence of all beings makes it possible to establish harmonious relations with everyone around us. When we suffer ourselves, if we recognize that innumerable beings are also immersed in suffering, we feel compassion for them and our personal sufferings are replaced by a much vaster perspective, and that gives us courage.

This change of attitude and the mind training that must accompany and sustain it might seem too difficult. However, as the great seventh-century Buddhist master Shantideva wrote, "There is no big difficult task that cannot be broken down into small easy tasks." Thus the way we must pursue this gradual transformation is step by step, moment by moment, thought by thought, emotion by emotion, in joy as well as in sorrow.

Our Advice for Times of Trial

Stormy-Day Advice   ALEXANDRE

- Practice in daily life. Don't wait to be at sea to learn to swim. Beginning to practice a spiritual way when everything is going wrong is like trying to score on a penalty kick at the time of the World Football Cup without having done any previous training.

- Take action. In the midst of suffering, what helps me is taking action. There's nothing worse than immobility. So this becomes a reflex: "What can I make happen here and now to start feeling a little better?" We should especially avoid closing ourselves off from others. Without others, without my family, without my companions in good, I wouldn't make it an inch further on the path of acceptance.

- Don't overreact. St. Ignatius of Loyola tells us that at times of despondency, when everything is going badly, we should not overreact but stay true to the everyday level of things—get through your day well. In the midst of torment, it is perilous to try to change everything. And it takes immense courage not to thrash about in the waves but just let the hurricane pass.

The Invention of Shoes   MATTHIEU

- Don't try changing the decor no matter what the cost. Shantideva wrote, "How can enough leather be found to cover the entire earth? With just the leather for one simple pair of soles, you achieve the same result." If we see the whole world as our enemy, trying to transform it so that it is no longer harmful to us is an endless task. It is infinitely easier to change our perception of things!

A Few Basic Messages that Are Not Necessarily Very Amusing   CHRISTOPHE

- First message: I see suffering as well as violence in the world. We all dream of having it go away, but we know very well that there's enough of it to last a good long while. Rather than getting upset or indignant about it, we should say to ourselves, "Okay, it's there. What can I do on my own personal level and then in my immediate environment? What can I encourage through my own behavior, by my actions, through my talents?"

- Second message: Stay connected with the world, in happiness as well as unhappiness. That connection is what will save you. Suffering cuts us off from the world. It deprives us of what we need the most—connection with people, the capacity to love, the ability to let everything around us nourish us—because we are focused on our suffering and on the idea that there's no solution to it. The most precious training, when we are not feeling too badly, is to cultivate this relationship to the world and other people.

- Third message: When suffering is there, stop, accept it, explore it, give it all the space necessary to observe what direction it is pushing you in. The distinction of Jon Kabat-Zinn's that I like the most is the one between response and reaction. When you are suffering, there is an impulsive *reaction* that comes from your history and from social pressures—it's an automatic pilot that sometimes crashes you into a wall. Then there is *response*, adapted and intelligent, which takes both the present and its context into account. But to respond, one has to have explored, one has to have accepted feeling what goes on in our body and in our mind.

Consistency

A Question of Fidelity

CHRISTOPHE How do we live in accordance with our aspirations? Can we say one thing and do another, as if normal requirements applied to other people but not to ourselves? Do people who commit themselves publicly to certain values behave consistently with what they profess in the intimacy of their hearts and their deeds? Consistency is a subject that touches me and that Alexandre and I talk about frequently. We are uncomfortable whenever we notice divergences between what people say and how they behave in private. When we see a politician revile fiscal fraud and call for administrative honesty and then not pay his own taxes, we clearly have a case of inconsistency. I'm not suggesting that we conduct witch hunts and ensure that all public personages are perfect. But at least public speech and action should be consistent with private behavior. If that's not the case, we should either admit our fault, or shut up and stop handing out lessons. In either case, we should go back to working on ourselves!

High-Fidelity People

CHRISTOPHE Why does consistency have so much value in our eyes? There are doubtless many reasons. The first line of reflection that comes to my mind is that of the difference between a master and a professor. A professor can teach various articles of knowledge and himself be distant from the perfection he teaches. Whereas one expects a master to be exemplary in both his speech and behavior. It seems to me that we can speak of consistency when there is a balance between different aspects of the same entity. We can speak of consistency in a rational argument, consistency in a person, consistency in attitudes toward life. For the three of us together here, what is important is being consistent with our values and ideals. But why is it difficult for many of us to remain consistent with our ideals, values, and commitments? I can hardly wait to hear what the two of you will say.

Fidelity is another form of consistency in relation to one's commitments. It's a question of resisting all the temptations, all the expedients, all the cowardliness, all the laxity that might take us away from our ideals. It's a little like so-called hi-fi components, which are called that because they produce high-fidelity sound. What we want is high-fidelity people, human beings capable of staying on track with regard to their ideals. Naturally there is not only the question of consistency or fidelity to our ideals, but also the question of what ideals we choose.

MATTHIEU Fidelity to oneself is a notion Michel Terestchenko talks about a great deal in his book *Un si fragile vernis d'humanité* (A very thin coat of humanity). Some people sacrifice this fidelity. They relinquish their fundamental moral principles by gradually making concessions, and they end up caught in an irreversible chain of events that leads them in the opposite direction from where they wanted to go. This is how the simple police officer Franz Stangl gradually became the head of the Treblinka concentration camp and ended up responsible for the deaths of nine hundred thousand Jews. Each time he tried to refuse a further promotion in the Nazi hierarchy, both he and his family were threatened. So each time he took a further step into ignominy. In the course of the seventy hours of interviews he gave to the journalist Gitta Sereny in 1971, he told her that he should have committed suicide in 1938, the first time he was forced to do something he disapproved of. Michel Terestchenko cites by way of contrast the self-fidelity of Father Trocmé and his wife, who decided not to go along with the least infringement on moral

Free Audio Programs!

The Self-Acceptance Project ($97 value)
Instant access to 23 respected spiritual
teachers and more than 26 hours of
transformational teachings on self-compassion,
especially during challenging times.

The Practice of Mindfulness ($15 value)
Download guided practices by Jon Kabat-Zinn,
Shinzen Young, Kelly McGonigal, Tara Brach,
Sharon Salzberg, and Jack Kornfield.

Meditation Music ($10 value)
Listen to nine inspiring tracks for healing,
relaxation, and releasing stress.

To download these **3 free gifts**
go to **SoundsTrue.com/Free**

800.333.9185

Dear Sounds True friend,

Since 1985, Sounds True has been sharing spiritual wisdom and resources to help people live more genuine, loving, and fulfilling lives. We hope that our programs inspire and uplift you, enabling you to bring forth your unique voice and talents for the benefit of us all.

We would like to invite you to become part of our growing online community by giving you three downloadable programs— an introduction to the treasure of authors and artists available at Sounds True! To receive these gifts, just flip this card over for details, then visit us at **SoundsTrue.com/Free** and enter your email for instant access.

With love on the journey,

TAMI SIMON   Founder and Publisher, Sounds True

SOUNDS TRUE
many voices, one journey   800.333.9185

ST330

principles, and who openly declared that they would protect Jewish families no matter what price they had to pay. They succeeded in saving thirty-five hundred people.

We have to know clearly what we want to remain faithful to. Can we speak of consistency in the case of somebody who is convinced that members of an "impure" race must be eliminated? If that person puts his beliefs into action, he will certainly be faithful to his aberrant view of the world, but unfaithful to his fundamental nature, which Buddhism calls Buddha-nature, which is present in every one of us, free from hate, desire, and other negative mental states that obscure the mind.

When I am asked what the main qualities of the Dalai Lama are, one of the first answers that comes to my mind is that he is exactly the same in private as he is in public. He behaves the same way with a head of state as he does with the people who clean his hotel room. He sees them first as human beings, which means he values them equally and gives them the same attention. At the time of the fiftieth anniversary of the Universal Declaration of Human Rights, to which he was invited by the highly respected French lawyer Robert Badinter—who was instrumental in the abolition of the death penalty in France and consequently in the European Union—numerous meetings were arranged for him with various officials. One evening, coming back from a conference, one of the motorcyclists escorting his motorcade, a woman, took a fall. As soon as the Dalai Lama arrived at his hotel, he asked for news of her. He was told she had suffered arm bruises. The Dalai Lama, who was scheduled to leave by plane the following morning, asked if he could see her again before leaving. She came about seven thirty in the morning with her arm in a sling. He gave her a book and embraced her. He seemed to be more concerned about her than the important people he had met.

> When I am asked what the main qualities of the Dalai Lama are, one of the first answers that comes to my mind is that he is exactly the same in private as he is in public.

One day he left President Mitterrand waiting on the porch of the Élysée Palace so he could go shake hands with a member of the Republican Guard who was standing twenty yards farther on. It was a way of saying we are all equal. He often says, "If you see me as the Dalai Lama, you create a gap between us. I am, first, a human being and you are human beings. Second, I'm a Tibetan. Third, I'm a monk. And fourth, I'm the Dalai Lama. So let's stay on the level of our common humanity!"

Should We Play a Role in the Social Theater or Tell the Whole Truth?

ALEXANDRE   Without a doubt you need a tremendous amount of courage to reach that point. I'm not sure I can get through half a day without reciting a whole rosary of pious lies. Who can claim to have entirely peeled away his social veneer and be carrying on naked? It's crazy the way, all day long, without a break, we tend to play a role in order to protect ourselves, in order not to disappoint, in order to meet expectations. In the long run, this comedy can wear us out, sap our strength. If from morning till night we put up a facade so as to play nice, how can we avoid ending up completely drained? That being the case, what better path to freedom is there than to imitate the Dalai Lama and the sages of other traditions and become who we really are? But where to begin? Maybe by daring to be a little more true, by rejecting all lying. But this major step, preliminary to any spiritual life—I always tend to put it off until later.

For example, I hardly dare say it, but I think I have never let myself appear 100 percent as a disabled person. I'm always trying to edit my performance, making efforts to hide who I really am. How can I live in acceptance if I am constantly disguising myself? To take off the masks, to stop playing the chameleon—that would be a radical conversion. Why should I not start now to identify the points at which I am

> How can I live in acceptance if I am constantly disguising myself? To take off the masks, to stop playing the chameleon—that would be a radical conversion.

only pretending to be sincere, when for fear of others' judgment I fully betray myself? Why not just laugh about it and, without establishing any fixed point, take off all the masks, one after the other? More than anything else, unconditional love vaccinates me against having to carry on this masquerading. With my near ones, there's no need for costumes or posturing. Feeling oneself deeply loved heals. Because of this, every day I am called upon to live much more simply, to stop living only for the eyes of others and instead love beyond all calculation.

Loving without calculation, without any reason, doesn't necessarily mean saying amen to everything. I can pardon a murderer without thereby condoning horrible acts. No person can be reduced to his acts—not the assassin, not any villain. Unconditional love does not stand in the way of proclaiming loud and clear that there are acts that are unacceptable—quite the contrary. And what freedom it is to drop the logic of quid pro quo!

> Somebody who spoke the truth—nothing but the truth—would surely pass for a nut case. But the hypocrite who from morning till night hides his background thoughts, isn't he, in fact, really the sick one?

In order to drop my masks, I found a master. One of my friends, a young girl suffering from autism, shares with the Dalai Lama this nearly superhuman power—she never lies. It's troubling to see that in our society this freedom is regarded practically as a defect. How do we react, for example, if we find the food at a restaurant totally disgusting? Somebody who spoke the truth—nothing but the truth—would surely pass for a nut case. But the hypocrite who from morning till night hides his background thoughts, isn't he, in fact, really the sick one? From time to time I catch myself telling little white lies, one after the other. I haven't slept a wink and I hear myself saying, "I'm fine, in great shape." Without failing to take into account the value of well-intentioned courtesy, I might just ask myself if I'm not falling into a state of self-compromise. I also have the freedom to take a vow to lie just a little bit less from today onward.

On the path of the spiritual life I see another danger, that of trying to play the superhero, pretending to have risen above injury. It may not be inappropriate at this point to recall Nietzsche's words, "One must still have chaos in one, to give birth to a dancing star."[1] It may seem to be a contradiction, but it is a good idea to see that our wounds can also become prime sources of creativity. Nietzsche's challenge is surely a liberating one: we should stop dismissing the wounds of the past as a bad thing and work to find in every moment an opportunity for making progress.

Trying to be at least somewhat consistent also means doing a bit of housekeeping—dropping outworn preconceptions the way we would throw away old clothes. We might begin this work by ferreting out the nostalgia that binds us to these hundredfold repeated errors. Attachment to the past, making an absolute of what is only transitory, reactivates our unhappiness. On this earth, everything is ephemeral, impermanent, even the teaching of the Buddha, which the texts tell us is like a raft that can take us to the other shore and can be discarded once you get there. Life is a series of stages. On the way, we have to throw out many reflexes, presuppositions, and many of those cathartic ideas that sustain us for a time but end up spoiling our lives. Before falling asleep I sometimes examine the opinions that I'm fettered by. What's the point of keeping all that paraphernalia in tow? I'm not saying we should throw out everything, but I can already see that the majority of my thoughts proceed from illusion.

What has struck me the most in spending time with masters is that I've never spotted in them the slightest desire to please. They radiate from their hearts a profound harmony with reality and an uncon-ditional love for every being. Whereas our wounds can turn us into beggars, avid for affection, ready to do anything for some consolation. But it's not with violence that we kill ego, but rather with gentleness, so we must accept our paradoxical aspects without harshness. Fidelity to the deepest part of ourselves is the approach that moves us toward consistency. Instead of pointing our finger, from moment to moment, at the slightest falseness in others, we should nourish ourselves with unconditional love.

So let's throw all our unnecessary accessories overboard, everything that prevents us from progressing in joy, peace, and love. And speaking of worn-out clothes, why not risk a little spiritual undressing? But all too often, instead of dropping our roles and daring to live nakedly, we undress the other person with our looks . . . On this path the Dalai Lama remains a model. As you say, Matthieu, he remains faithful to himself no matter where he is, whether in the company of a chief of state or a hotel maid. Let's hasten to imitate him.

MATTHIEU Being true doesn't necessarily always mean telling the whole truth, especially if it creates suffering, and as long as one is not lying to hide one's mistakes and faults or, worse, to deceive another person with malicious intent. Being true to oneself requires remaining in conformity with one's own ethic and with the profound, basic nature I referred to earlier. But that doesn't mean that one has to follow some inalterable rule or dogma at any cost. We must take into account the good or bad consequences for others that fidelity to our principles might have. If I rush to announce to someone that his wife or her husband is cheating on him or her, or that people are saying that that person is a complete imbecile, I might very well be telling the truth, but I am betraying my ideal of compassion and, at the same time, my basic nature.

Alexandre, you say that you are rarely able to just be 100 percent the disabled person you are because you are aware of always trying to correct something in order to be seen differently. Disability is an incontrovertible reality, but it does not define your true nature. Deep within, you are not disabled, just as the Dalai Lama is not the Dalai Lama, or a super handsome guy is not a super handsome guy. The Dalai Lama is first a human being, and on a deeper level he possesses, as you do, Buddha-nature.

Coming back to consistency, I can say that with my master Dilgo Khyentse Rinpoche, it was a quality one could discern in the least details of his life. I am not capable of saying what the depth of his wisdom and the extent of his compassion were, but during the thirteen years I spent with him—pretty much day and night, because I slept in his room to assist him because of his advanced age—I never saw in his behavior the least behavior that differed from what he taught. I never saw an act or heard a word that even remotely suggested malevolence. He could be harsh with his disciples, because coddling their egos would not have helped them progress along the path, but with all people who came to see him, from the kings and ministers of Bhutan and Nepal to simple farmers, he was always immensely kind and totally available. Seeing this level of consistency, I ended up feeling unshakable confidence in him.

Charlatans who conduct themselves in accordance with the principle "do what I say but don't say what I do," do a great deal of harm by discouraging people who are looking for role models. You see it in many sects. The guide puts himself forward as a model of virtue, whereas in private all his behavior betrays the ideals he teaches. This is also frequently the case, sadly, in politics.

CHRISTOPHE　These lies and pretenses, notably on the part of public figures, pose a very serious problem in my view. As a social species, humans have an absolute need for reliable and credible models. One of the most powerful tools of personal transformation, besides the messages and values one receives from a spiritual teaching, is the value of exemplariness, what is called in psychology "learning through imitation of models." It's not a question of transforming oneself into a Torquemada of personal rectitude, but rather establishing clearly the difference between what is merely on the level of imperfection—without being a betrayal of one's word and public commitments—and that which is all-out duplicity and deceit.

MATTHIEU　Lack of consistency is often connected with an exacerbated sense of self-importance. A person who insists absolutely on displaying a flattering or deceptive image of himself has a hard time admitting his faults and showing himself as he is. He tends to lie when his words and deeds are not up to the level of the appearance he wants to give.

This kind of attitude falsifies our relationships with others. Thus it prevents all inner progress. In Buddhism we say that the most compassionate master is the one who points out our hidden faults and thus allows us to correct our inconsistencies.

The Ravages of Intolerance

CHRISTOPHE   I see another problem in this area. I have friends who are very consistent with regard to their values, who have political, religious, and other commitments that I completely respect, but who are intransigent and sometimes express their convictions violently. I dimly perceive that deep down it is their consistency that is rigidifying them in their position. To what point can fidelity to our values be a guiding light in the right direction, and at what moment does it become something that prevents us from changing and opening? Now, Matthieu, I'm sure you're going to tell me that we must choose our commitments well and not deceive ourselves about what stars we hitch our wagons to.

MATTHIEU   There's a difference between, on the one hand, fidelity to our values and to applying them in a way that takes into account the circumstances and our behavior's effect on others and, on the other hand, dogmatic intransigence that fails to take the situation of others into account. That is the reason why the Dalai Lama often does not reply right away to ethical questions with regard to which you would think he has very definite opinions. In view of the circumstances, he takes the time to think over what seems to him the most appropriate answer and the one least likely to cause suffering. Francisco Varela used to speak of "embodied ethics," ethics that always take the particular context of each human situation into account. This is the contrary of the ethics of "duty" of the Kantian type, in which absolute principles must be applied in all cases.

Embodying an Ethic

CHRISTOPHE   Returning to the question of white lies that Alexandre raised, can we say to someone who has prepared a meal for us, "Sorry, but no, really, it's not good"? And if we're not going to lie, what can we say? In positive psychology we encourage our patients to put the accent somewhere else; not to reply to the question of whether or not it's good but to say instead, "It was a delicious moment in your company," if at least that was the case, or else, "Thank you, it was really a pleasure to share this meal with you." Maybe this is hypocritical, but it's also a means of partially maintaining your sincerity while not delivering a blow to your host.

As for practical work on consistency that I might set for myself, I have a vast area to work with respect to invitations. I am frequently invited to conferences, dinners, parties, and so on, and it would please me to be able to please. But, deep down, I don't want to say yes because I am tired or because it's not on the top of my list of priorities. Being faithful to my values is not hurting people who offer me invitations, but it's also not hurting myself. How shall I put it? Lying is the simplest solution, and I often have recourse to it. "Oh, I'm sorry, I already have an engagement." But more and more I reply, "I'm sorry, but I need some rest" or "If I had more time, I would be delighted, but in this case, I just can't." When I reply in writing, in general I formulate things this way: "I'd like to be consistent with what I write. I encourage everybody to take care of themselves, respect themselves, listen to themselves. I must do the same, and thus I cannot respond positively to your invitation. I like you very much, it sounds very nice, it's a good cause, but I can't." Sometimes, on days when I'm really in top shape, I follow the model of Jules Renard, who wrote in his journal: "A really free man is one who can refuse a dinner invitation without giving an excuse."[2] So I reply simply, without justification, "Thanks very much for your invitation, but it's impossible for me to come."

MATTHIEU Compassion provides a simple solution to problems of consistency. If the meal is bad, should we at all costs say the truth? Is it more important to have told a little lie or to have told the truth and hurt somebody? Lying and stealing are generally harmful acts and are thus reprehensible a priori. But one can also lie to save the life of somebody being pursued by a killer, or seize the food reserves of an egocentric potentate to save people who are threatened by famine from death. Here we are in the opposite camp from Kant, according to whom, for example, we should not lie under any circumstances, even to save someone, because in permitting ourselves to lie, we destroy the credibility of all speech in general, which constitutes an injustice toward humanity as a whole.

We come back to the notion of contextual—embodied—ethics, that is, ethics based on compassion. As the Canadian philosopher Charles Taylor says, "Ethics is not only what it is right to do but what it is right to be." A good person will spontaneously react in a compassionate manner. His behavior might take various forms, but from the point of view of compassion, it will always be consistent. It is only from a dogmatic point of view that it might seem inconsistent. We can, of course, behave awkwardly, lack discretion, be incapable of foreseeing all the consequences of what we do, but from the point of view of altruism, we will have acted in the way most apt to create the greatest possible good in a given situation.

Our Advice on Consistency

Living with Consistency (Even in the Smallest Things) and Avoiding Hurting Oneself   CHRISTOPHE

- It is more effective to work on embodying one's values oneself than to content oneself with talking about them and recommending them.

- Here is an example of an important practice I try to do. I do my best not to say anything bad about other people. If I end up doing so anyhow, I make an effort not to say anything I wouldn't say to their face.

- Ideals and concern for consistency must not be transformed into self-tyranny. Our scruples should be accompanied by compassion toward ourselves, tolerance toward our mistakes and our imperfections. Let's indeed present ourselves as people who are working to make progress on the path, but not as examples of those who have attained their goal.

Avoid Tyranny Toward Oneself and
Intolerance Toward Others   MATTHIEU

- Don't become attached to fixed dogmas. Since human situations are always complex, being too rigid can result in reactions that are out of sync with reality and that create more suffering than happiness.

- Prioritize compassion. That considerably simplifies the problem of consistency because compassion becomes the sole criterion that our thoughts, words, and deeds must answer to.

Try to Live Beyond Roles   ALEXANDRE

- Live from your inner being and send your social ego packing. Get rid of the desire to please and the thirst to succeed at any price. What a misunderstanding it is to associate our inner being with what we are ashamed of and has to be hidden! In our deepest being, there is no longer any ego, any mask. We become one with all of humanity.

- Surround yourself with spiritual friends. A real companion on the path doesn't take off when the weather gets grim. He also doesn't hold back from speaking the truth. His ultimate desire is to support you and help you move forward when war is raging in your heart.

- To move in the direction of greater health is also to integrate our contradictions and, in any case, to cease to regard them as our enemies. Who says you have to be 100 percent balanced in order to taste joy? There are a thousand and one ways to experience health and peace. Neither disability nor pain has the last word.

Altruism

Everybody Wins

ALEXANDRE   It takes tremendous courage to fight against the slope that makes us slide almost irresistibly toward selfishness. And the hearts of those who give their all for the good of their fellow beings are anything but sappy or weak. People already understand this, but it's difficult to get away from those notions. But that should not stop us from going ahead and nourishing authentic concern for others and from doing our best, without condescension, to be genuinely interested in them. In my view, the great challenges in life can be expressed in a few words: take very good care of your soul, of your body, and of other people.

> Take very good care of your soul, of your body, and of other people.

First, we should see that we are all in the same boat, and that's why there's such a great danger of shooting each other in the foot. Why the devil should we consider other people as our enemies, our competitors, and forget that all men and all women are fellow crew members who also aspire to happiness? For Aristotle, it's by practicing virtue that we become virtuous. Generosity, charity, and genuine love for our neighbor happen in ordinary everyday life circumstances. Very simply, we befriend our next-door neighbor, console a child, greet a homeless person without pity, and refrain in all circumstances from inflicting harm.

The Joy of Altruism

ALEXANDRE   Dostoyevsky jocularly reminds us that it is easier to love humanity as a whole than put up with our neighbor. But it is on the down-to-earth level that love is embodied. Real kindness embraces all of humanity. There is always the danger of doing a lot for unfortunates who are facing terrible difficulties while forgetting the person who for years has been laboring under a chronic illness. As if our heart's energy got worn out from contact with reality. . . . Let's not wait for catastrophes or blows of fate to develop tenderness. We can approach others starting now. Who says we have to wait for our world to be struck by major misfortunes to rouse our compassion? The most ordinary act can be marked by immense generosity: the way you say hello, the way you answer the phone, the quality of your attention to others—it all becomes a spiritual exercise. When we put on our pants in the morning, we can quite simply ask ourselves who we are dedicating this day to.

> Who says we have to wait for our world to be struck by major misfortunes to rouse our compassion?

MATTHIEU   When we speak of altruism, compassion, solidarity, good attitudes in general, it is true that we encounter all kinds of prejudices. Isn't it true that altruism is for the weak, the kind of people who tend to make stupid sacrifices, who are unable to get ahead? Isn't reality, as hard as it is, made for triumphant egos, for consuming passions, for destructive fits of anger? Some people think that altruism is no more than a duty artificially dinned into us by our family or our church. We must be good because that's what we have been told, because it's taught in the Holy Scriptures. Others think we can only truly be altruistic if it costs us, if painful sacrifices are involved. If you get joy out of it, it's fishy.

ALEXANDRE   Little repeated acts in everyday life help me infinitely more than great heaps of resolutions I never put into effect. The

Gospels tell us that there is no greater love than giving one's life for another. How, without necessarily dying as a martyr, can I answer this call day after day? The newfangled cynics really give me a pain when they try to pass altruism off for naive foolery. Your life, Matthieu, persuades me of the opposite. And what would the great saints say who devoted their entire lives to others? It's not selfishness that leads to happiness but rather this commitment, this generosity lived with joy and freedom.

Positive psychology labors under a certain negative judgment laid on it by cynical and jaded minds, folks who believe in unhappiness. You don't have to be a naive dreamer to believe in the power of generosity. On the contrary, the fight for social progress, the struggle against injustice, has always been led by great-hearted people eager to eradicate evil. I'm not sure that the indifference of the cynic leads anywhere worthwhile.

When we're riding on public transport together, I often say to my kids, "Try to spot the person with the grimmest face and ask yourself what you might be able to do for him or her." You might think this is a laughable exercise, but what could be easier than to smile at someone, hold a door open, give your seat to an older person, not succumb to anger?

Thank you, Christophe, for reminding us that there is an *almost* too-steep slope that forces us in the direction of egotism. If we were to let ourselves go, that would be the beginning of the end. Precisely in relation to that, it is all those little acts that make it possible to put us in reverse, to change our direction millimeter by millimeter toward generosity.

At the institute, my teachers urged me to be self-reliant, independent, but they themselves were so distant that I was unable to find the courage to start working to improve myself. By contrast, the people who brought me the most joy were the ones who loved me the most. It wasn't lukewarm, sappy love, but invigorating, demanding, unstinting love. Which reminds me of my master, who lavishes luminous teachings on me every day. Once he called me "the last of the real imbeciles." Yet there was such gentleness, such infinite kindness in his words that they gave me the strength to immediately drop a whole raft of stubborn misunderstandings, preconceptions, and fixations. This was absolutely nothing like the condescension or cruelty that we find pretty much everywhere. Watching television back in Seoul, I saw many of the featured performers providing a pitiful example of this. It used to be that if a critic was evaluating a book she didn't like, she put forward her arguments. Nowadays something else is in fashion: vomit on people, tell them off in public with a kind of false, contagious glee, that of the toreador planting his knives in his victim's flesh. We urgently need to rehabilitate altruism and compassion. Life is hard, we can't escape from that; so why add another layer to that with this gratuitous nastiness?

In Marcus Aurelius's *Meditations*, he suggests an approach I get tremendous benefit from: "Begin each day by telling yourself, 'Today I shall be meeting with interference, ingratitude, insolence, disloyalty, ill will, and selfishness.'" So we prepare ourselves for that. Just going one step beyond that, I could consider every encounter as an opportunity for self-transformation. Being with others becomes a chance to strip away my veneer, to drop all roles. To make ourselves available to others, it's enough to recall the miracle of life. One day a monk gave me this luminous lesson: "Can you imagine how many chances out of a billion it is that you would meet the very people you're close with, your friends, your family? Are you aware of this daily miracle? It's as though, in this infinite universe, there was an intergalactic train station and that *by chance* you have met these men and women there. These moments are brief, fleeting. Let's not waste them on meaningless reproaches. Let's not waste time on anger. Let's take delight in this short stopover at this station and be generous toward all the travelers."

When I say goodnight to my children, I like to remember that I'm kissing beings who are going to die one day. Thus I remember the extraordinary gift I'm being given, and I savor the joy of passing some time in their company in the great intergalactic train station. I also try to convert the way I look at things so that I regard every encounter, as ordinary as it might seem, as a miracle, the occasion for a teaching. And I never cease to marvel at the richness of human beings. In the subway I tell myself, "I'm never going to encounter this woman or this businessman side by side again. This moment will never be reproduced." Closing one's eyes to the richness of daily life is letting the joy of life pass by and only being half alive.

For a very long time joy aroused in me a kind of persistent sense of guilt, as though happiness put a gulf between me and those who suffer, as though I were spiting them by feeling good. Today I understand that it's not a troubled soul, crippled with wounds, who is best able to lend a helping hand to those in trouble. It is even my duty to do everything I can to root out of my heart anything that moves me to bitterness and sadness.

> We can give what we have not received, and that is one of the great things about being human.

Contemplating everything beautiful in my life delights and recharges me. But the moment I try to grasp and possess these gifts, joy leaves me almost at once. Appreciating without becoming attached—that's the whole challenge. We can give what we have not received, and that is one of the great things about being human. A father who has not been loved by his parents can lavish unconditional love on his children. The art of compassion is practiced in the present moment.

CHRISTOPHE As I see it, altruism lies in the attention we give to the needs of others and in the action we take to help them. It can come into play before suffering happens. There's no need to wait for a person to be in pain to come to their side and do something good for them. It's enough if they have need of it. In this attitude, there's no particular expectation of getting anything in return, such as acknowledgment or profit. Even if there is profit, the fact that it exists and that we appreciate it does not disqualify or contaminate altruism. But to the extent possible, profit should not be the primary motivation.

Compassion consists in being attentive to the suffering of others, wishing for it to be less, and trying to remedy it.

Where Does Concern for Others Come From?

CHRISTOPHE Today we know that human beings are hardwired for empathy. It is in our nature to be able to feel others' suffering. But compassion may perhaps require further learning—Matthieu is more knowledgeable on this subject than I am. I was struck a long time ago by what I saw in an animal documentary about two leopards, brothers, in an African animal reserve. They grew up together, playing, hunting. But one day a lioness attacked one of the brothers and crippled his pelvis with a bite. He was partially paralyzed and became a burden in the hunt as well as for the general survival of the pair. Initially the unimpaired leopard was very upset. He licked his brother and attempted to comfort him. But then after a short time, he began being aggressive toward him and finally abandoned him altogether. I had the sense of seeing the difference between empathy and compassion. The leopard had had empathy for his paralyzed brother, but it didn't reach the point of compassion; it wasn't strong enough for him to want to stay at his brother's side, help him, bring him food, even though, in the long run, it might not have changed things that much.

Human beings are hardwired for empathy.

MATTHIEU The leopard perhaps suffered a kind of empathy fatigue. I've heard of another case that turned out better. It concerned an elephant whose trunk had been badly cut by a trap and was no longer able to feed itself. Right away another elephant began to bring him tender reeds, which it put directly in its mouth. When the wound healed, the mutilated elephant discovered that it was no longer able to uproot tough plants and could only feed on tender reeds. What happened next was amazing. The entire herd (often around ten individuals led by a matriarch), which was normally constantly on the move, stopped roaming from place to place and stayed in areas where tender reeds were plentiful. The elephants were unwilling either to abandon their fellow or to force it to go places where it could no longer feed itself.

CHRISTOPHE So there must be a place in the evolution of species where the capacity for compassion appears—somewhere between leopards and elephants! Primates have this capability. Several works exist on this subject, notably a study of a group of baboons on an island near Japan.[1] Researchers discovered that a little female had been born without legs. In a compassionless species she would have been doomed because she was unable to contribute anything to the group. In this case, even though she had a very low ranking in the hierarchy, the other monkeys left food for her, accommodated her slow pace in moving from place to place, and showed her special and lasting attention. Thus she lived much longer than she would have been able to on her own.

In my own case, I came to compassion through luck. As a doctor, I always had the goal of helping my patients feel better, which, by the way, helped me feel better myself. However, my thinking about compassion was clouded for a long time by my initial understanding that compassion was bad for happiness since it meant taking on suffering, the suffering of others. But upon further reflection I saw that accepting into ourselves the suffering of others distances us from the blind and selfish happiness that in the long term is really counterfeit happiness. Compassion, it turns out, is an excellent tool for ripening our capacity for happiness in that it leads us to what I call *lucid happiness* or *mature happiness*, that is, happiness that doesn't isolate us in some random bubble but keeps us in contact with the permanent flow of suffering that passes through human lives.

Nature has worked things out well, because happiness gives us the energy necessary to come to the aid of others, to act, to change the world. This makes sense when you look at studies on the relationship between happiness and attention. Happiness enlarges our vision of the world, whereas suffering shrinks our attentional focus. By opening up this focus, we see what is going on around us and we confront suffering. In other words, if we're happy, we don't need to flee in order to avoid suffering ourselves, and we have more opportunities to succeed in relieving others.

> Happiness enlarges our vision of the world, whereas suffering shrinks our attentional focus.

One of my three daughters has a great capacity for compassion, which makes her suffer in a certain way. When she sees a beggar in the subway, or an old lady alone, or somebody who has fallen, she's on the verge of tears. "It's just too painful!" she says. A few years ago on a trip to Japan, we visited a Zen temple where an old woman served us some green matcha tea with all the ceremony. There all five of us sat with our bowls of green tea, but my three girls hate green tea. The two older ones took a taste but then, though they didn't want to offend, they pushed their bowls away. The old woman disappeared for five minutes to go get some cookies, and my third daughter turned to me and said, "Oh, Papa, I beg you, drink my tea! I don't want to hurt the lady!" She was very concerned not to cause the slightest unpleasantness for this person who had so beautifully served us tea. So I ended up drinking all the bowls of tea, which was fine because I love matcha!

I have another recollection concerning compassion, a very painful one, which shows how it sometimes automatically arises in us. It has to do with one of the most difficult moments in my life, when my best friend got killed in a motorcycle accident. We were both on vacation in Portugal, and we'd ride one behind the other, sometimes with him in front, sometimes me. On the way out of a village, he was in front, and he started to pass a farmer who was pulling a cart with a motorbike. Suddenly the farmer made a left turn, without any warning, with no signal. My friend slammed into the cart, rolled over horribly a couple of times, and crashed into some bushes. The farmer also fell. I stopped my cycle and ran toward my friend. I had my helmet on and my motorcycle boots, and I must have looked scary to the farmer who was in my path. He saw me coming, and I think he was very afraid I was going to hit him, when in fact I wasn't even angry, just shocked. He held out his hand to show that he too was hurt. And like an idiot I stopped to look at his hand. I smiled at him to reassure him, then I kept moving to go help my friend. I wasted ten seconds looking at a minimal wound while my friend was in the process of dying. He had an internal hemorrhage, probably of the aortic arch, and he died very fast. I barely had time to speak to him and kiss him. I was very guilt stricken. What strikes me in thinking about it is the automatic, almost mechanical quality. I looked at the wound of the man who had killed my friend rather than pushing him out of my way. I was on automatic pilot. It was not a virtue that was expressing itself at that point but a habit. You show me a wound, I look at it. Why was I unable to prioritize?

This is a question I've been wanting to ask Matthieu. Chögyam Trungpa sometimes speaks of "idiot compassion." It strikes me as terrible to associate these two words, and I feel that no compassion is idiotic. The compassion that I showed for the Portuguese farmer was inappropriate maybe, but I find this phrase "idiot compassion" sullies the word *compassion*. However, it appears frequently in blogs, on Buddhist sites, and in certain teachings.

MATTHIEU The example you give is very moving. Daniel Batson and other psychologists speak of altruism that is not suited to the real needs of the other person, even of pathological altruism. One day Batson gave me the following example: "Imagine that you are in India and that you meet a group of children and spend part of the day with them. Among them is one who has a nice face, smiles at you all the time, and sticks to you like glue. In the evening, before leaving, you give him a nice gift but you give just a little something to each of the other children." Batson's view is that in this case, the altruism is inappropriate because it doesn't take into account the real needs of the children. It is indeed possible that one of the other children had more need of your help than the one you gave a nice gift because you liked him.

In my humble opinion, in this type of behavior, it is not altruism that is in play but rather factors that are grafted onto it and distort it—partiality, lack of consideration for all the children who were there, and short-term vision.

As for what is sometimes called *pathological altruism*, this refers to people who sacrifice more than they are able to give emotionally and materially at the risk of compromising their own physical and mental health. But there also, it is not altruism that is pathological. What we are dealing with there is rather an empathic distress that derives from the fact that one overestimates one's capacity to help others and ends up being submerged by the effect that the suffering of others has on one's own feelings.

Altruism, Empathy, Compassion

MATTHIEU   People sometimes tend to lump altruism, compassion, and empathy together as pretty much the same. But behind these words are different mental states that have different repercussions on our behavior and consequently on other people.

Altruism, or altruistic love, is essentially the intention to do good to others. If I perform a generous act while calculating that I will derive advantages larger than the cost of my act, it is not altruism but selfishness in disguise of benevolence.

Compassion is the form altruism takes when it is confronted by the suffering of others. Buddhism defines it in a particular way, as "the wish for all beings to be liberated from suffering and its causes."

Empathy has two aspects: affective and cognitive. Affective empathy is the capacity to enter into an emotional resonance with the feelings of another person and thus become aware of their situation. If the other is happy, I myself feel a certain happiness. If the other is suffering, I suffer the other's suffering. Affective empathy thus alerts us to the nature and intensity of other people's feelings, especially their suffering. Cognitive empathy may consist in putting oneself in another's place: What would I feel if I was suffering from famine or being tortured in prison? Or else it can mean imagining what the other person feels without feeling the same thing oneself. For example, I might be sitting on an airplane next to someone who is terrified by flying, and I might help that person by imagining their distress even though I don't feel the same fear myself. So without empathy, it is difficult to know the situation of another person or be concerned by their fate.

It is essential for us to be able to distinguish these different states of mind. If, for example, I feel empathy without this empathy turning into altruism and compassion, I am in danger of falling into empathic distress, or burnout. In order for it not to lead to emotional exhaustion and depression, empathy has to open into the greater space of altruism. Altruistic love then acts as a kind of balm for the burnout and implies a warm-hearted desire to help the person who is suffering.

Altruism and compassion would be limited if they were confined solely to their emotional component. But they also have a cognitive dimension, which is spoken of less often. This is the dimension that makes it possible to perceive the needs of others, including people we consider strangers or enemies. It also extends our comprehension of their suffering. For Buddhism, the fundamental cause of suffering is ignorance, mental confusion, which makes us perceive reality in a distorted fashion. It causes a multitude of harmful mental events, ranging from compulsive desire to hate and including jealousy, arrogance, and all other negative emotions. If we are unaware of this cognitive aspect of altruism and compassion and focus only on visible forms of suffering, we will never be able to entirely heal this suffering.

One day I was in Bodh Gaya, India, with Rabjam Rinpoche, the abbot of my monastery. This place—which is Buddhism's principal pilgrimage site because it was there that the Buddha attained enlightenment twenty-five hundred years ago—attracts a lot of lepers, disabled people, and poor people, who solicit charity from the pilgrims. This is without doubt a full-time profession. They beg all day and go home to their families at night. Looking at them, Rabjam Rinpoche said to me that day, "When we think of suffering, we think of people like these unfortunates, but when we see a billionaire smoking a big cigar in a stretch limousine in New York, we don't say, 'Oh, the poor thing, how he must be suffering!' However, this rich person might well be quite miserable inside, maybe on the verge of suicide. Even if he is very pleased with himself and rolling from one success to the next, that is not what will make him truly happy. So he should be the object of our compassion in just the same way as the beggars of Bodh Gaya." The problem we all have, the Buddhist master Shantideva tells us, is that we aspire to happiness while turning our backs on it, and we fear suffering while rushing toward it. That is how Buddhism defines ignorance, which is the source of suffering.

ALEXANDRE Understanding that everybody is suffering also invites compassion. That didn't escape the Buddha, who put forth this fearsome and liberating diagnosis: everything is *duhkha*, everything is suffering. Even joy, which can always come to an end, has something painful in it for someone who clings to it. Instead of criticizing and looking down on others, all you need to do is stop being negative toward them, merely see that they are also rowing in the great ocean of suffering. Thus the politician, the tyrant, and the torturer, who seem to be thinking only of themselves, are not exempt from this terrible condition. Sooner or later, they will suffer. Moreover, can we even imagine a happy oppressor? Actually, I can't find any better antidote to jealousy than to consider the fragility of the daily life of us all.

Covetousness proceeds from an error of perspective, an optical illusion. It points the projector at one part of reality and forgets the rest. Never would I wish for the life of another person if I took it as a whole. There's always a squeaky wheel, something amiss. Every life holds its portion of suffering, its unhappiness. On a very concrete level, the moment I become jealous of a writer who just climbed to the top of the bestseller list, I remember that he too will die, that he is perhaps already suffering. Why not delight in his success? In short, working gradually, I can get myself out of the prison of ego mind and cultivate compassion. One day, a friend told me, "Ultimately, I'm only a member of Club Med for the sake of my ego. From morning till night, I exhaust myself entertaining it, providing it with food, spoiling it. I am the jester and the slave of a master who is never satisfied."

The Buddhist tradition, like the Gospel message, shows us a way out. Yes, we can emancipate ourselves from this slavery precisely by making ourselves available to our fellow beings and especially to the most helpless ones. This is what makes the notion of bodhisattva dear to my heart. Why not commit ourselves, with the means and forces presently at hand, to become genuine bodhisattvas, heroes of enlightenment who devote their lives to relieving all beings who are caught up in suffering, bogged down in samsara?

Humbly, amid the ups and downs of existence, I can already avoid imposing my ego and my hurts on those around me. The masters and spiritual fathers have given me the example because in their hearts I see an infinite patience with regard to human errors and weaknesses. I also find there an absolute demand, an urging to keep moving forward, to make progress on the path. A good parent, I daresay, knows how to bring together firmness with immense and unflappable gentleness.

Why not begin with this exercise inspired by the tradition of St. Ignatius of Loyola, which is to identify all our deficiencies of love and compassion without developing a sense of guilt. It's a bit like an artist contemplating his work at the end of a workday. Cultivating and arousing generosity is also, and especially, daring nonfixation: no longer binding the other person to what they were in the past, no longer fixing them in their deeds or reducing them to their errors, but loving them for who they are. Meister Eckhart helps us here: "God is the God of the present. Just the way he finds you, just that way is the way he takes you and accepts you, not as what you were but as what you are now."

Extending Our Capacity for Compassion

ALEXANDRE   Following the example of the bodhisattvas, we can extend our compassion to all living beings. On this path, it is tempting to stop midway and give our attention exclusively to those who are going through major crises. There's nothing like a car accident or an acute illness to bring out our empathy. Whereas giving our support with extreme compassion over the long term to a person who is close to us is quite another thing.

What can I do to avoid fatigue of the heart? Every morning I can renew my attention to others and particularly to those who pass unnoticed. Recently a doctor told me that he fled as from the plague from cases of incurable disease, the cases that forced him to see his impotence. He added, "The patients that I can't treat successfully tire me out. I try to get rid of them as fast as I can." Now there's something that is clear as can be, and shows that impotence creates fear. Developing infinite compassion, absolute love, means no longer taking the other's pain as a routine matter or habituating ourselves to it. We must abandon the idea that compassion is a cake we have to divide up. It's not a question of distributing a few crumbs here and a few crumbs there. On the contrary, compassion is an unlimited resource. You never run out of stock.

Suffering of any kind at all is too much suffering. It's something that can kill you, drain you of your last resources. If compassion does not embrace all of humanity, it dies out. And what should we say about the ratings of death on television? There again, we have flagrant injustice taking place. To be honest, I find that I am distinctly less touched by a catastrophe on the other side of the world than I am by an incident nearby, the least one of which throws me for a loop. But one death is always a death too many, and any hurt should mobilize me. Making up our minds to work a bit more for others is just expanding the completely natural love that arises in us from contact with those close to us. Starting now, I can turn myself toward all beings, particularly those who have been struggling for a long, long time.

CHRISTOPHE It is true that for most of us there is a big difference in the extent to which our compassion is triggered by African deaths as opposed to European deaths. I think this is human—and has to do with geographical and cultural proximity, as you were saying—but it's not a good thing. Compassion requires training, and if we don't work on it, we will simply have the reflex of being compassionate toward those close to us, perhaps only our fellow citizens. For others, our compassion will be vaguer and less dependable.

MATTHIEU When they hear the phrase "infinite compassion," many people think we're talking about some kind of Utopia. Jonathan Haidt, an American psychologist and philosopher, said to me one day, "The altruism and infinite compassion of which the Dalai Lama speaks is completely unrealistic. It is, of course, natural to be concerned for the people close to you and a few other people, but beyond that, it doesn't make sense." His words showed me that an intelligent person who writes extremely interesting things cannot envisage a wider vision of altruism and compassion, as though they were rare commodities that had to be divided up carefully, like a handful of cherries. But they are attitudes and ways of being characterized by the desire to be benevolent toward anyone who enters into our field of attention. By loving all beings, we don't love those close to us less. In fact we love them more and better because our love grows in scope and quality rather than being diluted. The more we express it, the more it grows and deepens. As Albert Schweitzer said, "Love doubles every time we give it."

Our altruism is not exhausted by the number of people who receive it. If ten people warm themselves in the sun, and if a thousand others come to warm themselves in the same area, the sun does not have to shine a hundred times more. That doesn't mean that we can nourish and care for every being on this planet, but that our intention can extend to everyone.

CHRISTOPHE To move into the anecdotal rather than the scientific realm, when I was a young intern I had the experience of what we might call "altruistic intoxication." I had realized that my place was no longer in the hospital among the psychoanalysts, and I began to step back from it a bit. In the morning I worked there, but in the afternoon I looked around for some other kind of training. That was the situation in which I met my master, for whom I was a substitute at a clinic. I loved to be the first to get there and the last to leave. Of course I was looking for approval, recognition, esteem, admiration—and I got it. The patients really liked me, and the nurses did as well, because I was available—when there was a little problem, they knew they could call on me. I did everything I could to learn and to be liked, but I think there was something else, something that resembles altitude sickness among mountain climbers. It's a kind of intoxication they get when they climb too high. It causes a kind of euphoria that puts them at risk of making careless errors. In my case, it was an altruistic drunkenness. I remember those summer evenings when I left at 11 p.m., when the day was ending. The patients waved goodbye to me through the windows. I was in a state of total happiness, doubtless with a narcissistic component, but also with this sense of fulfillment, a feeling of having done the job of being a human, a doctor. It was a feeling of having given everything I could in terms of listening, treating, being kind. The problem is that I was overheating and I forgot that time for rest was also needed. I became exhausted.

As Haidt said with regard to infinite compassion, I think there are physical limits on energy and the amount of attention you can give. It costs a lot of energy; it takes time away from sleep, leisure, the family. And if you don't take care of yourself, you put yourself in danger, and over time you compromise your capacity for future altruism.

True Altruism

MATTHIEU   When we perform a beneficial act for others with a vested interest, that is not truly altruism, because we have in mind promoting our interests. You can lavish attention on an aged person in the hope of inheriting their fortune, do somebody a favor in order to get complimented, or be generous in order to acquire the reputation of a philanthropist. We might also help someone in order to assuage our bad conscience, so we can have a good opinion of ourselves, or to avoid being criticized.

Reciprocal altruism is at the core of communal life. In the long run, reciprocity creates the texture of a harmonious and balanced community, in which each person is inclined to help the others and manifests gratitude when others help them. In a community where people know each other well, everyone takes for granted that the others will behave kindly toward them when the need arises. Reciprocal altruism makes it possible to find a just balance between the interests of each person and those of the community. If a member of the community doesn't play the game and uses the kindness of others without reciprocating, they will be ostracized. In Asia, in Nepal and Bhutan where I spend a lot of the year, the villagers render reciprocal service in terms of work in the fields and house construction. Without this being explicitly said, they all expect payback in kind for the services they have rendered. This reciprocity plays an important role in the preservation of social cohesion.

Altruism is disinterested when one helps others with the sole objective of doing them good, without making any distinction among them.

ALEXANDRE The Gospel of Matthew tells us, "But when you give to the poor, do not let your left hand know what your right hand is doing, so that your giving will be in secret." This is what ought to be made clear. It does away with the danger of navel-gazing while practicing generosity and pretending to be cool.

MATTHIEU When the "righteous among the nations"—who saved many Jews during the Nazi persecutions, often at the risk of their own lives—were honored years later for their heroism, for most of them these honors were unexpected, often embarrassing or even undesirable. The idea of being admired for their acts had never entered into their minds when they decided to do what they did.

True altruism is the simplest and most probable explanation for the helpful acts that are constantly taking place in our daily lives. We might call it the "banality of goodness." The American psychologist Daniel Batson, trying to get to the bottom of the matter, spent thirty years of his life creating experimental tests that would make it possible to determine without ambiguity the altruistic or selfish motivations of the subjects whose reactions he was observing. At the end of his patient and systematic study, he concluded that true altruism, which has for its sole motivation bringing about the welfare of others, does indeed exist, and that in the current state of scientific knowledge, there was no plausible explanation for the results of his study based on selfishness.

> True altruism is the simplest and most probable explanation for the helpful acts that are constantly taking place in our daily lives.

ALEXANDRE Spinoza gives us a magnificent clarification of this in his distinction between pity and compassion. In the latter, love is primary: I love someone, and to see that person stuck in some painful situation hurts me. Whereas in the case of pity, what is primary is sadness, even a narcissistic sense of guilt. On television, we see pictures of children dying of hunger and this pitiful spectacle sickens me by calling to mind what I myself might possibly suffer. But if I observe carefully, I see that I have very little concern for these unknowns whose hunger I see, and this is why it is so urgent to awaken our sensibilities and to let ourselves be motivated by love to struggle against injustice. Pity and compassion can cohabit in the same heart; insight and meditation permit us to separate the wheat from the chaff.

Why should we perceive ascesis as a duty, as a chore, when on the contrary it is part of an itinerary of joy? Observing all that I project on others, sniffing out the least sense of calculation, eliminating the vicious tendency toward quid pro quo—all that is part of a path to liberation. Meister Eckhart reminds us that to often say "I love you" to someone is nothing but a disguised way of signaling that I need that person. Encountering the other, really taking care of the other, supporting them with no expectation of return, without why or wherefore, is beginning to come close to unconditional love.

I remember the day when, at age three, I was taken to the institute for the disabled. The gentleness of my new companions provided relief from the abysmal misery and anxiety I felt at seeing my parents leave. When I felt abandoned in this new universe, I understood in my very flesh that compassion, solidarity, and mutual help were natural, like a response to being alive, a balm far from any calculation, whatever those embittered philosophers think who pretend that nothing in this base world is done selflessly.

CHRISTOPHE   For my part, I'm uncomfortable with trying to establish a hierarchy between compassion and pity. Of course we always say that pity is not good whereas compassion is. But whenever a person feels pity, tenderness,—that is, whenever a person becomes sensitized to another's suffering, whatever their motivation—it seems to me preferable to indifference. In other words, imperfect compassion is preferable to zero compassion.

MATTHIEU   You're absolutely right, but one can doubtless still distinguish different kinds of pity. Pity is sometimes embryonic compassion and is translated into good done for others. But it can also be a form of condescension or reflect some feeling of inadequacy, of the sort: "What a pity! It's so sad. Unfortunately there's nothing I can do about it."

Altruism Without Labels

ALEXANDRE The great traditions provide us with extremely effective exercises for entering the path of the bodhisattva or simply for situating generosity at the center of our lives. As a Christian, I can't live without the Buddha. Day by day, he teaches me the path of nonfixation, a wisdom and a science of mind that is directly applicable on the ground in daily life. If Buddha pacifies me, Christ consoles me and prevents me from sinking into the kind of disembodied compassion that just keeps churning. Because here what we are talking about is loving beings of flesh and blood, in person, and not remote abstractions. Unconditional love is expressed when I am with those I am close to, in the subway, at the supermarket, always and everywhere. Every morning when I get up, I can dedicate my practice and my efforts to all the people I am going to encounter that day. Loving without dependence, leaving behind all risk of idolatry, is the prerequisite for the great spiritual path. And I'm amazed every time I hear about someone attributing quasi-divine powers to a master, turning him into a god. In my view, there is nothing more contrary to Buddhism than this kind of deification, which blinds us.

On my way, I recharge myself again and again by rereading the Diamond Sutra. There the objective of the bodhisattva is to liberate all beings by showing very precisely that there is no being to liberate, because the ego, the individual, is only an illusion. Without getting into the realm of metaphysical debate, I can already experience that our little social egos—these bundles of illusions, reactions, habits, and preconceptions—are not what bring about authentic encounters. Everything happens on a much more intimate level. Helping my children requires me to take greater interest in their profound aspirations than in their very transitory whims. The notion of person, which Christianity exalts, is very dear to my heart. It reminds me that every human being is unique, singular, and that relationship beyond all social games is possible. And I love so much figures such as St. Francis of Assisi and Abbé Pierre, geniuses of charity, who commit themselves body and soul to take care of *persons*! It is easy to sink into a kind of compassion in bulk, to love everybody without actually pitching in and carrying out concrete acts.

In Seoul I met a Buddhist monk whose remarks shook me up a bit. When I told him that I wanted to find some friends, he replied, "Humans are like cactuses; if you get near one it sticks you." I very much admired this man who devoted his days to gathering food and medicine to send to India for the most unfortunate. I then saw that generosity has no label and that it implies immense freedom and a great deal of detachment. It doesn't matter whether the practitioner is a Buddhist, a Muslim, a Jew, or an atheist. What counts is authentic commitment, really helping people, getting your hands dirty in order to help men and women out of their misery.

Ecclesiastical disputes pain me greatly. I am sad when I see this popular activity that disrespects Christ by shutting him up in vile caricatures. What a heap of prejudices, which have ended up transforming the charity of the Gospels into sappy moralism—insipid or outright abject! The effect it has on me is to make me want never to have power over other people, to get rid of ego and love others here and now. Embarking on the path shown to us by Jesus requires tremendous courage and mad freedom. What an aberration to turn charity into a kind of condescension, a fix, a hypodermic of good conscience.

The reason the Diamond Sutra touches me so much is that it shows that altruism requires attacking the causes of suffering directly. It's not enough just to put some salve on the wounds, to momentarily soothe the pain and carry out part-time generosity. On the contrary, we are called upon to labor over the long term, to do the maximum possible to dispel unhappiness. Proper charity begins with oneself. How shall I dare to be compassionate if I've got my head in a vice from morning till night? Helping means detecting the origins of our torments: illusions, preconceptions, greed, attachment . . . This does not mean that we cannot at the same time improve our material conditions, ease our physical pain. The Gospels, when they call upon us to convert and live lives of love, give us incredible encouragement to go out and treat the wounds of those who are suffering. And the masters of the various spiritual traditions remind us that if we stay disconnected from our inner being, exiled from the ground of all grounds, we are doomed to discontent.

In Kathmandu—in your monastery, Matthieu—I came close to the experience of the presence of God. I had tears in my eyes and was filled with gratitude when a monk told me he had seen the cross that I almost always carry with me lying on the floor in my room. With infinite respect, he had picked up the crucifix and put it on my night table. He said to me with a very sweet smile, "You should take care of that and pray more." I have rarely seen such luminous freedom. It was so far from dogmatic quarrels, proselytizing, and prisons. And what more wonderful gift could there be than to invite another person to become what they truly and profoundly are! Thanks to you, I was also able to meet another monk, who with infinite compassion organized a healing ceremony. His gentleness and the kindness of his look, as well as his great wisdom, took me straight to the ground of all grounds. Nowhere else have I felt so strongly the need to read Meister Eckhart to purify my heart. I realized that I had to throw off ego and plunge into God. What more dazzling proof could there be of the benefits of sharing, tolerance, and mutual enrichment! Basically two Buddhist monks in Nepal brought me closer to my faith in Christ. We can lavish gifts on someone, but nothing is more precious than to guide them to freedom and joy. If the ego disappears in the act of altruism, it is not the ego of a Buddhist, a Catholic, or the corner grocer that practices generosity but rather the heart in its naked state.

That being the case, how can we protect ourselves from the narcissistic hijacking operation that tries to get us to proliferate our good deeds in order to magnetize the greatest possible esteem? The danger is devoting ourselves to generosity to make sure we go to heaven or in order to purify our karma. From there, it's only a short step quickly taken to exploiting others, making them our instruments, our stepping stones, not even caring if we mash their heads as we go by. Jesus reminds us to love without expecting anything in return those who remain on the fringes of our heart—the prostitutes, the publicans, or simply the people we don't like. I have been struck by the fact that in the Gospels, Christ never says anything to justify suffering. He acts practically; he helps, he heals. In this area, blah-blah-blah and inaction are criminal.

MATTHIEU   I was astonished to read an interview with Mother Teresa, who was one of my main inspirations when we began our humanitarian projects. She said that she had devoted her life to relieving the sufferings of others, but she did not aspire to eliminate suffering *itself*, since God had permitted it to exist. So how could she rebel against the will of her beloved God? It's completely logical from her point of view and compatible with her unshakable devotion to every suffering being.

The position of Buddhism is a little different because suffering is not considered acceptable *in itself*. It must not only be remedied by all possible means, but also, ideally, we should go out and find the means to eliminate it.

Every second, beings are murdered, tortured, beaten, mutilated, or separated from those close to them. Mothers are losing their children, children are losing their parents, and there is an endless succession of sick people in the hospitals. Some people suffer without hope of receiving care, others receive care without hope of being cured. The dying endure their death throes, and their survivors endure their mourning. Isn't all of that undesirable? Thus we must take into consideration the wish of every being to escape suffering, and we have to trace suffering to its very root.

Though suffering is absolutely not desirable, that still doesn't keep us from using it when it is there in order to make progress in our humanity and spirituality, to train ourselves not to be devastated by painful events, and to make our altruistic love and compassion grow. Tolerating illness, disability, hostility, treason, criticism, or failures of all kinds does not mean that these events don't affect us or that we have forever eliminated them, but that they don't hamper our progress toward inner freedom.

ALEXANDRE How can we come out the other side of the spiky problem of the existence of evil in one piece? How can we keep ourselves from dodging it by taking refuge in questionable and dangerous certitudes? On this terrain, this minefield, we should just remain completely silent. Especially, we should not trivialize suffering with lame explanations and dreadful justifications. I believe in a good God, and every day I see innumerable injustices in this world, intolerable cruelty. The mass of sufferings that assails us daily, the ever more flagrant inequalities that trouble the world, force me to strip away everything I project on God and not use religion as a crutch, as a tranquilizer. As far as charity is concerned, Mother Teresa reached the summit—even though we should avoid idealizing anybody, this saintly woman or the Dalai Lama, whoever. On a very concrete level, what we have to do is set aside the labels with which we decorate God and stop once and for all speaking in his place. Maybe, basically, we don't know that much about him. So why should we see the realm of quid pro quo everywhere? God is not a milk cow, to use the words of Meister Eckhart. Let's not make a caricature out of him, a human caricature, too human. Ascesis, conversion, requires that we drop everything, including our mental constructs.

> What we have to do is set aside the labels with which we decorate God and stop once and for all speaking in his place.

In any case, following Jesus is above all abandoning oneself to Providence and loving one's neighbor and supporting him or her fully and completely. Christ was a luminous example of this; Christ who healed, soothed, and liberated those who were bent under their burdens. Never did he give any lessons in theodicy, never did he urge his followers to throw up their hands and accept misery just like that.

Philosophically, we must distinguish, as Leibniz did, between metaphysical evil—that is, the imperfection of the world—and physical evil—that is, suffering. Illness, old age, earthquakes, and death are tragedies that render the human condition very fragile. From the time of birth, a human being runs head-on into impermanence and danger. And it doesn't stop there. As German philosophy makes clear, moral evil—malice, selfishness, injustice, poverty, ostracism, and the thousand and one torments—can ravage a soul. Though we have very little power over the inevitable trials connected with our condition, we do have the power to limit the damage brought about by our selfishness. In his *Manual*, Epictetus urges us to distinguish between what depends upon us and what does not. If I use up my strength in vain battles, how can I devote myself body and soul to works that actually bring relief, that really force misery and unhappiness to retreat?

The question "Why, if God is good, does evil exist?" never ceases to reveal the tragedy of life, its extreme precariousness, and the limits of our understanding. If I begin by asking if God permitted, willed, or even desired that I be disabled, without doubt I would ruin my life and not make an ounce of progress. Ultimately it is our vision of God that we are called on to revisit and question: Is he a potentate, a judge full of vindictiveness, an automatic distributor, a righter of wrongs, an impassive observer who watches us sink in the mire? There are so many caricatures that we have to set aside in order to drop our illusions one by one and descend into the ground of all grounds. Our preconceptions lead us to a hard life. The notion of karma hastily interpreted can result in an unwholesome fatalism, in a representation of the world in which the unfortunate have no choice but to wander in a universe devoid of pity and pardon, and in which the prerogatives—indeed, the abuses of the powerful—are legitimate. Decidedly, nothing can possibly exhaust this mystery—it is beyond us. In short, the crushing enigma of the existence of evil brings to light the impotence of our reason. In no case do I feel the need to point the finger of accusation at a Creator, nor even to find a justification. There will always be an epistemological gulf between God and the human being, which does not in the least prevent the two from being united at every moment on the deepest level. In the face of pain, engaging in discourse plays up how we are mistreated, whereas what is needed is to act without delay, to relieve the pain, to struggle against the injustices, and to attack the selfishness—the globalization of indifference, as Pope Francis puts it.

Along the way, the admirable book of Marion Muller-Colard, *L'Autre dieu: La plainte, la menace et la grâce* (The other god: The lament, the menace, and the grace), helped me a lot to mentally dislodge God from his role of super-protector. Little by little, I am learning to love him for nothing, as the book of Job says, to no longer turn him into a life insurance policy, an entity who will intervene in the twists and turns of life to eliminate tragedy from our lives. The job description of the Most High is not to pamper and take care of me full time, or in any case, not in the sense that my fears too often make me hope for. In the end, moving toward "the Other God" means leaving behind the certified-public-accountant mentality, spurning magical thought, and daring to love and live without why or wherefore. No, I have not signed an insurance contract with the Most High; it's a purely non–quid pro quo relationship. He doesn't owe me anything, and suffering and injustice remain ongoing questions that do not dampen my confidence. But, at the same time, the desire I feel to *revolt*, to *rebel* against injustice wherever I see it is not left anesthetized. Happiness is a grace, a gift, not something we are owed. And since I have given up looking for a guilty party to blame for everything bad that happens to me, I am getting along much better in life.

> Happiness is a grace, a gift, not something we are owed.

CHRISTOPHE   Two quotations guide me in my personal work on altruism. First, there is the one by Martin Luther King Jr. that says, "Life's most persistent and urgent question is, 'What are you doing for others?'" We should ask ourselves that every day, every evening. And we should be able to answer. Then there is the extraordinary phrase of Christian Bobin, already cited: "Whoever you're looking at, know that that person has been through hell several times." In other words, we should remind ourselves that all human beings suffer, even the billionaires in their stretch limousines. Compassion is our fundamental duty, even with people who don't seem to need it or deserve it.

Compassion should
be our default attitude
toward relationship.

Generally speaking, it seems to me that compassion should be our default attitude toward relationship. That being established, then we can adjust our intentions and expectations. We can back off, withdraw, or give more, but compassion is the best starting point from which to make genuine choices as a genuine human being.

How to Be Compassionate Toward Difficult People

ALEXANDRE   Let's come right out and ask that murderous question: Where can we find the strength to nourish compassion toward a real jerk? Because the hardest thing is daily life, with its disappointments, fatigue, and misunderstandings. Maybe we first have to recall the famous formula from the Diamond Sutra and tell ourselves that the jerk is not a jerk, that's why I call him a jerk. In any case, we should refrain from judging because how can we know what pains are tormenting that person's heart?

I often go to the public baths with my son. One day we ran into a super hard-ass guy who sneered at us in a really nasty way. At first I tried smiling at him, doubling down on generosity, but he cut me off: "Why are you looking at me like that, imbecile?" Since then, every time I see him I make every effort to behave very straight, to remain who I am without trying to flash him a smile or say something nice. In those kinds of moments, compassion takes a delicate course—just being totally straight, without trying to score points.

MATTHIEU   I am often asked the following question: "I want to be compassionate and kind, but how do I do that when I'm confronted with ingratitude, bad faith, hostility, and ill will? How do I feel altruism for Saddam Hussein or for the ruthless barbarians of ISIS?" In the Buddhist teachings, we are often given the advice not to inwardly own the wrongs that have been done to us. There is the story about someone who insulted the Buddha many times. The Buddha finally asked him, "If someone gives you a gift and you refuse it, who in the end is the owner of the gift?" A little disconcerted, the man replied that it's the person who is trying to give the gift. And the Buddha concluded, "Your insults—I don't accept them, thus they remain yours."

Dealing with ingrates, boors, and nasty people, it seems to me we have everything to gain by maintaining a compassionate attitude. By remaining calm, courteous, and open to the other, in the best-case scenario, I will disarm their hostility. And if they don't change their attitude, I will have at least kept my dignity and my inner peace. If I get into a confrontation, I will myself commit the faults that I deplore in the other. The usual pattern in confrontation is escalation. You keep shouting louder and louder, I reply shout for shout, the tone worsens, and the next thing you know, we're moving in the direction of violence.

In the case of organizations such as ISIS or Boko Haram, the idea is not to tolerate their unspeakable actions. We have to do everything possible to put an end to them. At the same time, we have to realize that these people weren't born with the desire to cut off heads or massacre all the inhabitants of a village. A combination of causes and conditions has led them to this ghastly behavior. Compassion in this case is the desire to provide an antidote to those causes in the same way a doctor might try to end an epidemic. That implies, among other things, rectifying the inequalities in the world, making it possible for young people to get better educations, improving the status of women, and so forth, in order to do away with the social compost in which these extreme movements take root.

When hate has inflamed someone's mind, compassion consists of adopting the attitude toward them that a doctor would adopt dealing with a madman. First we have to keep them from causing harm. But, as a doctor would attempt to cure the illness that is gnawing at the mind of a mad person without braining them with a club, we must also envisage all possible means to resolve the problem without ourselves resorting to hate and violence. If we fight hate with hate, the problem will never end.

CHRISTOPHE Yes, indeed, why is it difficult to be altruistic, compassionate, and kind when dealing with problematic people? No doubt, life has already provided us with enough grounds for suffering so that we have no wish to go rub against a cactus. But the problem gets to us anyhow when we have spiny individuals in our family, in our neighborhood, or in our workplace. Quite often we have little desire to do them good, to be nice to them, to do any of what we consider their portion of the work in hand. We think, "Everybody has to step up; I'm not going to cover for him!" And sometimes we even almost get pleasure out of it when that person has little problems. "That will teach him!" we think. This is what's called *schadenfreude*, this dark pleasure we feel at seeing other people in difficulty, and being as troubling and problematic as it is, it is the subject of numerous psychological studies.

One last point seems important to me here. You have to be feeling good yourself in order to be able to work with difficult people, whether what comes up is a confrontation (so you don't lose it when facing aggression) or a moment of compassion (so you don't become the victim of manipulation or exploitation). Sometimes it's better not to play the compassionate hero if you are not ready at that particular moment. I advise some patients to avoid such situations because I sense they're not able to deal with them.

ALEXANDRE   In order to gain in freedom and love, it's a good idea to identify the people who drag us down. We need neither flee them nor avoid them, but simply redouble our attention when they are around. This is especially important since certain people, because of our projections and memories, more easily arouse our anger, fear, and sadness. A friend told me that when he visits his mother, he takes all possible precautions. "It's almost as if I were going to Chernobyl. I expect waves of negativity to hit me in the face." And I can tell you that this son loves his mother. From his lucidity I draw a remarkable approach that permits me to attend closely to my inner compass at moments when many parasites are hampering a healthy relationship. To outmaneuver the mechanisms that are harmful to a true encounter, you have to drop the logic of combat, leave your boxing gloves in the cloakroom, and recognize your vulnerability with certain persons.

Stepping out of your preconceptions already dissipates the thick fog that separates you from the other and allows you to look at them without bitterness.

The philosophical tradition has some tools for us that might lead to understanding here. In the *Protagoras*, Socrates utters the famous sentence, "No one does evil willingly." We get the following analysis: The wrongdoer is above all a person who is suffering, who manifestly lacks peace and joy. Based on that, we can begin to see aggression and violence as so many alarm signals and calls for help.

Opting for gentleness and renouncing hate requires great strength. Why don't we just go on a word diet and keep our mouths shut, seeing that our attacks and accusations only exacerbate the situation? Here, ascesis consists in not overreacting and especially not adding anything further. It's also a good idea to remember that it's not necessarily a bad thing if all is not resolved on the spot. In spite of all our efforts, there will always be people who prefer to stew in their rancor and live in their rage. An acquaintance said to me, "Until my last breath, I'll hate him for that." When I suggested that she relinquish this anger a little bit, she replied that she was not a coward or a wimp . . . At times, to our great misfortune, we'd rather die than be wrong.

I agree with Christophe. It takes great strength to avoid the logic of war. When from morning till night we have to deal with a colleague who never stops complicating our lives, what can we do to avoid getting carried away by animosity? One thing is for sure—the more we have established ourselves in profound peace, the better able we are to escape the law of an eye for an eye. There is a famous exercise to allow us to swallow affronts: consider the person who is hurting us as a victim blinded by passion. It would never come to your mind to reprimand a blind person on the street who stepped on your toe.

MATTHIEU Socrates's statement that nobody does evil willingly has given rise to a number of different interpretations. It seems that according to another passage in Plato, Socrates was making a reference to the absence of free will. In fact, elsewhere in the *Protagoras* he says, "All those who do ugly and bad things do them in spite of themselves."

The question of free will is one of the most complex there is. Some neuroscientists say that at a given moment it is not possible to do anything other than what one does, because our act is the endpoint of a series of cerebral processes of which we are not conscious and therefore which we cannot control. We might reply that we do in fact have the ability to manage our emotions and neutralize our undesirable thoughts; and over the long term, it is certainly the case that we can transform our character traits by training our mind.

But it is evident that sometimes people do deliberately wish to harm others. The question, which is perhaps not the one Socrates was responding to, is whether or not there are people who do evil for evil's sake. According to psychological studies, the answer is no. The media and novels like to portray evil in its pure state. Many films show us monsters or mutants who want to do harm for harm's sake and rejoice in the gratuitous pain they inflict. But as the psychologist Roy Baumeister has shown in his comprehensive work *Evil*, absolute evil is a myth. Even those who have committed the worst atrocities are convinced they are defending themselves against negative forces or promoting a just cause. Those who commit acts of vengeance believe incontrovertibly that it is morally justified to get violent payback for the wrongs that have been done to them. Their interpretation of reality, as aberrant as it may be, nevertheless shows us that none of them seems to be moved by the sole desire to commit evil for evil's sake.

According to Buddhism, absolute evil does not exist because, as I mentioned earlier, all beings, no matter how far gone they may be in the commission of horrors, always have in the deepest part of themselves, in the fundamental nature of their consciousness, an inalterable quality comparable to a gold nugget that has fallen into the mud, or Buddha-nature.

Those who have given way to violence declare that their cause is just and that their rights have been violated. Even when what they say is a gross distortion of reality, we must pay heed to their motives if we want to prevent new eruptions of violence. Alexandre quotes Spinoza: "Do not weep. Do not wax indignant. Understand." That's the first thing to do. The police officer who supervised the interrogation of Anders Breivik, the fanatic perpetrator of mass crimes committed in Norway in 2011, was an advocate of "active listening." You have to ask the criminal how he explains what he has done. To prevent the recurrence of evil, it is essential first to grasp why and how it occurred to begin with.

If we observe how genocides come about, for example, we see that the perpetrators almost always begin by demonizing, dehumanizing, and de-individualizing a particular group of individuals. These people cease to be persons like you and me, with families, with joys and sorrows. They become all alike, differentiated only by their serial numbers. The perpetrators also desensitize themselves to the sufferings they are about to inflict by transforming murder into a duty or an act of public salvation. That is how people, little by little, reach the point of committing acts that previously they would have considered unthinkable.

CHRISTOPHE   I agree with you. Socrates no doubt meant that no one is evil in essence. Nobody is bad, of course; but people can be evil deliberately, deeply. Various terrifying deeds have been committed. I don't know if the cruelty they arise out of is voluntary, but it is total. I remember the story of two twelve-year-old children in England who kidnapped a five-year-old and tortured him in an abominable fashion. That brings up the problem of psychopathology. A certain number of human beings have a kind of biological incapacity to feel empathy. Their compassion is crippled. I don't know the story of these kids, but they were obviously orphans from the point of view of ideals, values, convictions concerning respect for human life; and these stories underline the necessity of teaching compassion. We can't hate them for what they were, but such people are potentially very dangerous for others. Our way of dealing with them can't be naive. In addition to the compassion that every human deserves, sometimes it is necessary to apply means of education, coercion, and so forth.

MATTHIEU   In any case, compassion should never be considered a weakness, a burden, or a sacrifice, but always the best option, even in situations that seem the most unworkable, such as the case of those nonempathic children. It is also the best way to preserve our own integrity and the inspiration that permits us to hold out in times of adversity. The philosopher Miguel Benasayag was tortured in the prisons of Argentina. He told me that what saved him was that, in the worse moments, his torturers did not succeed in breaking his basic dignity. One of the Dalai Lama's doctors, Dr. Tenzin Chödrak, spent twenty-five years in Chinese forced labor camps. He had no sympathy for his torturers, but he succeeded in not giving in to hate. After torture sessions, he was almost always able to regain his compassion. He said that his torturers were mentally deranged as they had been subjected to brainwashing, and they deserved his compassion more than his hate. That's what saved him. Above all, he feared losing his compassion, which was what gave meaning to his life.

The Courage of Altruism and Nonviolence

CHRISTOPHE   Seeing narcissistic people as "ego mendicants" who hold out their begging bowls to be recognized, to receive confirmation—that's a beautiful metaphor you suggested, Alexandre! When you said we should make an effort to see the other's anger as a call for help, it made me think of a way of looking at things that has developed for me. Often we tend to see kindness as a weakness, whereas I see signs of weakness in arrogance and aggression. The day when the people society regards as weak are no longer the kind ones but the aggressive, malicious, and arrogant ones, society will really have made some progress!

ALEXANDRE   We often come up with false arguments so we can continue to take refuge in our selfish approach. Who has never said, "I agree, but I'm not Mother Teresa" or "What, am I supposed to be Gandhi?" The underlying thought is you might be taken advantage of if you think a bit more of others. We find a whole host of proverbs that legitimize this kind of cowardice, like this one: "Every man for himself and God for everybody."

CHRISTOPHE Yes, and unfortunately there exist business cultures and family cultures where the individual creed is that if you show yourself to be compassionate, you put yourself in danger. I have a friend, a professor of medicine, whose motto is, "If you're going to swim with the sharks, make sure you don't bleed." If he thought of me as kind or nice, it's because I gave up my academic career and thus was no longer in competition with anybody. He thought that at his level of responsibility, at his status level, that was an impossible approach. Was he perhaps right? Objectively, there are circles where kindness and compassion are neither easy nor valued nor understood.

The misunderstanding surrounding compassion seen as weakness also reminds me of the book by Thomas d'Ansembourg, *Being Genuine: Stop Being Nice, Start Being Real.* This title poses enormous problems for me, even though the book is good and I like the author a lot, and even though it responds to a need people have to understand that being nice is not all you need to do to change the world. Why does it bother me? Because it encourages us to withdraw from being kind or nice and put in place of that a kind of authenticity that is excused from being nice. I have timid or socially phobic patients who suffer from the feeling of "having been had" because they're too nice and who think that the only solution is to be less nice. I try to explain to them that it's not a unidimensional or zero-sum situation. It's false to think that if we go too far on the side of being nice, we automatically lose on the side of being strong. In other words, we can very well stand on a high level of kindness and niceness *and* a high level of strength. The point is not to take anything away from your kindness and niceness, but work harder on your assertiveness.

MATTHIEU In my opinion, the only way to be genuine is to be kind. Kindness is in harmony with our deepest inner state, which is free of confusion and of mental poisons such as ill will, arrogance, and jealousy. By contrast, ill will tends to distance us from this harmony with ourselves. Kindness and happiness both proceed from a synchronization with ourselves. Plato said, "The happiest man is he who has no trace of evil in his soul."

I would like to come back to this weakness that is often associated with kindness, patience, and nonviolence. In truth, it takes a great deal of courage to be a nonviolent protester facing a company of soldiers ready to fire. *Satyagraha*, the name of the nonviolence movement started by Gandhi, means "the force of truth." In 1930 Gandhi undertook what was known as the Salt March to defy the British authorities. Starting from his ashram with a few dozen disciples, Gandhi covered four hundred kilometers on foot all the way to the shores of the Indian Ocean. During the march, they were joined by many sympathizers. The British army tried to bar their route. They were beaten by the soldiers, but at no time did any of them respond with violence, and they continued to march under the blows. The forces of order finally let them pass, and it was a crowd of several thousand that arrived at the seashore. There Gandhi took a bit of salt in his hands, thus violating the monopoly of the state that obliged all Indians, including the poorest, to pay tax on salt and prohibited them from gathering it. The crowd followed his example and took salt water in their hands. When this news became known, everywhere in the country the inhabitants evaporated water and collected the salt from it right under the noses of the British. Tens of thousands of people were thrown in prison, including Gandhi. But the British viceroy finally gave in, in the face of their determination. This march was a turning point in the nonviolent struggle for the independence of India.

> The only way to be genuine is to be kind. Kindness is in harmony with our deepest inner state, which is free of confusion and of mental poisons.

It is truly a pity that we tend to consider nonviolence a weakness. The Dalai Lama has repeated for forty years that there is no question of having recourse to violence against the Chinese. "We are neighbors forever," he said. "We must find a mutually acceptable solution through dialogue." It is sometimes said, "The Dalai Lama is great, but we're not going to resolve the Tibet problem that way." Should the Tibetans then carry out bomb attacks? Should they hijack planes, commit slaughters that will provoke still more terrible Chinese oppression, pitiless persecution, and thus a hostility that is still more unresolvable than at present? If the international community would do everything necessary to crown the Dalai Lama's approach with success, it would serve as an example for the interminable conflict between the Israelis and the Palestinians, to mention only that. But, unfortunately, the international authorities are more likely to mobilize their powers when communities start killing each other.

CHRISTOPHE To continue on the subject of the pressure from the social and cultural environment, I'd like to tell you how I myself was shaken in my commitment to altruistic values. I come from a family strongly attached to the ideology of Communism. My grandfather was a Communist militant. He took me with him to the gatherings of the *Parti communiste* and bought me *Vaillant* (Valiant), the Parti communiste weekly for children. There one read about positively engaged heroes who worked for the benefit of those around them—Doctor Justice, Rahan . . . I adored these characters. However, they didn't transform me into a saint. I was a feisty little boy, not always nice, not always altruistic. Nevertheless, I had the feeling that these characters were the real thing.

Later, these ideals were shaken by the psychiatric and psychoanalytic orthodoxy that was dominant at the time I did my medical studies. In the psychiatric treatises, the word *altruism* was systematically associated with the word *neurosis*. They talked about the "altruistic neurosis." In other words, as soon as someone's level of altruism went beyond the average, it was a neurosis. Basically it was trying to compensate for something, to obtain recognition. Or worse, it masked tendencies toward sadism or egotism . . . Fortunately, through reading you, Matthieu and Alexandre, I saw that I should again place these values at the center of my approach to treatment. This tale also tells you how I became convinced of the major role played by public discourse in the promotion (or denigration) of values such as altruism in society.

Fatigue, Helplessness, Discouragement

MATTHIEU   Is our capacity for altruism unlimited? Eve, the daughter of Paul Ekman, for example, works in emergency services in San Francisco, with people who are in danger of dying if they don't get immediate help. They are brought to a calm place, they are given help washing, shaving, etc. They are helped to develop clean habits, they are fed, and they are kept for a time. But at the end of two weeks, in the absence of funds, they have to be put back on the street. Eve confessed that she ended up feeling a sense of total helplessness, since the interventions she participated in, which required a huge emotional investment, did help to some extent but ultimately did not solve the problem.

What should be done in situations like this? What should we say to people whose physical pain torments them without respite? What should we say to the parents of a mentally disabled child? To people whose parents want to be euthanized? Altruism here can only be accompanied by humility, especially when there's no obvious or immediate solution. We can advise others to practice mindfulness of pain, but when the pain is horrendous and no end is in sight, such a solution is a bit flimsy.

In such cases, more than advice, a mere loving and warm and wholehearted presence can bring some comfort. Homeless persons will know they are not alone, that there are people who are sincerely concerned about their fate even if they can't provide all they need. Those who suffer, who are desperate, who are dying, will know that someone loves them.

It is possible to tolerate physical pain, even acute pain, if you know that it will only last for a certain time. But not to know how long it's going to last and having no way to control it is intolerable. Such a situation saps our inner strength and resilience. Athletes voluntarily put up with the pain associated with their training, but when their pain is accidental, unexpected, and meaningless—when a cyclist takes a fall on the road, for example—the pain is much worse because it serves no purpose.

CHRISTOPHE   You're right to bring up the problem of the caregivers. All caregivers must prepare themselves to deal with situations where they are in the position of Sisyphus. Their efforts produce improvements, and then when the patients leave treatment, they relapse. That's unfortunately the case with people suffering from drug addiction, personality dysfunction, or schizophrenia. We often confront this question when we are leading or supervising a team of caregivers because we know it's a major obstacle in maintaining motivation to care for the patients. One of the ways we can give some comfort and also provide food for thought is to say, "Nothing you do is useless. If for two weeks you have made it possible for a homeless person to keep clean, dry, and warm, and get some attention, kindness, and compassion, even if he goes back to how he was, you have offered him two weeks of a decent human life. That is perhaps much more precious for now and for the long term than we can imagine when we do it." It is definitely difficult to disengage from fixating on the results, hoping for some satisfaction for the little bit we're able to offer, and I think often in those cases of Camus's Sisyphus, who constantly has to push his rock up to the top of the hill only to see it fall back every time into the valley. These efforts seem absurd from the outside, but as it says at the end, "we must imagine Sisyphus to be happy."

Without rummaging around in the realm of mythology, when I'm discouraged by the feeling of the uselessness of the efforts I've made on behalf of patients, I say to myself that the time I give them, the moments in which they feel some respite—all that is better than their just having to face their difficulties alone, no matter what happens later.

ALEXANDRE I like to recall the powerful advice of John XXIII in his *Journal of a Soul*, where he invites us to accomplish each action as though God created us only for that. This intuition harmonizes with a major principle of Zen: give yourself entirely to what you are doing here and now, without distraction.

MATTHIEU From the point of view of Buddhism, there's no room for discouragement. The bodhisattva takes the vow to work for the benefit of beings, not only for a few moments, days, or years, but for innumerable lives, for as long as there are suffering beings.

The courage generated by compassion is one of the principal qualities of a bodhisattva. His sole reason for existing and being reborn in samsara, the world conditioned by ignorance and suffering, is to help others liberate themselves from it.

CHRISTOPHE Further to our reflection on this subject, I want to point out that certain services or missions can only be carried out for a certain number of years. We know, for example, that in pediatric oncology, where one has to watch children die, it is necessary for caregivers to leave after a certain time because it is impossible to give the best of themselves in this regular confrontation with such heartbreaking situations. Moreover, the need for exchanges and mutual support between the teams is immense. When I was in Toulouse, I was supervising a group of SOS Amitié listeners (Friendship SOS, a phone and internet hotline for people in trouble). They sometimes experienced a sense of helplessness. Their clients are at the end of their tethers, and the listeners try to improve their morale. The clients hang up, and you don't know if they've killed themselves or they're better. So the listeners need to comfort each other, share their experiences, give each other advice.

ALEXANDRE The idea of a "self-made man" has something frightening about it. Treading on a spiritual path, practicing meditation and prayer—all that is extricating ourselves from worldly concerns in order to love others genuinely and so that we can grow up together. So many hurts and frustrations prevent us from being fully what we are and from being totally in love with humanity . . . Leaving behind the dimension of calculation and appearances, taking one's pilgrim's staff in hand and committing oneself here and now to a more altruistic existence, has nothing superhuman about it. The vocation of the religions and the great spiritual ways is to plunge ourselves into the ocean of gratuitous and unconditional love that comes from the bottom of our hearts. In doing that, the looks of my children are very helpful to me. By their side, I learn to love and never cease to marvel. Their father's disability, his clumsiness, his thousand and one fragilities—all these shadows are as though illuminated by the sun of their love.

If I come to the end of my Korean adventure, I would like to found a retreat place where the practitioners meditate a large part of the day while at the same time devoting themselves to helping disabled persons or people going through crises, in very concrete ways.

MATTHIEU That's what Jean Vanier, for example, has done with his communities of L'Arche, more than a hundred of them in the world, where volunteers live with the disabled, particularly the mentally disabled, as in a big family.

ALEXANDRE And that is a magnificent thing. Too often the practice of meditation risks cutting us off from the world. Nicely tucked away in a corner, secluded, we pursue our own benefit and forget those who are in need. That is why I have this dream of one day creating a place where solidarity and spiritual practice go hand in hand. Fortunately there are magnificent examples such as L'Arche communities, groups of contemplatives who devote themselves to others, and so many others who give up their individualism. The monastery of Lopburi is also an island of compassion in the middle of this ocean of suffering.

> There's no need to wait for tragic circumstances to spread peace, joy, and love.

Two hours' train ride north of Bangkok, this temple has taken in more than three hundred victims of HIV from the time the epidemic began. During the times when many were dying, the monks surrounded the sick with infinite tenderness. When there were no more drugs available, they surrounded them until the end with total love, offering them herbal teas, playing heartfelt music for them, being there. Emmanuel Tagnard made a magnificent documentary about these heroes of compassion.

What more beautiful gift, when medicine can do no more, than to lavish human warmth on the unfortunate, compassion without limit. And there's no need to wait for tragic circumstances to spread peace, joy, and love.

Engaging in altruism is finally escaping from prison, freeing oneself from the ego. It's not a misfortune to throw away this ball and chain. Before establishing my sainthood, I can spare five minutes, or even a little more, to devote to relieving others, to work for the benefit of beings. This project goes well beyond the capacity of one's little ego, which is incapable of climbing over this mountain. So committing oneself to others is already leaving our neuroses behind and working to discover joy and love in the heart of our lives. Every morning we can retake the bodhisattva vow, escape from samsara's infernal laws, and rush to the aid of those laboring under their burdens. By practicing meditation tirelessly, I can learn to swim in the immense ocean of suffering and reach out a hand to those who are sinking in it. Basically the spiritual life helps us float and offer help to those who are struggling. The great wisdoms are so many temporary rafts to get together on through the great storms. The urgent thing is to offer some relief to the person who has been struggling for a long, long time and has taken it for a life sentence.

Practicing Compassion

MATTHIEU In Buddhism there is a practice that seems paradoxical at first but that is very powerful. In that practice we begin by realizing that when we are suffering we are not the only ones suffering. There are others who are suffering a lot more than we are. So we say to ourselves at that moment, "Instead of becoming indignant, why not also embrace the suffering of others with love and compassion?" We often tend to think that we have enough problems already, without increasing our load with the suffering of others. However, it's just the opposite that happens. When we take the suffering of others upon ourselves, and then when we transform and dissolve it mentally by the power of compassion, not only does it not increase our torments but it also makes them lighter.

How do we do this practice? We begin by feeling profound love toward someone who is suffering, first someone dear to us. We offer that person our happiness and take their suffering on ourselves, using the coming and going of the breath. With the outbreath, along with the air going out, we send that person our joy, our happiness, and all our good qualities in the form of a white nectar, refreshing and luminous. Then we think that if that person's life is in danger, it has been prolonged; if they are poor, they obtain whatever they need; if they are sick, they recover their health; if they are unhappy, they find joy and well-being. Then gradually we extend the practice from this one person to all beings who are suffering.

When we breathe in again, we imagine that we are taking on all the physical and mental ills of these beings, including their negative emotions, in the form of a dark cloud. This cloud comes into us through our nostrils and dissolves without a trace in our hearts, which we visualize as a mass of light. This exercise can be practiced at any time, in the course of formal meditation sessions or in the course of our regular activities.

This is not a sacrificial practice, since the suffering is transformed by compassion. I knew an old monk who carried out this practice until his last breath. A few hours before his death, he wrote a letter to Dilgo Khyentse Rinpoche in which he said, "I am dying, taking joyously on myself the suffering of all beings so that they will be liberated, and I am giving them everything I have in me that is good as well as all the good I have accomplished in my life."

Now consider the fact that one day I heard someone recommending just the opposite: "When you have a great deal of suffering in you, when you breathe out, your sufferings are expelled into the universe." This makes me feel like saying, "Oh, thanks a lot. You're just too kind!"

CHRISTOPHE   Yes, by acting like that you add to the existing pollution, if only symbolically. When I lead mindfulness sessions with my patients who are coming back after an initial cycle of eight weeks, I have them practice a meditative exercise in the movements of which compassion, love, and the breathing are associated. Breathing in, we take on the suffering of others, not to store them but to expose them to the light of our love. It's a little like a conveyor belt on which these sufferings pass before the lamp of our affection, our love, our tenderness. But be careful—at this moment we are not like a cooking filter that filters out the fats! We do not keep the sufferings in ourselves, but we add our love to them, we illuminate and soften them with our love, then we let them move on. In this way the participants understand in their very bodies the infinite and precise nature of compassion. They understand that we never suffer alone, and that we can always work with the suffering of others, not necessarily finding solutions to it or suppressing it, but just trying to provide little acts of love, thoughts of love, loving intentions. And when you connect that to the breath, it's very strong, very soothing. You can then, of course, apply the same thing to yourself and your own suffering in the framework of compassion and kindness toward yourself.

> We do not keep the sufferings in ourselves, but we add our love to them, we illuminate and soften them with our love, then we let them move on.

Compassion Toward Oneself

MATTHIEU   In the beginning, before I knew specialists such as Paul Gilbert and Kristin Neff, when I heard references to the notion of compassion toward oneself, I thought it was a co-opting of compassion by narcissism. I was wrong. I had also underestimated the number of people for whom the idea of extending compassion to others is very painful, because they are suffering so much themselves. I was unpleasantly surprised to learn that 10 to 15 percent of adolescents in Western Europe engage in self-harm behavior, including self-mutilation, especially girls, a great number of whom have had traumatic childhood experiences. I realized that the ability to love others is connected to the ability to love oneself, and that people who want to hurt themselves find it very difficult to conceive of love and compassion toward others. I also became acquainted with the work of the American psychologist Kristin Neff, who has shown that the development of compassion toward oneself has numerous benefits but without also resulting in an increase in narcissism.

How is the concept of compassion toward oneself related to compassion as envisaged by Buddhism? Compassion toward oneself answers the question, "What is really good for me?" The logical answer: "A decrease in my suffering." Thus we become interested in means to alleviate our own suffering. Once we've gotten past this stage, it becomes easier to say to oneself, "In the end, others are in the same situation I am. It would be good if they could also stop suffering."

People suffering from contempt or hatred toward themselves have to become aware that they are not unworthy of the love of others, that there exists within them the potential for change, that one day they will be able to experience inner peace and that their unhappiness is never fixed in stone. This kind of reconciliation with oneself is the essential prerequisite for opening to others.

CHRISTOPHE Yes, it's important that the messages we are sending not be misunderstood. We are talking about the importance of being altruistic, but sometimes we are talking to people who, as you just said, have not gone through the prerequisite stages and for whom this is a mission impossible or at least an overwhelming mission. Many people's first reaction toward self-directed compassion, as you described in your own case, is one of distrust: "What kind of weird number is this that's going to make people even more self-centered?" And then, once this reflex has passed, you look into it further. You talk to theoreticians, experimenters, clinicians, and you discover that self-directed compassion has several dimensions, which include gentleness and respect toward oneself. We often say to our patients, "Be respectful toward yourself as you are toward your best friend." When a friend of yours experiences a setback, you don't say to him, "You are the king of idiots!" Instead you discuss what happened with understanding.

In psychotherapy we frequently encounter people who are terribly violent toward themselves. Thus what is essential in self-directed compassion is becoming aware that suffering is part of the human experience, and that when we suffer, we're suffering along with a ton of other people who are also suffering. The idea is not to say, "There are worse sufferings than yours," nor "It's not only you who's suffering"; and we also don't try to prevent the suffering of just existing. Instead, the object is to understand that, in the end, suffering is a universal human experience and so, in fact, when I am suffering, I am neither alone nor abnormal nor isolated. I am just part of the shared experience of humanity.

For that reason, over the course of the time I've been practicing psychiatry, I've become convinced that it's better to treat people in a group. At St. Anne Hospital in Paris, in the department I work in, we try to do group therapy as much as possible. I am always amazed to see people suffering from phobias, depression, and obsessions, coming into the groups with the absolute certainty that they are the only people who experience such weird, intense sufferings, and the only people who are incapable of getting them to go away. In short, they have a terrible feeling of loneliness and abnormality. And suddenly we begin our group work and everybody tells their stories and sees that the experience of suffering is universal. They see that it's not a sign of being a bad and incompetent person but rather a characteristic of being human.

Our Advice for a More Altruistic Life

Freeing Ourselves Somewhat from Self   ALEXANDRE

- Retain the capacity to be touched, moved, by others.
  The danger when one has really had to struggle in life
  is to become hardened, even to cut oneself off from
  others entirely. Thus we should imitate Buddha and
  Christ, who lived without itineraries. We should leave
  room in our schedules, remain open to what life might
  bring us here and now, remain open to encounters.

- Be generous without letting yourself be consumed by
  the desire to please. It is a sacred duty to discover one's
  inner freedom. How can we do that if we live at the

beck and call of ego, if we are totally at the mercy of what people might think of us? Move from the desire to please to pure love that expects nothing in return, and immediately perform some acts of altruism.

- Extend the love that you bear toward your near and dear ones to all of humanity. There is a life *by* others that proceeds from a desire to please; and there is a life *for* others that requires freely giving of oneself, joyously and without second thoughts. The words of Jesus bring us close to this: "If anyone would come after me, he must deny himself and take up his cross and follow me."

It Is Possible to Be Compassionate Toward Others Without Conditions MATTHIEU

- Don't be frightened by the practice of unconditional altruism and say that it is beyond your reach. Don't ever think, "The suffering of others is none of my business."

- Don't blame yourself for not doing what is beyond your strength, but do reproach yourself for turning away when you can do something.

- No matter what level we start from, kindness and compassion can be cultivated just like any other physical or mental aptitudes.

- We should make use of our natural ability to be compassionate toward those near us as a starting point for extending our compassion beyond our family and those we love.

The Good Use of Compassion   CHRISTOPHE

- Don't forget to be compassionate toward yourself!
  That makes it easier to be compassionate toward others.

- Observe what happens in yourself, in your mind, in
  your body, when you are compassionate, gentle, and
  kind. And by contrast, observe what you feel when
  in a state of conflict. Your entire body never ceases
  to remind you of the obvious: "See how I suffer from
  conflict; and how soothed and happy I am when I'm
  gentle and compassionate." It's a very clear teaching!

- Grant yourself permission not to be compassionate!
  When you have the feeling that compassion is
  impossible for you or is impracticable in a given
  situation, don't demand perfection. Do your best,
  and if it's too difficult, drop it, protect yourself, be
  content to not feed ill will and aggression, not to add
  to them; perhaps it's not the moment, it's too hard for
  you, or too hard for anybody, to try to change what's
  happening. Sometimes it just happens that we are in
  horrible situations—in the family or at work. You
  can't get through it by means of compassion and love,
  but only by fleeing, getting the heck out of there and
  saving your skin so that you can be compassionate
  with other people at other times. I sincerely feel that
  there are moments where one does not feel strong
  enough to provide long-term compassion and where
  one is just in danger of getting hurt.

The School of Simplicity

CHRISTOPHE This subject fascinates me because I feel I have a lot to learn in this area, both as a human being and as a caregiver. Our Western logic goes against simplifying in the sense of stripping away the inessential, because it is a logic of accumulation. We accumulate possessions, knowledge, and even relationships—for example, in the social networks—quite beyond what is reasonable and sometimes beyond any possibility of real use.

"The sage: don't ask what he has more of than you, but what he has less of." This little thought, picked up by chance in my reading, has affected me strongly. Being wise is often going in the direction of less, toward simplicity and detachment.

The Diogenes Syndrome

CHRISTOPHE In my profession, all my patients touch me emotionally, but my "accumulator" patients particularly move and intrigue me. Because of obsessive-compulsive problems, they don't throw anything away; they keep absolutely everything—newspapers, boxes, empty bottles, used-up toilet-paper rolls, old clothes. We speak sometimes in their regard of the Diogenes syndrome. When these "accumulators" live in big houses, the neighbors complain because their gardens are full of old tin cans. When they live in small apartments, it's no better. I do behavioral therapy and therefore I sometimes go to people's homes to work with them. I've seen apartments transformed into labyrinths with newspapers and shoe-boxes piled all the way up to the ceiling.

MATTHIEU It's amazing that you speak of a Diogenes syndrome here, since Diogenes disdained material possessions. It's said that when he was in Athens he contented himself with sleeping in a barrel on the street.

CHRISTOPHE Yes, it's something of a contradiction because if Diogenes lived in the manner of a street tramp, he certainly didn't accumulate much. But however that may be, these patients of mine suffer a great deal from accumulating, which inevitably leads me to ask myself, "How about you? They may be in an extreme state, but aren't you somewhat like that yourself?" I'm not at all good at getting rid of things. I don't like throwing anything away. I have my excuses, my justifications—my parents were major accumulators, adepts of "just in case," of "I'm not going to throw away this piece of string because it might come in handy" or "these old newspapers might be just what we need if the car leaks oil." I always felt that the extent to which that approach cluttered up their heads and their lives far outweighed the use they got out of all the accumulated stuff. But I have the same reflex regarding things I like. For example, I have a terrible time throwing away books, and it's almost impossible for me to throw out some old outworn item just because somebody gave it to me as a gift. I encounter total paralysis when it comes to getting rid of my daughters' old drawings and toys—my wife knows she can only throw them out when I'm not looking.

In general, divesting ourselves of objects that have emotional significance for us is painful. I remember the time I spent with my mother rearranging the house after my father died. Throwing things away was very complicated for me, and even more so for her, because I had the feeling I was throwing away parts of my father's life. In the end, why are we so attached to our memories? Of course they give a feeling of cohesion to our personal identity, the impression of knowing a little better who we are, where we come from. But if you think about it, memories can be more of a burden than a support. At a certain point, accumulation ceases to be good for us.

It seems I'm not the only one with this problem. I look around me and see this kind of attachment taking other forms, like the obsession some people have with taking photos—at family gatherings, on trips. We see more and more photography freaks, people who don't participate in parties so they can capture images of them. And what's going to happen? They will accumulate a ton of pictures that will just die on their hard drives because people actually look less at those pictures than at the photos in paper scrapbooks where there are only a few chosen images.

The obsession with being connected to the greatest possible number of people on the social networks, sending hundreds of texts or photos in real time—this all comes from the same tendency toward accumulation, toward not wanting to lose or throw away anything that is part of our lives. Our era is obviously very different from earlier times, when the connections both with objects and people were sparser but more intense. We live in a society that is extremely toxic, absolutely malignant, because it incites us to buy, to possess, to accumulate. And after a short time it pushes us to throw things away, not for the benefit such stripping away may bring us but rather to make room to buy more because the old stuff is no longer in fashion or is obsolete. This is demonic—consumer society has identified the fact that throwing away, stripping away, even in a mechanical way, is an indispensable, essential need, but it appropriates this and transforms it into a need to keep acquiring more.

In the world of psychotherapy, there too I have the feeling we are focused on the process of compensating for deficits. The depressed person doesn't have enough vital energy—how do we give him more? The fearful person lacks social skills—how can we teach him more? The hyperemotional person doesn't have enough emotional control—how do we give him more? How do we teach a drug addict more self-control? The meditative practices have opened my eyes to the fact that we can also guide people in the direction of less: less brooding, less thought, less attachment, less desire for control, etc. This was a very new thing for me, which has proven very fruitful in my practice and in the conduct of my personal life.

At this moment I keep on my desk Meister Eckhart's book on consolation. I brought it with me, and I'm going to read you a passage from it that's wonderfully appropriate to the notion of stripping away: "If God wants to give me what I desire, I possess it and I am fulfilled; if God does not want to give it to me, it is through privation that I receive it in this same divine will, which is precisely that it does not want to give it. And thus it is in being deprived that I receive, it is in not taking that I take."[1] I've also copied down a quotation from St. Augustine, which reads, "Create emptiness, in order to be filled, learn not to love in order to learn to love, turn away in order to be turned to. To say this in brief, anything that would accept or be receptive must necessarily be naked and empty."

ALEXANDRE   Hearing these words, I almost never want to speak again. In the matter of stripping away, I'm a complete beginner who often gets into trouble with it. Not long ago, on the advice of a friend, I canceled my Facebook account. Quite counter to my expectation, it didn't bother me at all. On the contrary, it was like being freed from an addiction, from chains, and this little victory gave me the strength to deal with more serious challenges. And it turns out I was going to have to do just that.

It was during a retreat called "Zen and the Gospels" that I discovered the pleasures of stripping away. These weeks spent on the study of a sutra and the practice of the Gospels were one the most beautiful times of my life, a time that transformed me entirely. Starting at dawn, we meditated six hours a day and we studied a sutra in detail. The evening Mass, which was an occasion of extraordinary purity and simplicity, would bring me back to the heart of that inner space where everything takes birth. Every time we did it, I had an experience of boundless gratitude and found the strength to say yes from the bottom of my heart to the tragic quality of life and to welcome in the thousand and one gifts of daily life. One night, when I went back to my room to take my night's rest, ascesis took an unexpected turn. I showered and rinsed out my clothes because I had brought only the minimum along. As I was washing my things I experienced an immense joy, a limitless thanks toward all that we receive day after day. It was as though stripping down my needs to the essential caused a completely new joy to arise, profound and without reason. It may sound crazy, but in the bathroom, I came to the point of saying thank you to my body, to the sink, to my clothes, and even to the toilets that rendered me a sacred service. I discovered, as if for the first time, all these everyday objects, which in my hurry and haste I had forgotten. On all fours, under the water jet, I understood that joy was an acquiescence to life, and that prayer comes down to these essential words: "yes" and "thank you."

Detachment and Opening to Others

ALEXANDRE   Who says that to be happy we necessarily have to be free from all lacks? I believe, on the contrary, that it's possible to know profound joy along with our deficiencies, our frustrations, amid all the ups and downs of life. If I need my car, my computer, if I'm hooked on the social networks, I will suffer sooner or later, and all the more so because the attachment to them is flawed. Wholeheartedly I can begin to track my attachments and recognize that they deprive me of lightness. Listening to you, Christophe, I begin to understand that behind my dependence on emails and texts, the illusion of security is hiding. As if having a bunch of online friends protected me! In this case too I have to learn to accept with compassion this desire that wells up from the depths of a wounded heart, but also not to be its slave. By the way, since we have been together, already two or three friends have written me: "Why don't you answer your emails? Are you dead?" It's for sure that this pressure, kindly though it might be, does not encourage detachment. It is urgent to learn that another kind of connection with others is possible, more profound, more free. And why should we always evaluate love on the basis of how much we might miss that person? What misunderstanding makes us believe that the more somebody misses us, the more they love us? Spinoza opens up an amazing horizon with a simple question: "What does love attach us to?" What is helpful for me is seeing that my wife, my children, my friends, and my master are there, even in the bad times. They never judge me. There is a consolation that the material world could never provide.

The big step forward might be seeing that happiness comes from stripping away and moving in the direction of *less*. Always we have to descend into the ground of our being, the ground of all grounds, to heal. Amassing, accumulating, heaping up, conquering don't lead to anything. Often when I'm caught up in avid greed, I ask myself, "What is it that I lack here and now?" Not very much, it turns out! The question immediately appeases me, and I immediately see the fullness that is present there in the moment. Here and now, I lack for nothing, but as soon as imagination and conceptual mind get going, I begin living in a conflicted and dependent state. That is why it is worthwhile to dare to take little miniretreats to reimmerse ourselves in the experience of nothing lacking that exists in the ground of being of us all.

In order to suffer less, there is a big temptation to harden ourselves, at the risk of becoming completely insensitive. We must not be fainthearted about stripping away our shells and vain protections. When I moved to South Korea, I experienced a certain solitude. There I don't have friends falling all over each other trying to see me . . . A Buddhist monk helped me with a lot of the administrative details involved in moving. One day, as we were separating, he bluntly served notice: "Don't count on me to contact you; if you need me, call me." The danger of remaining at a distance from others once you devote yourself to a spiritual life is always lurking. But detachment does not at all entail being cold. It's not a barrier between others and myself, but rather a letting go of myself, a bit of freedom with regard to my ego. If I meditate or pray in my little corner and expect serenity from that without performing acts of solidarity with others, I'm surely mistaken. That is why friendship and genuine encounters are important. We are all team members on the road to happiness.

Thanks to you, Christophe, I understand that detachment begins with very concrete acts. Divesting oneself of everything superfluous also passes by way of the material level. The cause for our packing up and heading for South Korea was a friend of ours. One day he came to our house, and when he saw the books piled up everywhere, he gently commented that our decor was not exactly Zen, nor was my whole lifestyle. Then he asked me a murderous question: "What is your greatest wish?" I answered, "My wife doesn't want to, but I'd like to get some training in South Korea that will put the spiritual life smack in the middle of our everyday activity." Suddenly I heard a voice cry out, "But who told you I was against it?" In a few weeks, we packed our boxes and left for Seoul.

So it was a simple discovery like that that led me to journey to the "Land of the Morning Calm." In preparing for the trip, I had to divest myself of my books, and in doing that I found that I got more pleasure out of giving them away than running out to the bookstore to buy the latest publication. So I called a prison to tell them that I had a bunch of books to give them, and thus it was with delight that I dropped off suitcases full of them at the Lausanne Penitentiary. I smile at the idea of some prisoner coming upon the works of Meister Eckhart, Spinoza, Rumi, etc. . . . In short, it's joy and the practice of spontaneous generosity that detaches us from our worldly goods and artificial relations. Learning to make good use of the garbage can, that great instrument of liberation, is also something that takes time. In my view, throwing things away, abandoning them, is connected with death, with fear. That is why we are

> If I meditate or pray in my little corner and expect serenity from that without performing acts of solidarity with others, I'm surely mistaken.

strongly tempted to hang on to things . . . The spiritual exercise for today is learning that, as to the essential, we lack for nothing. Material things can never fulfill the aspirations that lie deep in our hearts. For example, my desk is piled high with drawings by my children that I never take the time to look at properly. Lately I've remedied this by creating some order. I take time to appreciate them, look them over in detail, and then I toss them out. This is a way of taking note of the fact that my children live, die, and are reborn every day; that little baby Augustin has already departed and left in his place the young boy who smiles at me today. My three children are given to me anew every moment.

Being Content with Simplicity

MATTHIEU   At this point, our subject matter clearly doesn't apply to people who live in precarious conditions or in a total state of deprivation. We all need to have roofs over our heads and enough food and comfort to stay in good health. And we should do whatever is necessary to come to the aid of all the people on earth, numerous indeed, who are still deprived of these things. Remedying the inequalities and the poverty in the world is an essential duty.

But what we're talking about here is the need of getting rid of what is superfluous. I have to acknowledge that that is easier for me. I have taken monastic vows and possess neither house nor lands nor car. I have chosen a lifestyle that makes it possible for me to leave on a moment's notice for the other side of the world without shirking my responsibilities to a family or to work colleagues. I can do it without slighting anybody.

That said, the notion of lack and privation is very relative. For thirteen years I slept on the ground in my master Dilgo Khyentse Rinpoche's bedroom, wherever he was in the world. In the morning I folded up my sleeping bag and put it in a sack with my toothbrush, my towel, and a few other small items. After Dilgo Khyentse Rinpoche died in 1991, I slept in his anteroom on a carpet. In the morning I stowed my things in a little cubby. After three years of this, somebody said, "Wouldn't you like a room?" I accepted and it was rather nice. But at no time did I consider my previous situation a privation. Quite to the contrary, what was foremost for me was the joy I felt at the extraordinary good fortune of living close to Dilgo Khyentse Rinpoche, of benefiting from his presence and receiving his teachings.

I still use the same sleeping bag today. There's really no reason to be attached to this sleeping bag, which is losing its feathers, but I see no reason to replace it as long as it still keeps me warm in the winter.

Attachment complicates life. One day, at the end of a conference, as I was signing books, I found myself with a Montblanc fountain pen in my hand. I looked around. No one claimed it, so I kept it. The problem is, I tend to lose pens. With ballpoints, that's not a big deal, but a Montblanc, on the other hand, is no ordinary fountain pen—it would be a shame to lose it! So since then, it sleeps in a drawer and I never use it. I would do better to give it away. But is it a good thing to give away a fountain pen that represents 5 percent pen and 95 percent meaningless attachment?

It's not objects, people, or phenomena themselves that pose problems but the attachment we have to them. A great Indian Buddhist master said, "It's not appearances that enslave you but your attachment to them." The story is told of a monk who was so attached to his begging bowl that he was reborn as a snake coiled in that bowl and let nobody come near it. So stripping away is not a question of wealth or poverty but rather how strongly we cling to things. Even the richest man, if he is not attached to his riches, is not enslaved by them and can use them for the benefit of others.

That said, it's unbelievable that in spite of myself I end up hoarding. I have a small room, which is three meters by three meters, in the Shechen monastery in Nepal, and a retreat place in the mountains that is even smaller. In each of these places I have a shrine with some books and a few statues, and beneath them, two small storage spaces. And I end up accumulating more than necessary. Then, once a year, I take out all the garments I have stored there and give away those that I have two or three of. At my workplace in the monastery, I take enormous pleasure in throwing out old files, which go to feed the fires in the kitchen.

Today, when people talk about a financial crisis in the rich countries, it usually means a crisis in the realm of the superfluous. If everybody contented themselves with only the necessary, we would never get into such crises. Recently in New York, I ran into a five-hundred-meter-long line composed of hundreds of people waiting patiently in the street. Intrigued, I asked somebody what it was all about. "A floor-sample sale of brand-name scarves. They're selling for $300 dollars instead of $500," I was told.

I couldn't help but think that at the same moment in Nepal, women were standing in endless lines in the street to buy a few liters of kerosene to cook food for their children. A financial "crisis" obviously looks different in different places in the world!

According to a Tibetan proverb, "Being satisfied is like having a treasure in the palm of your hand." The truly rich person is one who is not greedy for superfluous things. A person who lives amid opulence and wants still more will always be poor. If you think that having always more will lead to your being satisfied, you are deceiving yourself. It's like thinking that by drinking ever more salt water, a time will come when you will no longer be thirsty.

In Tibet it is said that the true hermit leaves behind only his footprints when he leaves the world. In consumer societies, we accumulate, accumulate, and always want to keep it all for ourselves. My dear mother says that our civilization is centripetal because we always draw more things to ourselves. Traditional parts of Asia still contain many examples of centrifugal civilization, in which people share. I know a Tibetan nun who says when you give her a gift, "Thanks. I'll be able to make offerings and give to the poor!"

The Freedom of Nonattachment

MATTHIEU Not being attached doesn't mean loving others less. On the contrary, we love them more, because we are less preoccupied by the need to receive their love in exchange for the love we give them. We love them as they are, and not as they would be seen through the distorting lenses of our egos. Rather than being attached to others for the happiness they bring us, we are concerned for their happiness. Instead of waiting eagerly for gratification, we are simply happy when our love arouses love in return.

I prefer the term *nonattachment*, which evokes the image of not being glued to things, to *detachment*, which makes you think of being painfully torn loose from them. Nonattachment consists in fully appreciating beings and situations but without trying to own them, without coating them with the glue of our possessive desire.

Nonattachment is thus not hanging our hopes and fears on external situations. In Tibetan Buddhism, we speak of "one taste." That doesn't mean that we don't make any distinction between mustard and strawberries and everything becomes equally insipid. Rather, we are capable of preserving our inner peace in all circumstances, whether it's cold out or hot, whether we are comfortable or not, whether nice things are being said about us or unpleasant things. Once this inner peace has been found, we are like a boat with a well-shaped keel: even if a gust of wind tips us, we don't capsize, and we are quick to regain our balance.

> Not being attached doesn't mean loving others less. On the contrary, we love them more, because we are less preoccupied by the need to receive their love in exchange for the love we give them.

As to inner simplicity, this is one of the cardinal virtues of spiritual practice. It goes hand in hand with great freedom with regard to mental stewing and chewing, with regard to the hopes and fears that often complicate even the simplest situations. In Tibetan, the word *simplicity*, in the most profound sense, means resting in the nature of the mind, free from all mental fabrications.

CHRISTOPHE But in simplifying in the sense of stripping away, no matter what one may say on the theoretical level, there is a relative loss of comfort. Living in a big room with a beautiful view seems to me more comfortable than living in a very small room that gives on a wall or a parking lot . . . Even if we know that what is essential does not lie in this, comfort is initially a facilitator. Then little by little it becomes an obstacle if it turns into an imperative priority.

MATTHIEU I'm not sure stripping away is less comfortable than excessive ownership. Based on my experience, I would opt without hesitation for felicitous simplicity. The situations you mention, Christophe, are not merely uncomfortable. In the case of one's view being a wall, what you are talking about there is not really stripping away but a situation that is unfavorable to our well-being, at least until we reach a certain level of inner freedom. The simplification or stripping away that I'm talking about does not consist in putting oneself in a miserable situation but in getting rid of useless things associated with superfluity. Superfluity is like the icing on the cake—the more there is of it, the less good it is for your health.

Dilgo Khyentse Rinpoche used to speak of the suffering of possessing too much. If you possess a horse, you have the suffering connected with this horse—the problem of providing it with shelter and food, of keeping it in good health, of sadness if it dies, and so forth. If you possess a house, you also have the suffering connected with this house—taxes, repairs, maintenance, fire, flood, and so on. It is undeniable that the more things one has, the more problems and suffering one has connected with these things.

I might cite the unexpected example of a very wealthy person who deliberately simplified his life. I'm talking about Pierre Omidyar, the cofounder of eBay. One day he said to his broker, "Stop making my money grow. I have enough of it." With his wife, Pam, he created a foundation that aids hundreds of thousands of women in India, among other beneficiaries. I was intrigued by his story, and I met him in Vancouver at a roundtable with the Dalai Lama. When I met him again in Paris, he came by metro. His mother had said to him, "You're often in Paris, you might as well buy yourself a car." He went to an automobile show where he saw all kinds of beautiful cars. He looked around and then he said to himself, "I could buy all of them, but do I even need one? No." He was quite content to leave the show by metro.

ALEXANDRE That's terrific!

MATTHIEU I could also cite the case of Gérard Godet, today deceased, who was a great patron of Buddhism and supported many charitable organizations. He did a nine-year spiritual retreat. He was also rich, but he lived simply and dressed so modestly that one day when he had taken refuge from the rain under an awning and stuck out his hand to see if it was still raining, a passerby put a coin in his hand.

Lightening Up That Pacifies

MATTHIEU   Renunciation is, in fact, not a privation but a freedom. At first glance, it doesn't make you think of anything very pleasant, but imagine that you are walking in the mountains and your backpack feels too heavy. During a break, you open it up and you see that some joker has put a pile of stones underneath your provisions. At the moment of throwing away the stones, you are not depriving yourself of anything; you're simply making your life easier. Real renunciation is like that. All you are doing is distinguishing what in your life is a source of profound satisfaction from that which is only a source of problems.

If an alcoholic father decided to renounce alcohol for the good of his children, the withdrawal would without doubt be difficult, but we could not say that it will diminish or impoverish this father. Renunciation does not mean depriving yourself of that which brings you joy and happiness—that would be absurd—but putting an end to that which creates endless suffering for you. In truth, we are all suffering from an addiction to the causes of suffering. Let's drop artificial euphoria and canned happiness. Without forbidding ourselves desire, let's embrace what is truly desirable from the point of view of our growth and development.

Being constantly preoccupied with praise and blame, fame and anonymity, richness and power, deprives us of our most precious possessions—our time, our energy, our health, and even our lives. Seneca said, "It's not that we have too little time, but that we waste so much of it." The phantoms that we pursue are not so much ways of improving our lives as ways of ruining it. We could throw so many activities overboard and as a result live better lives rather than being so scattered in superfluous things. As Chuang Tzu said, "He who has penetrated life's meaning no longer troubles himself with things that do not contribute to it." Nonattachment has a joyful taste of freedom.

Stripping oneself is also freeing oneself from the wandering thoughts that never cease spinning in our heads. It's leaving behind those mental preoccupations, those hopes and fears that usually fill our mental landscape, crowding out love, compassion, and inner peace.

CHRISTOPHE   Is there a Tibetan word that positively describes this process of lightening? Stripping away and renouncing are words that have a negative aspect.

MATTHIEU   The Tibetan word that we usually translate as "renunciation" in fact means "determination to liberate oneself." It refers to a staunch resolve to liberate oneself from the samsaric ocean of suffering, conditioned by ignorance and suffering, and thus to leave behind everything that weighs us down and makes us sink in this ocean. We speak of the relief of someone who puts down a heavy burden or who escapes from a pit of burning coals. The state that results might be called happy and wished-for simplicity, which recalls somewhat the "happy sobriety" of Pierre Rabhi.

Stripping Away in Daily Life

CHRISTOPHE   It's very complicated to recognize the need for stripping away solely by the power of intellect. We have to get there through concrete experience.

Retreats, for example, are an extremely precious aid. When you do a retreat, you are stripped of the possibility of telephoning, sending texts, reading, watching television, and so forth. You are deprived of these external crutches and all your usual little possessions. You are immersed in a monastic environment, closely attuned with people who have made the choice of an entire life stripped to simplicity. They are not even aware of this quality of being stripped, just as a fish in water isn't aware that it is in water. If you get into phase with them, you get a lot of lessons about your attachments.

Another practice that is instructive in this area is fasting. I've had the experience of fasting in a way that was closely connected with the notion of stripping down. We see that it is quite possible not to eat for a period of time, that it isn't dangerous, it doesn't make us suffer. Through fasting we acquire a great deal of insight about our relationship with food—we do a much better job of distinguishing between real hunger and the urge to eat because the food smells and looks good, because of the habit of eating at a particular time, for the pleasure of it because we like to eat. For me, fasting was a lightening laboratory, a renunciation laboratory, something that went well beyond the simple act of fasting.

I'd love to hear about all the types of efforts you two have made. I think there is a methodology of stripping away. I need (and I think our readers may also need) you to say more about this, since you are more advanced on the path.

ALEXANDRE When I was leaving for Korea, I began to see the thousand objects that I had accumulated little by little. So I launched into a little ascesis, which was to ask myself why I was so attached to these objects around me and from where they drew their value. My parents had made my ears sore telling me ceaselessly to clean up my room. Today, thanks to Zen, I understand that a cluttered environment ends up polluting our mind and distracting it. So I very painstakingly rid the house of everything that wasn't useful. It's very simple: only those objects that have a real use for me get into the room. I pushed this exercise to the extreme by keeping only one book on my nightstand. Creating order in the house begins by asking the question: What is essential? Since I first did that, it's practically become a game. When I go shopping I ask myself, for example, if the garment I'm about to buy really suits me or if I'm just following a consumerist impulse. And the very latest computer technology that tempts me, do I really need it? More than anything, giving liberates.

One day, my wife gently brought me back to order by pointing out that I was more willing to get rid of paperbacks than hardcover books. She simply said, "If you're really going to do your exercise, go the whole hog and start with your Pléiade editions (fine leatherbound classics on very fine paper)." By showing me that the best intentions in the world are not enough, that real, concrete deeds are necessary, she really made me laugh at myself.

In Seoul, with the children, we sometimes do a little spiritual exercise. As soon as we set foot in a big-box store, we challenge ourselves to get out of there empty-handed. When Socrates would take a stroll in the marketplace, he took pleasure in seeing how many things there were there that he could do without.

> As soon as we set foot in a big-box store, we challenge ourselves to get out of there empty-handed. When Socrates would take a stroll in the marketplace, he took pleasure in seeing how many things there were there that he could do without.

MATTHIEU   I heard the Dalai Lama say that in his whole life he's only been into a department store twice. Both times he made a short tour, and after having looked at all kinds of things, saying to himself, "Hmm, I could buy that," he realized he had no need of it and he walked out empty-handed.

ALEXANDRE   Why don't we imitate him and take another look at what tempts us? The moment I go into a department store, I hear a small voice, like an alarm going off, that stops me right away. I resist the frenzy that makes me believe that happiness is in having, and there are a thousand and one ways to resist the temptation. For example, by observing, by contemplating, and especially by taking pleasure in the exercise itself. Remaining attentive to others helps us make progress. So at the cash register, let the old lady who has trouble walking go first. More than any effort, it's attention to the present that sets us free. It's not privation, frustration, or lack that leads to detachment but rather fulfillment and joy. What helps me give and strip down is taking full advantage of life and reading with relish the one book that is waiting for me on the nightstand. Becoming detached is paradoxically learning to enjoy and move on.

Listening to you, I think again of the words of Thoreau, who raises this marvelous challenge: "Simplify, simplify, simplify." His motto, his remedy, serves as a compass in my everyday life. Coming back to the essential, stripping down our lifestyle, pacifying tortured relationships, is a practice, an ascesis. Here it is not a matter of deceiving ourselves but of considering with infinite candor all the needs that dwell in our hearts. One by one, sever the attachments so as to take flight into freedom. That is the path I can recommend, along with St. John of the Cross, who tells us that a bird may be tied by only a gold thread, but this tiny bond will prevent it from flying.

CHRISTOPHE   A trip through the supermarket as a spiritual exercise! This is something I've done with my patients who are compulsive buyers. This is known as ERP therapy, exposure with response prevention. You expose people to the environments that tend to trigger their pathological responses, and you help them to not carry out those responses. You go to the store with them, they breathe very deeply in front of everything they have the urge to buy, they don't buy it, and you leave with the feeling of having done some good work. The exercise must be repeated regularly because we are regularly recontaminated, repolluted by advertising and the consumer society.

MATTHIEU   I remember being at my retreat place and thinking to myself, "If a fairy offered me three wishes regarding material things, what would I ask for?" Considering the size of my retreat space, the possibilities were limited. No way to fit a hi-fi system or even a computer with a big screen into that place. I have a shrine with a few statues, about twenty books, a few articles of clothing, and some utilitarian objects. After a short time I burst out laughing because I could find nothing to wish for that wasn't more of a burden than an improvement. Hence the famous mantra, which is

Recite it ten times: I need nothing, I need nothing, I need nothing, and so on.

immensely soothing if you recite it ten times: I need nothing, I need nothing, I need nothing, and so on.

A great Tibetan master Dudjom Rinpoche said that when you have one thing and you want two of them, you are already opening the door to a demon. As soon as you are incapable of being content with the essential, there are no longer any limits. The whole earth wouldn't be enough. I remember a film I saw on an airplane. It was the story of a vast scheme organized by a man and woman who succeeded in embezzling billions of dollars from a banking system by wrongly resetting clocks. And so on. At the end, the woman wanted to be the smart one and get away with the whole amount. The man, played by Sean Connery, foiled her scheme and asked her, "What could you do with four billion that you couldn't do with two?" If you want to use a sum like that for the welfare of others, to wipe out malaria, or feed the hungry, doubtless you could do a lot. But for oneself, nothing.

CHRISTOPHE   I love this celebratory mantra, "I need nothing!" It's not a brainwashing or an autosuggestion technique but rather a kind of mental massage that softens up our psychological attachments to our false needs and progressively creates a taste in us for something else, another way of life and a way of responding to temptations. When you say it with sincerity, stripping away preconceptions, something happens, just like when Alex raised the question, "What am I lacking?" Such a question is ineffective unless you really stop and let yourself be struck by it.

Teaching Simplicity to Children

MATTHIEU   The teaching of stripping away should begin with children. From the beginning, you must have the decency not to condition them to become consumption junkies. In his book *The High Price of Materialism*, the psychologist Tim Kasser cites remarks by the CEO of General Mills, one of the biggest food enterprises in the world: "As for targeting consumers from an early age, we use the

THE SCHOOL OF SIMPLICITY

model 'from cradle to grave.' We think that you have to catch children very early and then keep them their whole lives." By way of combating this cynical project, Kasser suggests prohibiting all advertising aimed at children, as has been done in Sweden and Norway.

How do you teach simplicity to children? By sharing with them joy in simple things. To come back to Tim Kasser, in Bangkok, where we were for a conference on "Buddhism and Consumer Society," he told us, "This morning I had a wonderful moment with my son in a park. We discovered all kinds of tropical flowers and multicolored birds, and we were enjoying the beauty and calm of the place. Imagine that instead of doing that, I had taken my son shopping in a Thai supermarket. Imagine that when we came out, we took a 'tuk-tuk' rickshaw and that it had a collision with a car. We maybe would have had to take the driver to a hospital, a fine would have been levied against the delinquent driver, and all that would have been much better for consumption and for the GNP of the country, but not for our profound satisfaction."[2]

During an excursion in the French countryside, a friend reminded me that when we were children, during cherry season we used to be in the orchards enjoying the fruit. Today those cherries stay on the trees. Children don't climb trees anymore. Most of the time they're glued to their computers. Between 1997 and 2003, the percentage of children between ages nine and twelve who spent time playing outside together, hiking, or gardening fell by half. Games are more and more solitary, virtual, violent, without beauty, wonder, camaraderie, and simple pleasures. Now studies have shown that greater contact with nature has a significant positive effect on the cognitive development of children.

CHRISTOPHE The question of children is of the highest priority. I did a scientific analysis of Joel Bakan's *Childhood Under Siege: How Big Business Ruthlessly Targets Children*, where he shows in detail the way in which our society targets children, manipulates them, turns them into addicts, and also manipulates their parents. It's terrifying!

MATTHIEU And fundamentally immoral. We are dealing here with selfishness that is institutionalized and completely cynical, because these commercial enterprises know perfectly well that they are harming children.

CHRISTOPHE I think the same as you, Matthieu, and I also think that all forms of advertising aimed at minors should simply be prohibited, whatever the product—whether it's toys or sugary drinks. There's no reason that could justify encouraging children to consume that stuff. Their vulnerability is cynically exploited, which is unacceptable, as I see it.

And here's another area where we parents are responsible. I often have the sense that the gifts we give our children serve to compensate for the guilt we feel for the time we don't spend with them. For years, I was still living in Toulouse and my wife, Pauline, was in Paris. Every week I'd take the plane to go see her, and I spent a lot of time in airports. These are places where there are a lot of stores and, if you look carefully, also toy stores, which is somehow rather surprising. These shops target the dads—and more and more also the moms—who feel guilty about being far away from home and who, when they pass in front of the shop windows, are heartbroken thinking about their children. They salve their consciences and hope they will bring their kids pleasure by buying a toy, whereas ideally they should ask this question: "Is this because my child lacks toys? No, I'm unhappy because I'm not with him enough." And what do we do? Yielding to expediency, we go into the store, buy a toy, and give it to the child, who is pleased after all, because he more or less takes it as proof of love. I've done this, we've all done it, but it's like giving a child a soda to drink instead of teaching him to drink water—you're not doing him a favor.

The best thing we can do for these children is, once again, set an example. If you buy a new watch every six months, if you manically go to every sale, if your family weekend trip is a trip to the supermarket, what is the message you're sending them?

But I have hope because I think that the human species is intelligent and adaptive. I see this new generation of children—who grew up in an overstuffed environment from the point of view of stuff (toys, clothes)—beginning to immunize itself against consumption. The children I know well—my daughters, my nephews, the children of close friends—have, if not a sense of distrust, at least a kind of indifference or growing independence with regard to possessing stuff, and at bottom they give away what they possess much more easily than we did. I have the feeling that at some point this hyperconsumption society, which fans our desires and creates artificial ones, will end up quite naturally secreting in our brains the appropriate antibodies. Increasingly we see the emergence of parallel economies, economies of sharing, where instead of buying, we borrow—a chainsaw from a neighbor, for example. We might well be evolving toward other models that will prevail, where children lend their toys, their books, etc.

Our Advice for Traveling Light

Three Ways to Lighten Up   CHRISTOPHE

Here are three pieces of advice I try to follow (I don't always succeed).

- Lighten up materially. I recommend Matthieu's mantra, "I need nothing." Or if that's too hard, "I don't need all of that." When you go shopping or are just hanging out in the stores, before buying, ask yourself, "Do I really need that? Will that make me happier today? And tomorrow, in a month, in a year?"

- Lighten up activity-wise. We do too much stuff, engage our children in too many activities. Do we need all these leisure-time amusements, all these activities? What if we did less, so as to live better? What if we kept some time for doing nothing, for contemplation, just to breathe?

- Lighten up psychologically. We could lighten up our load of fears—fears for the future, fears about our social image, fears regarding our security. Alex talks about it often: there is a great deal of housekeeping to do on the psychological level.

What is Essential?   ALEXANDRE

- Free yourself of labels. Meister Eckhart constantly urges readers to rid themselves of self. Thus a hundred times a day, I can experience the fact that I'm not a certified worrier, not a temperamental hothead, not a philosopher, not a disabled person. Ascesis means stripping away these identities that we reduce ourselves to so we can allow ourselves to die and be reborn every moment. The more I reduce myself to a label, the more I suffer. Let's immediately drop this mentality of fixation that binds us to something rigid and solid every instant—that's the big challenge.

- The price of peace is stripping away. Profound joy requires us to do less. Meister Eckhart urges us to clear the temple of our mind. Today, here, right now, what can I concretely strip myself of? How can I make room in my agenda?

- Ask yourself what is essential. Learn to clean house, do the shopping—those are the areas of life where progress can emerge. Thus we can consider the supermarket as an immense practice ground where we can find out what our real needs are. Because we look for happiness where it is not found, we pass up what is essential. Nothing is more precious than a lifestyle that has been stripped bare, that helps us make ourselves available to joy and peace. So why not begin to put some order in our lives in the simplest possible way?

Simplify MATTHIEU

I'll use Thoreau's phrase again: "Simplify, simplify, simplify."

- Let's simplify our thoughts by avoiding cluttering our minds with useless thoughts, vain expectations, and unreasonable fears by ceasing to chew on the past and to anxiously anticipate the future.

- Let's simplify our speech by avoiding turning our mouths into meaningless gossip mills that keep running all the time. The words that come out of our mouths are sometimes heavy with consequences. So let's stop propagating attachment and animosity. Let's speak gently, and if firmness is necessary, let it be marked by compassion.

- Let's simplify our actions by not letting ourselves get caught up in ceaseless activities that eat up our time and bring us only minimal satisfaction.

10

Guilt and Forgiveness

ALEXANDRE Go forward, always make progress, agreed! But how do we get rid of those balls and chains that often keep us from moving forward? How do free ourselves a bit from the past? Guilt, resentment, grudges, and the whole parade of mental poisons really play terrible tricks on us. Once again, Meister Eckhart provides us with a powerful antidote when he distinguishes two kinds of repentance. One, the temporal and sensory one, makes us wallow in despondency and despair. By pulling us down, it imprisons us in a sense of helplessness; it floors us. The other, the mystical call of the divine and supernatural, gives us wings in a way. It elevates us toward God. It turns us away from evil and forcefully redirects our will toward the good. In short, without wiping away all feelings of fault, it makes it clear that we have to drop our narcissistic guilt, which far from making us better, paralyzes us. Above all, we must commit ourselves to a sense of forward motion; we have to get on with things. Even if I stumble and hurt myself, I remain a *progrediens*, a being who picks himself up and moves forward toward liberated joy. Until our last breath, we have the opportunity to advance, to say yes—even if we can barely move our lips—to what is happening.

Lightening the heart and letting the soul breathe perhaps requires us to return to the spirit of childhood, return to the innocence that the sages never lose. Laying down and leaving behind those kilos of worry, those bundles of bitterness and resentment, would certainly get us past a lot of blockages. Because basically what we have to do, with great patience, is let ourselves be what we have to be. A person who is macerating in self-contempt will never be able to rise very high. The example of the Zen masters helps us move forward here: in facing difficulty, the mind doesn't lose itself in speculations. When a problem comes up, we have to go into action. On the moral level, it's very simple: When I do something wrong, instead of letting myself get lost in "Oh, I never should have . . ." and "Oh, if only . . . ," I just have to figure out in concrete terms what I can do to make up for my wrongdoing. And instead of chewing on my screwup, I have to help the person I hurt. Perpetuating self-castigation, overwhelming oneself with a thousand reproaches, never helped anybody. In the end, all that does is lay down another layer of suffering.

An End to Guilt

MATTHIEU   You are talking about a sense of guilt that weighs very heavily on us, but there is also simple regret, which makes it possible to recognize the mistakes we have made and the harm we have done through our lack of understanding and lack of consideration for others. This is a form of healthy regret that is accompanied by the wish to not repeat the same errors and to repair the wrongs we have done to others and ourselves. In any case, that is the pragmatic view of Buddhism. Even if it seems paradoxical, this type of regret can lead to optimism because it turns into the desire to change. It is the starting point for self-improvement.

ALEXANDRE   In a superb book dedicated to Plato, the philosopher Alain exposes a false conception of freedom. I don't have the freedom to have married my wife before I did in the past, but I can choose to love her now every moment with all my heart. The horizon that opens up is a joyful one. The challenge here is to exercise our freedom now in the midst of obstacles: I didn't have the freedom to decide whether or not to be disabled, but I can decide to make the fact that I am a ground for practice, an opportunity to make progress on the path. After all, there is no better time than the one I am given here, right now, to become a more loving husband, a more attentive father, a more joyous disabled person . . . Regret fixes us in the past. Instead, let's live fully in the present.

In guilt I detect a kind of interiorization of the regard of the other, as if reproaches that I heard a thousand times ended up generating a self-accusation in me that is permanent and unhealthy. Regretting the past, stagnating in remorse, eats up a lot of energy. Why not simply acknowledge our mistakes and try to draw the lessons from them? What is the use of second thoughts such as "That isn't worthy of me. I'm a better person than that!" Between severe self-recrimination and total permissiveness lies a path. Step by step we can move forward on the way of nonfixation and love.

MATTHIEU It's true that if regret degenerates into guilt, it can lead to self-abasement, a feeling of being afflicted by a fundamental vice. We believe we deserve the others' blame, and we doubt our capacity to change. This form of regret leads to despondency and despair and prevents us from being clear-minded. It does not serve as a starting point for self-improvement. Moreover, by pushing us to put the focus on ourselves, it prevents us from thinking of others and making amends for the suffering we might have caused them.

In the West, the sense of guilt is influenced by the notion of original sin. In the Buddhist East, we speak, on the contrary, of "original goodness." There is nothing basically bad in us, and faults are considered to have at least one quality, that of being reparable. Every person possesses the potential for perfection, which may be forgotten or veiled but never lost. Our faults and defects are just so many accidents, temporary deviations. They can all be corrected and in no way spoil this potential. In this context, regret is not a feeling that fixes us in the past. On the contrary, it is what permits us to leave our mistakes behind and make a fresh start.

A few years ago, at the invitation of a few of the prisoners, I and a friend paid a visit to a penitentiary in southern France. We spent the afternoon with about twenty prisoners. They were all serving long sentences, at least twenty years. The thing that seemed most unreal to me was the feeling I had of having tea with a group of people who couldn't have been more normal, apart from one prisoner who remained in a prostration on the floor most of the time. After a long discussion, one of them said to me, "The idea that we have the potential to bring out the best in ourselves is reassuring; it's a source of hope. Most of the time, the spiritual advisers who come here tell us that we are sinners twice over. First, we're just born sinners, and then on top of that we have committed a serious wrong. That's quite a heavy load to carry. You feel crushed by it."

One of my teachers, Jigme Khyentse Rinpoche, gave an amusing example to illustrate the difference between regret and guilt. If you run a red light, you are stopped by the police and you get hit with a fine. Regret prevents you from running any more red lights and from being punished again. If, instead of that, you are overwhelmed by a sense of guilt, you're going to drive off thinking that you're a lousy driver, that you're distracted all the time, and, on top of that, that you have rotten luck because you're always getting fined. Absorbed in your thoughts, you fail to notice the next red light, you run it, and you're fined yet again!

Feeling neither regret nor guilt can be serious; in fact, that's a characteristic of psychopaths. They know the difference between good and bad, but they pay no attention to it. When their misdeeds are successful, they feel satisfaction, but when they fail or are exposed, they feel neither shame nor regret; they just wait for the next opportunity to do more of the same. Punishment has no redemptive effect on them and does nothing to prevent recidivism. When they are caught, they try to justify themselves, to minimize the impact of what they've done, and to put the blame on others—generally, their victims.

Intimate and Painful Feelings

CHRISTOPHE   I have a vision that's a bit different from yours in the way I define these phenomena. It would be interesting to compare our points of view. In psychology, we lump together the phenomena of regret, guilt, and shame in the family of "intimate and painful feelings" toward events and acts of the past. These feelings constitute a continuum that I will do my best to present a clear picture of. There is an evolutionist explanation for all that. The reason we are equipped with the capacity to go back to the past with our emotions and thoughts is that it is an extremely useful function. We often make mistakes, either deliberate or involuntary errors, "by action or omission," as is said in Christianity, and all these painful emotions help us to not make them again, or possibly even to wish to make amends for them.

The classifications of these emotions include several dimensions. First, does the deed that generates this emotional and psychological discomfort involve only me or does it involve harm to others? Here I would distinguish regret and guilt differently than you do, Matthieu. I don't necessarily feel *guilty* if I run a red light, because if the policeman catches me, I've only hurt my wallet. But I can *regret* running it. I can even not regret it, but just be annoyed, without the uncomfortable feeling connected with regret. By contrast, I might regret having done something that made me lose money, or regret some negligence that resulted in my house catching fire—but if I live alone in the house, I won't feel guilt. In psychology, guilt is a painful feeling in relation to a past act that caused suffering or pain to someone, while regret does not necessarily imply either pain or suffering.

We also speak of *shame*, another member of this big family, when we have an emotional feeling that is much more intense, much more painful. There is a dimensional difference here too. Often I feel shame about what I am, shame about my whole person, when the guilt is linked to a precise act or focused on a significant mistake that caused harm to others.

MATTHIEU It's true, we don't give these words the same meaning. In Buddhism we also talk about shame, but, again, as a good quality. We distinguish two kinds. The first is the discomfort we feel when we have gone against an ethical rule we have set ourselves. This is an intimate feeling that we can keep secret. It is considered beneficial because it encourages us to correct our attitude so we can feel better. The second kind of shame is the shame we feel before others, generally before a person we respect. This is a more noble feeling than the simple worry over what people might think of us. It helps us improve ourselves, taking as criterion what someone thinks of us whom we consider better than ourselves. So Buddhism simply suggests a positive approach to these feelings, seeing them as serving what we consider the most noble end, which is liberation from confusion and suffering, both for ourselves and others. Finally, guilt also has a healthy aspect. It can shake us up because we have harmed somebody, even involuntarily, and thus suddenly cause us to recognize the unacceptable quality of the harmful acts we have committed.

CHRISTOPHE Psychologists also take an interest in feelings that are much less intense, such as feeling awkward or embarrassed. For example, if I break a glass, I haven't hurt anybody and the glass itself isn't worth much, and breaking it is far from being a moral fault; but I'm embarrassed because it's an unsuitable act. All these emotions are feelings of what we call "self-consciousness," which require me to acknowledge responsibility for my actions.

In addition to the emotional side, there is also the cognitive side. When we brood about our past actions, we feel pain that is often vestiges of shame, guilt, embarrassment, or regret. We dwell on what happened more than might be considered necessary. Experts believe that one of the virtues of these painful emotions connected with deeds we have done in the recent or distant past is to activate a train of thought, which in turn activates a process of self-questioning, and this in turn might activate certain resolves. Matthieu, you described this causal chain, which Buddhism also tries to set in motion.

But some of these emotions can be excessive and pathological. Instead of feeling a little regret, a little guilt, instead of reflecting about how to make amends, I can sink into excessive and dispropor-tionate guilt, even into a sense of absolute shame. And the cognitive side, reflection, thinking things over, can go astray into brooding. In this brooding we go well beyond reevaluation of what happened, we rechew, we dwell—and we suffer.

Often in therapy we advise people to ask themselves three ques-tions to find out if they are reflecting or brooding. Since you have been thinking about that problem: (1) Has it helped you find an interesting or applicable solution? (2) Even if you haven't found any solution, do you at least see the matter a little more clearly? (3) You haven't found a solution and you don't see the matter any more clearly, but has thinking about it brought you any relief?

If you reply no to all three questions, you've been brooding. In that case, the best ways to break out of your brooding is go for a jog, go do something nice for someone, or go talk to a friend—not in order to cobrood on the same subject but to talk about something else.

In psychology, the two problems that come up with regard to painful feelings are excess and default. Guilt in itself is not a problem. But when it becomes excessive, that means that the alarm system is not regulated properly. You know this theory? Emotion is an alarm signal, especially "negative" emotion. If it is regulated properly—that is, if it goes off at the right moment; not too loud so as not to terrify the neighborhood; not too long, so I can begin to see what to do about it—it's perfect. If it is improperly regulated, it can be set off by insignificant stimuli, which creates a dreadful mess, and that means that we have a problem. Just as an alarm might be improperly regulated at the factory that makes it, our alarm can be thrown off by the education we have received, or it can be thrown off by thunder (that is, by the impact of serious traumas), and in such cases we have to change it or repair it.

So feeling guilty just because we have contradicted or annoyed someone we are fond of is without doubt excessive, even if it might help us reconsider the manner in which we expressed our disagreement. But to be tortured by guilt for several days for that same reason no longer makes any sense, because the weight of the emotion has gone beyond an appropriate level and might dissuade us later on from giving sincere advice (we don't want to cause others pain because we don't want to suffer ourselves). This tendency can come from an over-empathic temperament or from our education.

To take this a bit further, some patients suffering from obsessive-compulsive disorder have what we might call "guilt insanity." The least act, the least thought, represents a source of guilt. Such excesses come from causes related to individual life stories, to upbringings that create a tendency toward guilt, but there is also the weight of the Judeo-Christian civilization as a whole. Nowadays the impact of this is much less, but formerly guilt was used to control people's behavior. I would like to know if in your opinion, Matthieu, the Buddhist religion gives better protection from this kind of aberration.

MATTHIEU Since the Buddhist attitude is simpler and more pragmatic, it is less liable to this kind of abuse. There is no notion of original sin, no hereditary fault that could be experienced as something wrong with you. There is only the effect of actions you have committed yourself in either a recent or distant past. Thus we only speak of personal responsibility and the possibility, which is always present, of amending one's condition by avoiding the kinds of mistakes made in the past. Inner practice permits anyone to gradually see by themselves how the causality of action and the process of liberation work. Thinking, and then gradually discovering experientially, that we have Buddha-nature in ourselves provides fundamental confidence.

CHRISTOPHE On the other end of the guilt spectrum, we have default. Deficiency or absence of guilt are absolute catastrophes. If we lived in a world where nobody felt guilt, regret, or shame, it would be hell. People would walk all over us and not give a damn. They would do evil things and sleep just fine.

We find such traits of personality, which in themselves are not necessarily pathological, in the vague area known as *selfishness*, in a quality of being very little inclined to feel regret or responsibility for harm caused to others. Narcissists are even a notch worse here. They don't feel the harm they cause others and don't even recognize it. The extreme level you were talking about, Matthieu, are the psychopaths. In their case, we even suspect a deficiency in the neurobiological apparatus for feeling empathy. Since, obviously, to feel guilt we have to feel empathy and understand that we have caused others harm.

It seems to me that we were formerly in a period where guilt was overemphasized, and that today we are perhaps in a period where guilt is not emphasized enough. We tend to find excuses. We have a form of what philosophers call *anomie*, excessive distrust of rules and constraints. We seem to be saying that ultimately there is perhaps no basis for guilt, nobody is deliberately evil, everybody harms others, etc. But sometimes it seems to me that it wouldn't be such a bad thing to feel guilty, not permanently but by way of a sharp reminder. That's how the ancients saw it: *errare humanum est, perseverare diabolicum*. In other words, to err is human, to persevere in error is diabolical or demonic. And I would add that feeling guilty is human, but too much is too much!

MATTHIEU   In this respect, Buddhism suggests a happy medium. Shame and regret are considered necessary, but there is no real danger of distortion because these feelings do not serve as means to devalue oneself but as pathways to the adoption of wholesome, altruistic behavior.

Regrets—the Replay Button

CHRISTOPHE   Sometimes we'd like to have a "replay" button for the movie of our lives so we could rearrange things differently. This is a vast area of regret, which has been abundantly studied by scientists because it constitutes a source of energy loss on the psychological level. There are several ways to understand regret. First there is hot regret, which occurs immediately after one has acted; and cold regret, which we experience a day, a month, or several years afterward, when we suddenly realize something—for example, people who when they become parents recognize their own violence toward their own parents.

Also we distinguish regret for action from regret for inaction. I might regret having said something, but I can also regret not having said it. Researchers have shown that regret for action ("I did something that didn't work, was bad for my image, bad for my interests, sometimes bad for the good of others") leads to hot regret because the situation is immediate: I acted, failed, I feel the pain of failure. And then often, in order to avoid feeling hot regret, some people take refuge in inaction, because one way of not experiencing hot regret is to not do anything. But this does not protect against cold regret, since we can also experience regret for inaction: I could have done this, I should have done that, and I didn't do it. To make a long story short, when we ask volunteer subjects to evaluate what were the worst things in their lives, most often they regret things they didn't do rather than things they did do. In a human life, there is a multitude of things that one did not dare do, did not have the courage to do, and that is what brings regret over the long run; that opens much bigger oceans of virtuality than regrets over actions. For example, if I didn't dare approach somebody I liked, I might dwell a long time on my regret over that ("If I had dared and it had worked, my life would have changed"). But if I did approach that person and was turned down, I don't have a lot to dwell on. It's done, reality expressed itself, and I just have to turn elsewhere.

MATTHIEU Personally, in the realm of cold regret, it has often happened to me to regret deeply not having been considerate, attentive, or generous enough. If it was a case of a chance encounter, I no longer have any means of finding that person again to be more compassionate toward them, and that pains me. Even if I didn't, properly speaking, do them any harm, I am reminded of what Martin Luther King Jr. said, that the inaction of good people—he was speaking in particular about situations of violent oppression—is no less hurtful than the harmful actions of bad people.

CHRISTOPHE Yes, that's the definition of responsibility in the face of violence. Not intervening in the face of violence makes us accomplices to the violence.

What It Means to Forgive

CHRISTOPHE How can we resolve the feeling of guilt? By asking for forgiveness, very simply. And that is much more complicated than it appears. There are so many situations where people are quite reluctant to ask forgiveness, because while they know that they have hurt someone, they feel that the other person is coresponsible, that they provoked the act in question, that they also were at fault. Asking forgiveness does not mean that you are the only guilty party, nor that you are lowering yourself in relation to the other person. It is just a recognition of the harm that you caused, the wish for the other to accept the apology that you are offering. That seems to me to be a logical conclusion of guilt. When it happens, I also recognize that forgiveness is a gift.

In the end, what does it mean to forgive? If I have suffered hurt, if I have been attacked, if someone has wronged me, what does forgiveness mean? Often there is a misunderstanding. When we speak of forgiveness in psychotherapy, the first things that people understand by it are absolution and, in a certain way, submission. Studies on the psychotherapy of forgiveness show that, first, forgiveness only has a meaning if it is free from all forms of constraint—it must be a free decision on the part of the injured party. Second, forgiveness is an intimate act, completely dissociated from legal action. A psychotherapist who wants a person to move in the direction of forgiveness explains to them that forgiveness does not refer to a public reconciliation in front of everybody; rather, it is a matter of forgiveness in itself. That has nothing to do with forgetting about or denying the injury. It is the intimate and personal decision to liberate oneself from suffering. Forgiving is an act of liberation that permits us to free ourselves from resentment, from the wish for the other person to be punished and suffer in their turn.

> Forgiving is an act of liberation that permits us to free ourselves from resentment, from the wish for the other person to be punished and suffer in their turn.

MATTHIEU   I agree with your point. Forgiveness is not absolution. How can we wipe away with a gesture the harm committed and its consequences? It is also not a form of approbation, which would be an encouragement to repeat the deed. It is also not denying the resentment, anger, or even the desire for vengeance that were aroused in us by the conduct of the other. Moreover, it is not minimizing the gravity of the acts committed and forgetting about what has taken place, nor a prevention of measures necessary to keep the harmful action from being repeated. Forgiving is renouncing hate and resentment and replacing them with kindness and compassion. Thus it is breaking the cycle of vengeance. Doing this does indeed have a liberating effect because these feelings poison us and, in the end, destroy us.

If one applies the law of an eye for an eye, one is never at peace, since one must oneself adopt a negative attitude that will undermine one's inner peace, even if vengeance does for a moment appear to bring satisfaction. Gandhi said that if we practiced the principle of an eye for an eye, a tooth for a tooth, the whole world would be blind and toothless.

I heard an edifying BBC reportage concerning Ameneh, the young twenty-four-year-old Iranian woman who was disfigured by a rejected suitor whom she hardly knew. One day, the man approached Ameneh, looked at her laughing, and sprayed acid in her face. Horribly disfigured and without any financial means, she undertook a campaign to get her attacker punished in accordance with the law of an eye for an eye and have acid poured in his eyes. She won her case, and she was called to a hospital one day for the execution of the punishment. At the moment when, in the presence of a judge, her uncle was about to pour the acid, Ameneh relived the excruciating and terrifying effects of this action and called out for it be stopped. After a moment of stupefaction, the condemned man fell to his knees at Ameneh's feet and cried out in tears that he was sorry for what he had done. Afterward, Ameneh declared that people like this man could not be made more human by being punished with horrible pains. As she saw it, thanks to her forgiveness and kindness, her tormenter had regained his humanity. She added that she was happy and relieved that she had not had the sentence carried out.

From the point of view of Buddhism, you can't trick the law of causality, karma, which designates both deeds and their effects. People who have committed odious crimes will sooner or later end up suffering themselves. They, just like their victims, should be the objects of our compassion.

As I said before, it is important to dissociate the person from his or her acts. A person who is afflicted by a serious illness cannot be identified with his illness. We say, "I have cancer," not "I am cancer." Well, hate, cruelty, indifference, and the other destructive mental states are comparable to serious illnesses. A doctor attacks the disease, not the person who has it. Our enemy is not the person acting in the grips of hatred, but the hatred itself.

In his book *La bonté humaine* (Human goodness), Jacques Lecomte tells the story of Larry, an American who was a militant anti-Semite who had persecuted a Jewish couple with hatred and insults. The couple decided to invite the man to meet them. He finally accepted and was amazed by their total lack of animosity toward him. In tears, he ended up blurting out that he didn't know what to say to them, that he had been so awful to them and to so many others that he didn't know how they could forgive him. The man and woman assured him of their forgiveness and added, "Nobody can excuse cruelty, but it's different to forgive somebody who has been cruel but is now overwhelmed with remorse."[1]

> A doctor attacks the disease, not the person who has it. Our enemy is not the person acting in the grips of hatred, but the hatred itself.

Can one forgive on behalf of others? That's the dilemma faced by Simon Wiesenthal, who tells his story in *The Sunflower: On the Possibilities and Limits of Forgiveness*. He was a prisoner in a Nazi camp, where during the day he was sent to work in a hospital. One day he was told that a young member of the SS who was dying wanted to confess to a Jew. Simon went to the bedside of the young man, who must have been in his twenties. He had done horrible things. He had, for example, set fire, with his squad, to a house in which a large number of fleeing Jews had taken refuge. He asked Simon Wiesenthal to forgive him. Simon listened in silence, sponging away the sweat beading on the man's forehead. But he couldn't say the word forgive. This man had done him no harm, but he had harmed many others, and Simon felt incapable of pardoning him in their names. Later he always wondered if he had been right. For sure, one cannot offer forgiveness in the place of someone else, but that shouldn't have prevented him from doing something to break the cycle of hate. Cruelty is a pathological state. A sick society in the grips of a blind fury against a certain segment of humanity is nothing other than a group of individuals driven mad by ignorance and hate. Contemplating the horror of the acts of violence committed by people should strengthen our compassion rather than fan our resentment.

CHRISTOPHE Listening to you, I have an anecdote that comes to mind, less terrible than Wiesenthal's story. Some time ago a woman wrote to me and told me that her daughter had died by suicide, that she had thrown herself from the fifth floor of the institution where she was hospitalized. The woman wanted to see me to talk about this. At first I tried to put her off, send her to one of my colleagues, but she insisted and I finally gave her an appointment. She told me what had happened—a succession of medical errors. In theory, since it was a psychiatric institution, the windows should only have been able to be opened slightly so as to avoid accidents. On top of that, at 3 p.m. the girl had spoken to her mother of her intention to commit suicide, and her mother had warned the staff. That evening, the mother felt quite uneasy and she called the caregivers, who could not find her daughter. She had thrown herself out the window in the afternoon, and her body was hidden in the bushes below. But the caregivers told the mother not to worry, they would find her daughter. Anxious, the mother called back several times, but, as she told me, they finally basically told her to get lost. During the night, since they couldn't find the girl, they called the police, without telling the mother. And at dawn a gardener found the body in the bushes.

The ensuing encounter with the mother did not go well. The whole staff (doubtless feeling guilty and very embarrassed) took a clumsy approach, without warmth, without compassion, and she was very angry at them. That's the reason she came to tell me this awful story. I was so devastated by this woman's suffering and by the series of mistakes that had been made that I asked for her forgiveness in the name of the doctors and the caregivers (I could have been negligent the same way myself): "I'm so sorry about what happened; it's terrible. I ask you to forgive us." I didn't see anything else I could do. I felt so bad, helpless, impotent, and sad for her. I saw her several times after that, and I saw all the suffering she experienced as a result of losing her daughter and because of her personal regret ("Could I have avoided that? Could she have been saved if she'd been found in time?") But the third source of her pain was that she had been related to so badly. The head doctor called her afterward, but it was too late.

I would like to state another fundamental point. When one is dealing with extremely fragile people, the words *forgiveness* and *acceptance* can be problematic. Those are quite lovely expressions as long as you are not a victim, as long as you have not been badly hurt. I'm very cautious when I begin a therapy focused on acceptance and forgiveness. I avoid saying the words, and I work on developing the recognition that resentment makes the victim suffer even after the event. I try to make the victims understand that liberating themselves from this resentment will do their whole being good. Little by little, they understand themselves that forgiving is in order. In the word *forgiveness* we have the particle *give*, which seems inconceivable in relation to a person who hurt me, who did me violence, who destroyed me . . . This is an example of how the work of therapy differs from the work of teaching.

MATTHIEU　And if we moralize, forgiveness becomes a kind of obligation instead of a process of healing.

Small Pardons

ALEXANDRE　I would be best off keeping quiet after such luminous examples and get started following them right away. In my view, forgiveness restores to life its purity, its sweetness. It makes it possible to continue to flow without ever stopping. Forgiving is liquidating all fixation and killing ego. I wouldn't be surprised if such freedom were good for the health, because what could be worse than stewing in mean-spiritedness? Nonetheless, forgiving day after day might be rather tiring.

The notion of original sin comes with a host of misunderstandings. Even so, it is water to drive our mill. It's not a matter of denigrating our nature by calling it evil but rather bringing into focus our tendency toward withdrawal and egotism. How hard it is not to try to be the center of the world! With joy, every day, I can drop the mechanisms that keep me from remaining open, available, kept alert by others. The idea of original sin, far from overwhelming me, renews me. It's a matter, every day, of avoiding sliding down the slope that leads to the hell of indifference. Better than that is to rejoin the fundamental ground of all grounds, or for the believer, to find God, the source of infinite kindness.

To avoid exhaustion, Jesus recommends forgiving seventy times seven times. This is a way of saying that I can never establish myself in a fixed pose. I am always asked to do the hard work again.

MATTHIEU It's true, our basic nature, that of awakened mind, is free and lies beyond the duality of good and evil. Selfishness and the other mental poisons are deviations that can be characterized as accidental or adventitious because they are not part of our profound nature.

ALEXANDRE Forgiveness demands so much of us, it's almost subversive to speak of it. Forgiving requires incredible audacity, almost superhuman courage. First you have to get away from any and all rigidity, bid adieu to any possibility of hate or rancor. When Jesus in the Gospels invites someone who's been slapped to turn the other cheek, it makes me realize that I almost always prefer being caught up in the spiral of vengeance. You need a good dose of ascesis and some heavy-duty compassion to drop the insane logic of retribution. Why does someone who has wronged me necessarily have to suffer for it?

Why in the world do we persist in this reluctance to forgive? It's as if forgiveness trivializes the injury we suffered and vindicates the person who betrayed us. Going from there, it's only one step further to clinging to resentment in the hope that, in the end, the other person will recognize his evil ways. Forgiving has nothing to do with denial; rather, it is something that restores life to the heart haunted by vengeance. Let's remember that, in the end, it's a joy to liberate oneself from the past, to drop our grudges and move on. Like you, Matthieu, I had the opportunity, with my friend Bernard Campan, to talk with some prisoners. I was struck by the fact that I wasn't necessarily any better than these men—far from it. For the most part, I would have been ready to give them my complete trust and confidence. Our reason, like our heart, often follows a binary logic: the challenge is to forgive the worst of criminals while at the same time letting it be known loud and clear that crime remains unacceptable.

> Forgiving has nothing to do with denial; rather, it is something that restores life to the heart haunted by vengeance.

CHRISTOPHE You speak of the reluctance to forgive. Sometimes we're afraid that forgiving will encourage the other person to do whatever they did again. That's a mistake, but maybe, in a way, it's not that far off. It depends how you formulate your forgiveness. The very specific work of forgiveness emphasizes the fact that forgiving is not saying, "It's nothing, I forgive you," but rather, "I suffered, but I forgive you." This is associating your suffering with a movement of forgiveness. Whereas simply erasing the behavior that created the problem might indeed trivialize it.

ALEXANDRE By all means, we ought to go right ahead and totally forget our resentment and dare to offer a grand, complete pardon. But in the meantime, little pardons, if that's what we have strength for at the moment, repeated a thousand times, will keep moving us in the direction of peace. Dropping guilt grants us the right to make mistakes and to cease, for example, reproaching ourselves for not being up to unsustainable demands. Alongside the aspirations that move us forward, we have a ton of expectations that paralyze us permanently.

In the realm of marital life, it's easy to fall into resentment: "You remember that nasty comment you hit me with on June 20?" Instead of keeping an Excel spreadsheet on those things, we can try to start fresh each morning, wipe the slate clean. There's nothing like the unspoken things hanging on for screwing up a relationship. In love, there are no debts, everything is free every moment. What burning relevance we find in that passage in the Gospels where the people are about to stone a poor adulterous woman! Everybody knows those famous words of Jesus's: "Let he who has never sinned cast the first stone." Who might we be getting ready to stone today? Instead of looking down on that woman's accusers, I can recall all the times I allow myself to do stupid things; or more simply, I can just look at the domestic nastiness that has almost reached the point of being taken for granted. Forgiveness requires the most radical of inner conversions: you have stop imprisoning the other person in the past so as to give them a chance to be fully what they are here and now.

Our Advice on Daring to Forgive

A Question of Training   CHRISTOPHE

- Training exercise: Every "I shouldn't have" is without interest unless it is followed by a "What am I going to do from now on?" The two processes go together. If you turn too quickly to action without having accepted the sting of regret or guilt, it's not as good. If you remain dwelling on the sting of guilt without turning to what you're going to do, it's also not as good.

- Small acts of forgiving, little pardons, are exactly the kind of training we try to do in therapy. Little minipardons—of our spouse, of our near ones—provide the fresh starts that teach us to stop clinging to "Who's right? Who's wrong?" If I've slighted the other person, even though I might have been right, and if I'm in a relationship of trust that I want to continue, I should consider that the minipardons granted or asked for are means of reparation for all the mini-injuries that I inflict on a daily basis.

Some Steps Toward Forgiveness   ALEXANDRE

- Imperfect and happy. At the beginning of every Mass, there is a moment where the believer is invited to acknowledge himself as a sinner. This step frees me from burdens, expectations, and unwholesome perfectionism at the same time as exposing a lively desire to improve. Who says that you have to be perfect in order to be loved? It is within our fragility that we grow. Every day, going beyond constantly judging myself, I must die, give up everything, and be reborn completely.

- Seeing (sorry for the labels) the certified jackass who does us harm, the nasty tongue-waggers who malign us, the imbecile who ridicules us as creatures doomed to misfortune—we must drop our resentment. Nobody becomes evil by choice. We are all in the same boat, and in the face of life's precariousness, it's easy to get mixed up. What if we were to consider a person who has wronged us as a sick person, an injured party, and what if we were wish her or him happiness unreservedly and from the bottom of our heart?

- Send all resentment packing. Forbid yourself going to bed with a heart full of rancor. Each evening, wipe the slate clean and do all you can to avoid carrying on with unspoken bitterness and reproaches.

Separating Forgiveness from
Moral Judgment   MATTHIEU

- Don't morally judge people but rather what they have done.

- Don't be at all indulgent toward misdeeds. Counter them with all possible means, but without animosity and in such a way as to avoid, as much as possible, any further suffering.

- Forgive those who have harmed us. Think of them as victims of an illness and realize that they are suffering or will suffer for what they have done. All suffering is worthy of compassion, and compassion can only call for forgiveness.

- Remember that forgiveness is beneficial to all. It permits victims to regain inner peace, and for guilty parties to bring out the best in themselves.

True Freedom

What Can I Liberate Myself From?

ALEXANDRE Often I get dizzy just seeing the roller-coaster of mind. All the ups and downs, all the dramas tire us and, in the end, leave us as though wrung out, drained, exiled from serenity. I get up feeling great, and an email, almost insignificant, does the job of ruining my morning. The diagnosis is absolutely clear: emotional instability. It's not for nothing that I devote myself assiduously to zazen. If there had been no antidotes, long ago I would have declared myself defeated and turned up my toes. The good news is that this state of serious agitation is not incurable. Discontent can also pass away. So the quite urgent question arises, before what remains of my hair catches on fire: How can I stop being the plaything of circumstances, the puppet of emotions? In a word, how can I get a shot at a bit of freedom? Here-abouts, finding a state of balance is not easy!

Urgency Without Haste

ALEXANDRE The first thing is not to make too big a deal out of our troubles, except to discourage ourselves from getting into them further, while at the same time doing the maximum to get out of them alto-gether as quickly as possible! At the very moment of waking up, I can have the courage to do this exercise: identify the clouds that are keeping me from being joyful and from loving without expecting anything in return. Without haste, I can pierce this cloudy layer that is separating me from peace. How? Already you can do some of the job by seeing, as Epictetus did, that I am "a slave in the process of being freed," and then you can move on directly to attempts at escape. But trying to force the conclusion doesn't lead anywhere. If you focus on the result, you're a hopeless goner for sure. Every little step counts. And there's no need for heroic gestures when a small, well-calibrated effort can get the job done.

In order to move faster, slow down.

Zen has a very simple exercise for us: *kinhin*. This meditative walking technique teaches us to concentrate entirely on each step we take, without fleeing into distraction. When my mind is right on the edge of exploding, I come back to this practice that roots me immediately in the here and now. As I do this, I remember the words of a teacher: "In order to move faster, slow down."

Basically it's a matter of changing lifestyle. Sadness, anger, and fear become signals to leave the domain of ego, to skedaddle right out of there. Since change brings fear, remember the Buddha's analysis: if we cling to our states of mind, we are doomed to suffer. Hence the remedy par excellence—nonfixation.

MATTHIEU Having an ardent desire to liberate oneself from suffering doesn't mean rushing madly ahead. We simply have to show perseverance. You speak of slowing down. As far as our thoughts, words, and frivolous activities are concerned, it's a good idea to slow down, but it's even better to drop them altogether. On the other hand, once we're sure we're on the right ship, driven toward a worthwhile destination by favorable winds, why reduce the speed? If there really is a way to dispel suffering, let's get a move on. Let's not drag our feet! What *is* a total waste is to agitate ourselves with impatience, to commit ourselves imprudently in wrong directions, or to exhaust ourselves prematurely through excessive efforts. In other words, we should not confuse diligence, defined as joy in the form of effort, with haste, impatience, or caprice. There's a story about a disciple who asked a Zen master, "How long will it take me to attain *satori* (enlightenment)?" The master replied, "Thirty years." The disciple kept pushing. "And if I'm in a big hurry?" The master replied, "In that case, fifty years."

Our attitude should be a happy medium between effort and excessive laxity. The Buddha had a disciple who played the vina, a string instrument resembling the sitar. The disciple told the Buddha one day that he was having a lot of trouble meditating. "Sometimes I make a lot of effort to concentrate, and I'm too tense. At other times I try to relax, but I relax too much and fall into torpor. What should I do?" The Buddha asked, "How do you tune your instrument to get the best sound?"

"The strings have to be neither too tight nor too loose."

"It's the same for your meditation. You have to find the right balance between effort and relaxation."

We have to have a clear awareness of the goal, which is to liberate ourselves from ignorance and the mental poisons in order to give the right direction to our practice. If we don't, it's like shooting an arrow blindfolded toward a target whose size and location we don't know. But this awareness of the goal must not become an obsession to the point where it pretty much becomes an obstacle to its own accomplishment.

Disobeying a Frivolous Ego

ALEXANDRE In a very down-to-earth kind of way, liberating oneself is committing acts of disobedience to our cumbersome ego. Why should we think that freedom consists of always doing what it wants without constraint, just doing whatever we feel like? Often renouncing a whim takes us a few giant steps closer to joy because there's true pleasure in saying no to something that drags us down. So, for example, if my ego is scared of the dentist, I should listen to what my heart really wants, which is to go to the dentist gladly. That is what moving forward—life—calls me to. That's what

> There's true pleasure in saying no to something that drags us down.

I'm endlessly explaining to my children. A simple question can serve us as a compass: "What will really do me good?"

On this path, meditation takes better care of me than reason alone. Meditating is going to the school of surrendering the mind of ego, despite the fact that at the same time our will is insisting fiercely that we make a beeline to the full mastery of life. Sometimes, in the course of zazen, when I'm not expecting it, anxiety subsides, my timorous ego fades a bit *in spite of myself.* "You mustn't be afraid"—advice of this type has something oppressive about it. Directly touching the experience of letting go and letting be—that is what heals.

MATTHIEU When you talk about disobeying ego, you are certainly not talking about a whim or an adolescent revolt, but rather a flash of common sense that pushes one to emancipate oneself from the influence of an impostor. This is a bit like renunciation, which does not consist in depriving oneself of what is really good for one, but in leaving behind everything that leads to suffering.

ALEXANDRE Being of a rather anxiety-prone nature, as soon as fatigue takes hold of me, catastrophic scenarios begin to plague me. At that point I prescribe for myself a large dose of meditation, during which my anxiety subsides little by little. For hours at a time, thousands of times, I let things pass. A few years ago I adored a boy to the point of fascination. I would have given anything to trade my crippled body for his. That ended up turning into an obsession, an infernal dependency. Thanks to my spiritual father, to zazen, and to my wife, I watched this *idée fixe* disappear and reappear for months. At the beginning, it assailed me from morning till night, without giving me the least respite. Today I am so well-trained in letting it pass that it only lasts a fraction of a second. What fantastic encouragement to persevere! It is enough, without rejecting or denying anything, simply to observe. If my spiritual father had demonized this idolatry, had urged me to fight fiercely against it, I am not sure I would have been healed of it. On the contrary, he reassured me, "Be extremely patient with yourself. Freedom is found millimeter by millimeter." And to make a long story short, I would have cracked if I had listened to all those people who gave me magic formulas: "Stop thinking about it," "Move on to something else," and so on. Basically my wife and my spiritual father simply gave me the confidence that I didn't have and the patience to wait for the problem to resolve itself by itself.

But how can we initiate patience when our mind is torn into a thousand pieces, when it wants progress on the spot? Not by force. In my childhood I was battered the livelong day with repetitions of "Be patient!" In a time of trial, waiting seems almost superhuman. Are you going to subject somebody who's drowning to discourses on the art of floating? A life preserver is all he needs. I arrived in Seoul loaded with fears. The first day, when I took a shower, I was even afraid a rabid bat would fly out of the water spout! At no time did my master lose patience. He always reassured me, "There's no danger. I will repeat that to you a million times if need be, but don't get mad at me if I laugh, because your imaginations are really, really far-fetched." Then, gently, he would add, "You're ruining your life with fears, mental tempests that haunt you and prevent you from having a moment's peace."

Liberating Ourselves from What Ruins Our Daily Lives, or the CCL File

ALEXANDRE   Sometimes I'm just a hair's breadth from giving up. How is it possible not to abandon ship in the face of so many obstacles and the force of inertia: habits, passions, and the nearly indestructible tendency to repeat mistakes? The bodhisattva ideal gives me a boost here. This challenge, infinitely beyond my capabilities, is not a challenge the ego is going to take up. I can only take it up with my whole being.

I am learning to free myself from the tyranny of "later," which is enabling me to make progress bit by bit. When life becomes unbearable, it's tempting to grasp at the future: "Later, I'll feel better." But fleeing from reality and waiting for forever does us damage. Can someone who has struggled so much have the courage to lay down his weapons and enjoy life? The psychiatrists and the contemplatives should get into this juicy question . . . Why, when we are at the top of the mountain, can we not appreciate the landscape below instead of anticipating getting to the next peak? Living each phase thoroughly and fully is the way to avoid exhaustion. In order to escape from this curious frenetic quality—it's as though I was trying to recapture lost time, make up for all the injuries of the past—I am beginning to live in the present and take concrete action day by day.

MATTHIEU It's true. I was speaking in terms of general guidelines, but the rest is a matter of method. Once again, Shantideva said that there is no great task that cannot be divided into small easy tasks.

ALEXANDRE I met a gastroenterologist, who after he had examined me in every possible way, assured me that there was nothing wrong with me. He then gave me some precious advice: "From now on, you should have a CCL file. Couldn't Care Less. Next time some anxiety is bugging you, drop it in this file." This terrific doctor not only did everything medically possible to detect any illness I might have had, but he also emptied me of anxiety. Without trivializing my fear or falling back on the catch-all concept of "psychosomatic problem," he really helped me. Why don't we all follow his advice and create CCL files into which we throw all our meaningless hassles? This exercise is done in the present and in the first person; forcing it on somebody suffering from anxiety is ineffective and cruel. Becoming initiated into the path of patience also means progressively discovering confidence in life. On this path, our companions in the good sustain us when we falter.

MATTHIEU With regard to thoughts that constantly hound us, you deftly and vividly described how we can free ourselves little by little from the grip they have on us by letting them pass once, ten times, a hundred times, until a moment comes when these thoughts are no longer a problem for us. Whereas at the beginning the least obsessive thought was like a spark falling into a pile of dry grass, in the end it becomes like a spark that leaps into the air and vanishes.

This method is at the very heart of the practices that enable us to manage thoughts and emotions and achieve inner freedom. As we have seen several times, a great number of methods for attaining this freedom exist. We can, for example, get rid of the thoughts that trouble us by calling up thoughts or feelings that are diametrically opposed to them: kindness versus hate, patience versus irritation, and so on. A thought of love and a thought of hate can't exist in our mind at the same time. But the method of letting pass is a more subtle and more powerful method. One quickly realizes that preventing thoughts from arising is a lost cause. They arise anyhow. What's the point of trying to block them when they're already there? The real question: What shall we do with them? Do we just let them wander around and reproduce until our mind is completely submerged in the thoughts that they generate, or do we simply let them pass by without giving them the chance to proliferate? In the second case, we could compare them to birds that pass through the sky without leaving a trace, or to drawings made on water that disappear as we draw. This is what's called "liberation of thoughts as they arise."

Letting pass is one of the best methods, not only for skillfully managing thoughts that trouble us but also for gradually weakening our tendency to let thoughts get hold of us at all. If, for example, we give free rein to anger, not only do we fall into its power for now, but we also make it increasingly easier for us to get angry again. If on the other hand, we learn to leave anger to itself, without giving it the slightest weight, it will evaporate by itself. Thus for the present we avoid being gripped by it, and in the long term, the accumulation of little successes of this nature will eventually dissolve our tendency toward anger altogether. A day will come when hatred and the other mental poisons won't arise in our minds anymore. They will simply no longer be part of our mental landscape.

Freedom Inseparable from Responsibility

CHRISTOPHE   The first dimension I think of is freedom as a natural need. It took us a long time to understand that animals in captivity, even if they are well treated, are deprived of something fundamental—their freedom, the possibility of developing in space and moving around naturally—and that that literally makes them sick. In cages or in zoos, they are unhappy and suffer from absurd neuroses they never would have had in nature. It's the same thing for humans. They have a natural need for a space of freedom, of movement and speech.

But humans have added another dimension to that of the biological need: freedom as a right. In the United States' Declaration of Independence, we find three inalienable rights: to life, liberty, and the pursuit of happiness. Very intelligently, the expression is not "the right to happiness" but "the right to the *pursuit* of happiness." The implication is that happiness is an individual matter, but creating the conditions for this happiness (freedom, security, justice, education, etc.) is the role of the state.

Nevertheless, we cannot think of freedom as an absolute entity, autonomous and unquestionable in the same manner as the right to life, but rather as a relative entity, coupled with the notion of duty and especially responsibility. This pair, freedom-responsibility, in my view, is an indivisible one. Moreover, in Article Four of the Declaration of the Rights of Man and of the Citizen, which is part of the French Constitution, freedom is defined as the power to do anything that "does not harm others."

In theory, everyone agrees on this point. The problem is the natural movement of our psyche, which wants to take us back to our ego, to our needs, to our own belly button! We have the responsibility to consider others. If I see my liberty as a piece of turf in which I can do whatever I want, sooner or later frictions with other human beings are bound to appear, unless I'm living on a desert island. This is an obvious point that must be borne in mind and must, above all, be worked on. Freedom cannot be conceived of without consideration of the freedom of others and without giving others the same rights as ourselves.

As one of our friends, Mark, reminded us yesterday, there are three spheres of freedom: freedom of thought, freedom of speech, and freedom of action. We tend to think that the freedom of thought is absolute, but we should never forget that it is anything but innocuous. There exist thoughts that are toxic, dangerous, and injurious for the persons thinking them. And these thoughts are the breeding ground of action. Dwelling on certain thoughts is pretty strong preparation for action. Certain thoughts push us toward courageous and altruistic actions, but we harbor, without being aware of them, other thoughts—of the order of resentment and self-denigration—that have an immense power over our speech and action.

Freedom of speech is even less innocuous. Some people think that only actions count. But words have an essential value for our human species. If I may make an academic distinction, I would say there are two types of speech: private speech and public speech. I'm struck by marital conflicts, where one of the spouses, often in the grips of emotion, says horrific things to the other. This is very serious, especially when insults have become a habitual way of purging emotions. It's too easy to say afterward, "I'm sorry. I was upset." Freedom of speech implies responsibility, constraint, and obligation, especially in the area of how it is formulated. We stress that in couples counseling or therapy. We tell them, "You can say many things to your spouse, but not in any old way. Don't use hurtful terms. Don't generalize, stay with particular actions," and so forth. Freedom of speech is unthinkable and dangerous without constraint in the area of formulation.

But there is another level of speech, and that is public speech. According to the philosophical current known as consequentialism, the moral value of an action should be judged by its consequences. When we speak in public, we have not only to consider whether we are right, whether we are (according to us) in the truth, but also, and especially, what will be the consequences of our words for others. Some people speak of self-censure, but I think it's vital to take time to reflect on all forms of public speech. In France, we like activism, but we are not in the habit of screening our words from the point of view of consequentialism. Take, for example, the unbridled admiration people had for Sartre in the 1960s and 1970s, and the relative scorn of which his unfortunate rival, Raymond Aron, was the butt. Aron was a consequentialist, a prudent and responsible man who said, "Every time I come out with an opinion, every time I write something in the newspaper, I not only ask myself if I'm right, but also what the collateral damage might be of making my position public." Sartre loved to pose as the hero of freedom. His priority was to defend the values he was attached to, without necessarily taking into account the consequences they would have on the ground. Thus he supported, with what amounted to blindness, execrable political regimes. With historical hindsight, we see that in their activism Aron was much more lucid than Sartre. This was not because he was more intelligent (both men were great minds) but because he was prudent and responsible. Every time one takes a position in public, it is important to ask oneself, "How much impulse is at play here as opposed to responsible thought?" Human beings are more than just bundles of impulses, and even if reflection is not guaranteed, it seems to me it could eliminate a certain number of injuries and aberrations.

The Proper Exercise of Freedom

CHRISTOPHE   In conclusion concerning my views about freedom, four last points strike me as important.

First, the notion of *inner balance*. Doubtless this is connected with my outlook as a psychotherapist and psychiatrist, but it seems to me that if one hopes to lay claim to a personal freedom that is respectful of others, the first stage is the understanding and regulation of one's own emotions. This refers to the disturbing emotions of which Buddhism speaks (anger, envy, etc.) but sometimes also to the positive emotions (joy, love), which can impair our freedom and make us forget the needs of others. Amorous attachment, for example, can make us dependant or push us to reduce the freedom of the other. Our expressions of joy can be painful for people who are in difficulty at the moment we are happy.

The second important notion is *awareness of others*, of their needs, their frailties, their values. Basically the practice of individual freedom has to deal with a considerable number of constraints, which might seem paradoxical. To be authentically free in a way that is respectful toward others, I must accept certain limitations. This won't necessarily make me feel I am giving up my freedom, but rather that I am giving up the parts of my freedom that were meaningless, without foundation—like masks or false noses—or which were the causes of others' suffering.

The third point. During retreats in a monastery where, seen from the outside, one was subject to a great number of constraints, I often had the feeling of considerable freedom. Some people might say I was happy because I was in a state of submission, and voluntary submission to rules has a relief aspect in the sense that it frees us from decisions and responsibilities. That's possible. Nevertheless, accepting the constraints of life in a monastery can temporarily give us a feeling of immense freedom because it helps us *rid ourselves of nonessential questions* such as, What time is it? What am I going to do tomorrow? And the constraints bring us back to the essential, simple, stripped-down actions—meditation, prayer, reflection.

The fourth point is the notion of *courage*. Freedom is sometimes a matter of finding in oneself the courage to say certain things that are going to upset others. One can hurt others in a manner that is useful and meaningful. Sometimes you have to give somebody a piece of your mind. I like the Christian idea of "fraternal correction." When we see a brother or a sister doing something wrong or making an inappropriate use of their freedom, our duty is to put them back on the right path, but for that we need courage and motivation. Sometimes we say to ourselves, "Let him work it out; after all, it's his problem. I can't right the wrongs of the whole world." Sometimes we're afraid to create conflicts, to violate a connection that seems more precious to us than whatever the mistakes that are happening might cost us. In my case, I tend to respect the freedom of others too much or to lack the courage to correct something inappropriate. That's something important I have to work on.

> Freedom is sometimes a matter of finding in oneself the courage to say certain things that are going to upset others. One can hurt others in a manner that is useful and meaningful.

In conclusion, as a behavioral therapist, I have often, along with my colleagues, been characterized as a restricter of freedom because our therapy is based on teaching. We teach patients ways of thinking, behaving, or managing their emotions that life has not taught them and that we feel are basic. Our adversaries have sometimes called us "dog trainers." They are confusing teaching with training or indoctrination. For example, when we work with timid subjects who would like to say no but who don't dare, we show them how to go about it. We train them to stand up to pressure, for example, using role-playing. We teach them to say no, but we don't tell them *what* they should say no to. That's up to them.

ALEXANDRE Listening to you, Christophe, I'm reminded again of the houses of prostitution that I mentioned before. You give us a lot of leads to follow. The challenge occurs in the infinitesimal instant in which the disturbing emotion or the impulse arises. When I observe men entering into those sad houses, I have the sense that there is always a microsecond in which we still have a choice. Afterward, it's too late—the whole thing's already happening. So it's all a matter of not blowing it in that microsecond. It's crazy how one minute of inattention can determine a life, wreck it. Each person has to know for themselves the things they have to watch out for: anxiety, anger, sexuality, money, obsession with what others think, etc. In order not to screw up one's life, one has to learn to identify the mechanisms that render one's efforts futile.

Freedom arises out of this exercise: track the determinisms and the influences that weigh on our choices, our opinions, and dare to revisit them and call them into question, challenge them. Encountering the other, dialoguing genuinely, provides a royal road for getting out of our ruts and stopping being men and women "under the influence."

The Ultimate Freedom: Liberating
Oneself from the Causes of Suffering

MATTHIEU There are, in fact, different kinds of freedom that we mustn't jumble all together in the same basket. As a counterpoint to what you've said, I'd like to add a point or two.

In Buddhism we speak of two forms of freedom: the one that allows us to devote ourselves to the spiritual path, and the one that frees us from the yoke of suffering and its causes. The first one consists in ridding oneself of anything that could stand in the way of advancing toward enlightenment, in particular, preoccupations and frivolous occupations that only distract us day after day till we die. The second one is freedom from the mental confusion and negative emotions that afflict us and obscure our minds. From that point of view, the ultimate freedom is synonymous with enlightenment.

But there we are far from the freedom to do anything we feel like doing. I often recall the remark of a young girl interviewed by the BBC: "For me, freedom," she said, "is doing whatever comes into my mind without anybody having to say anything about it." For her, then, it amounted to being a willing slave to all the wild thoughts that came into her mind. Her point of view was radically individualist, since she was claiming the freedom to do everything she wanted without the slightest consideration of what others might want.

> True freedom consists in mastering one's mind rather than letting it drift around at the whim of thoughts.

True freedom consists in mastering one's mind rather than letting it drift around at the whim of thoughts. This is like a sailor being free to sail to the destination he has chosen by being in charge of his boat and not letting it drift at the whim of winds that would blow it onto the reefs. In other words, being free is having emancipated oneself from the dictatorship of ego and the habitual tendencies created by our conditioning.

To come back to two of the points Christophe raised, some people think that subjecting oneself to a discipline—when one is doing a meditation retreat or is staying in a monastery, for example—is losing their freedom. But then they must also think the same thing about an athlete or artist who trains for hours at a time rather than spending their time sunning themselves on the beach. Is the novice mountain climber sacrificing his freedom when he spends hours working on a rock-climbing wall under the tutelage of an instructor? For me, in any case, it's a joy to spend time in a hermitage working on cultivating compassion and controlling my mind and not doing things that lead to further confusion and suffering.

As for calling therapists, whose effectiveness has been amply demonstrated, bear or dog trainers under the pretext that they call for intervention, practice, and training, those partisans of the path of least resistance would do better to show more compassion toward their patients instead of imposing their mental fabrications on them.

Freedom is sometimes envisaged in a purely individualistic perspective. Individualism has several faces. It can refer to respect for the individual, with the idea that the individual ought not to be used as a mere instrument of society. This notion gave birth to the notion of the rights of man. This type of individualism confers moral autonomy on each person and permits them to make choices in complete freedom. But such freedom, as Christophe pointed out, should not eclipse the duties of the individual toward society. If this is not the case, the individualism is transformed into an egocentric desire to do away with all collective consciousness and give priority to each person for her- or himself.

The notion of rights implies reciprocity. Extremists, religious ones in particular, demand unconditional respect for their beliefs and react violently if they feel these are being disrespected. Unfortunately, they think they are not required to respect the beliefs and opinions of others, which they grant themselves the prerogative of denigrating and persecuting. Their idea of respect is one way. The Taliban were very proud, for example, of having destroyed the Buddhas of Bamiyan. But some time later, when a copy of the Qur'an was burned in the old quarter of Delhi, we don't know why or by whom, the violent protestations that followed caused the death of about ten people.

Compassion as a Compass

MATTHIEU   We are all completely in agreement that freedom can only be exercised to the extent that it does not harm others, but this position is often challenged by the exercise of freedom of expression. How is it possible to evaluate and foresee the negative consequences of what we say or write?

After the tragedy of *Charlie Hebdo* in January 2015, I participated in a debate on freedom of expression organized by the BBC at Davos. Among the speakers were the director of Human Rights Watch; the former chief rabbi of Ireland, David Rosen; and Sheikh bin Bayyah, who is noted for having declared "war on war" and is one of the few sages and scholars of Islam to be respected by all its branches. The speakers affirmed unanimously that at the level of the state, restriction of freedom of expression should never be accepted, but that, by contrast, individuals must exercise this freedom judiciously and responsibly.

During the debate I said that if I was a cartoonist and I knew that my drawings were likely to cause the death of fifteen people in Pakistan, Afghanistan, and Nigeria, I would consider publishing them to be an unpardonable lack of compassion on my part. The fired-up crowds of protesters are comprised, for the most part, of people with little education, who perceive what has been said or published as a serious offense to what they respect above all things. They care nothing for our freedom of expression, a concept that eludes them. In such cases, rather than offending these people, our efforts should take the long view and be directed toward helping them receive a better education and nurturing their evolution toward a greater level of tolerance.

Claiming the right to freedom of expression often requires great courage, especially in totalitarian countries. But once that freedom is obtained, it is up to individuals—journalists, writers, shapers of opinion—not to consider it a prerogative to say whatever they're thinking at the risk of provoking uncontrollable reactions. Taking that approach, we would end up with a kind of dictatorship of the individual, which often reflects a lack of compassion.

In the exercise of conditional freedom, it's better to consider consequences rather than principles. We should avoid clinging to the dogma of an unconditional freedom of expression that is disconnected from the effects it might produce. Certain deviations, such as racist rhetoric, inciting violence, or denying the existence of the Holocaust are punishable by law, but it is impossible to legislate for all the subtleties that might arise with regard to the exercise of freedom of expression. Thus the only possibility is for each person to decide the proper usage of this freedom on the basis of compassion. Compassion here does not mean taping your mouth shut or breaking your drawing pencil, but simply opening your heart more to others.

CHRISTOPHE Matthieu, you were speaking of the cause of freedom and the selfish motivations that sometimes hide behind it. Here are some concrete examples that occurred to me: the freedom to talk very loud on the phone, disturbing a whole carful of train passengers; the freedom to turn your music all the way up in your car and drive down the street with your windows open at three in the morning; the freedom to make jokes about Belgians, Jews, disabled people, Arabs, blonds, etc. What should we do? The solution is not simply prohibition, but also education—or more precisely a combination of the two. And where shall we draw the line? What is the aim of the behavior for which we are claiming freedom? Does that aim involve only one's personal pleasure or does it in fact have something to do with the common good? When the freedom in question is that of talking very loud on the phone: (1) Is the purpose of it the satisfaction of my own desire, my personal pleasure, or does it involve some contribution to the common good? And (2) Are there other ways of proceeding?

If we pass claims to freedom through these two sieves, we see clearly that the freedom to talk loudly on the telephone on the train does nothing to contribute to the common good but rather detracts from it and serves only for the satisfaction of my own personal needs. Moreover, the possibility exists of going to some private space to make my call. The verdict is clear: talking on the phone however I like in the train car is a selfish freedom, and thus should be controlled.

Our Advice for Exercising Freedom in Everyday Situations

Practice of Freedom   ALEXANDRE

- Liberate yourself by means of attention. Learn to track all
  disturbing emotions from the moment they arise, so as not
  to fall into their infernal spiral. Be aware of the thunder
  before it breaks.

- The CCL file. Create a CCL (Couldn't Care Less) file and
  put in it all the unwholesome ideas that bug you—fantasies,
  illusions, and deliriums. Don't dwell on the stream of
  useless and harmful thoughts that pass through our minds
  from morning till night—get out of that fog.

- Liberate yourself from the past. Liberating oneself, for
  Spinoza, is revisiting our past, examining our history. What
  are we getting out of it? What are we holding on to from
  it? Prejudices and traumas? Identifying the influences and
  automatic mechanisms that we are dragging around with us
  will speed us toward freedom. It took years to shape us, so let's
  take the time needed to free ourselves from the after effects of
  our history, from betrayals, from deficiencies. The challenge?
  Revisit the past not to find excuses in it but to become better.

For a Just Freedom   MATTHIEU

- Outer freedom is mastery of your life, and inner freedom
  is mastery of your mind.

- Inner freedom is acquired through training the mind,
  which becomes free from the yoke of confusion and the
  mental poisons.

- Inner freedom has kindness and compassion as natural parts of it, and they should be the guides for our outer freedom.

The Four Keys to Freedom   CHRISTOPHE

- Always think of freedom in stereo: freedom *and* responsibility. As soon as you separate freedom from responsibility, you are on the very slippery slope of selfishness, on the drifting boat that Matthieu was talking about.

- Don't forget morality. Freedom needs to be regulated in two ways: inwardly (individual responsibility) and outwardly (rules and laws). Once laws have been established, you come back to the individual, because the question is not just what's legal but also what's moral. Even if the law allows me to do certain things, it's not always desirable for me to do them.

- Pass my freedom through two filters: (1) Is the freedom I claim aimed at attaining my personal pleasure, or does it offer something for the common good? (2) If this freedom that I claim, even though it is aimed at the common good, causes problems for others, are there other ways that I can reach this goal?

- Decline freedom in the plural. It is a common possession, and every time I insist on something for the sake of my own freedom, I am making a big mistake— I should be thinking about *our* freedom.

12

Our Daily Practice

ALEXANDRE When I arrived at your monastery in Nepal, Matthieu, what amazed me was seeing to what extent spiritual life and the dharma shone at the heart of your daily life. When you welcomed me, you gave me *The Hundred Verses of Advice* by Padampa Sangye, which had this luminous dedication: "May the duration of your practice be that of your life." This means I have to believe and experience that every moment provides an opportunity to advance. No, nothing gets in the way of enlightenment, of union with God, not even the stubbornness of our little daily problems. Everything can become practice, including, and perhaps especially, the things that make us stumble. If I make no attempt to transform the bricks that fall on my face into something good, I'm finished, I've had it. And why not begin with the school of virtue: "Hey, that guy is really beginning to get on my nerves. Excellent! There's no better opportunity to get rid of my damned impatience!" And when anxieties surround me like so many nasty wasps, I immediately go meditate. No incident, no difficulty, however big, ultimately stops the mind in its work of liberation. On the contrary, disturbances can serve as alarm signals, telling you it's time to get to work, time to dare nonfixation or simply to ask for help. But when life's alarms begin to go off, I often prefer to ignore them or outright flee from them. Once again, it's dangerous to wait till you're in the middle of the ocean to learn how to swim. So let's begin right now!

Turning Daily Life into a Practice Ground

ALEXANDRE   Maybe this is the time to look at what constitutes the essential quality of daily practice. Since this is something that we will be pursuing our whole life long, we might as well be as diligent as possible about it. So here are some guidelines that serve me day by day.

The first step, without doubt, is to dedicate the day to others, and especially to the most helpless, and to those who are suffering. As we sit here talking, there are people who are finding out that they have cancer, others are losing children, many are dying of hunger. We must bear in our minds and hearts the thought of the billions of beings who are struggling in the immense, engulfing ocean of suffering; and day after day every one of us violates our freedom and dignity. We must constantly remember that we are not practicing to pamper our egos but (to use the expression of Father Arrupe) in order to become men and women *for others*, in order to become people devoted to loving others and relieving pain.

Of course you might say, "A hell of a lot of good it does those people who are at the end of their tethers that you're dedicating your day to them!" But after all, if a mobile phone can connect with an antenna, just a crappy piece of iron that emits waves, why not imagine that at the heart of our innerness there exists a profound link with all beings? It's not falling into occultism to understand that everything in this world is interconnected. I am convinced that placing our day under the sign of generosity makes us better. This practice waves bye-bye to that tenacious egotism that is so hard to uproot.

In the beginning, I flooded my master with questions: "Who is God?" "Why do people suffer?" "When am I going to heal from my pains?" With infinite gentleness, each time he invited me to return to the here and now, where eternity is found. He showed me in a masterly manner that getting lost in vain discourse on the nature of ascesis leads nowhere, that nothing else is worth as much as the practice of generosity.

Very concretely I try to follow four essential practices. The first picks up on the invitation of good Pope John XXIII: perform each act as though God has created you only to do that. For example, when I meet someone, I remind myself that at this moment that person is the most important person in the world. Similarly, when I brush my teeth, I devote myself to it wholly, without letting my mind get lost in thoughts. Master Yunmen summarized this great art in a magnificent formula: "When you sit, sit; when you walk, walk. Above all, don't hesitate."

A great misunderstanding is that a sage feels no emotion. On the contrary, he experiences emotions fully, and he knows how to let them evaporate before they cause harm. In short, if he feels anger, he doesn't feel obliged to throw dishes at the wall. Experiencing fully and thoroughly what is troubling us, without denying any of it, and going forward with great gentleness—that is the challenge. For a long time I was horrified by the notion of acceptance. Often we think that it's a matter of amputating our emotions, wringing their necks. But accepting them is above all seeing them without judging them, taking them in as though they were our children. So when grief visits me, I don't take to my heels. Experiencing this sadness completely makes it possible for me to move on to something else, to turn the page. When I was little, I never let myself go totally in the face of pain. I always resisted it to the point of exhaustion. Today, by contrast, when I'm laid low, I try to flow with it for awhile, not to resist. I see that I can float, even in the midst of agitation. Seeing that emotions don't kill gives me great confidence in the end. I would almost say that, in a way, storms help us. Nothing conflicts more with joyous yea-saying than denial with regard to something troubling us.

The second practice, the one that nourishes me the most, consists in letting pass—a thousand times a day, letting anxieties, fears, emotions, pass like so many bees buzzing around us. The more we try to shoo them away, the more it stimulates them. Just simply let them depart, without reacting in the least.

With a simple phrase, the Diamond Sutra gives us a powerful tool for converting ourselves moment by moment. It can be summed up as follows: "The Buddha is not the Buddha, that is why I call him the Buddha." That is a third practice that I work with nearly full-time and that helps me deal with the highs and lows of life. When I'm not doing well, I take this book out to find in it not weapons but tools for life: "Disability is not disability, that is why I call it disability." The phrase reminds me not to solidify anything and to see at the same time that a thing can simultaneously be a calamity and an opportunity. The point is to abandon binary logic, to exit the prison of duality. At every moment I can experience my disability differently. When conceptual mind tries to reify things and paste labels on everything, a thousand times a day, I repeat to myself, "Alexandre is not Alexandre, that is why I call him Alexandre." What is powerful in this formula—what is magical in it—is that it helps never to dwell on our wounds but not to deny them either. It's a question of recognizing that we plaster a lot of preconceptions onto this reality and later have to pull them off one by one. So without deceiving myself, I can call a cat a cat, knowing that reality is much denser than I think. The exercise that I practice—I've been doing it for years now—is detaching myself, trying to break away from all my egotistical fixations, and constantly joining in with the movement of life. So saying, "My wife is not my wife, that is why I call her my wife" is discovering that every day I am living with someone new, and ceasing imprisoning her in my conceptions of her. Seeing that a constant stream of thoughts and emotions is flowing in my mind is already enough to make me stop taking seriously everything that goes through my head.

And lastly, I take a practice from a text in the Old Testament that builds a magnificent bridge to Buddhism—Ecclesiastes. With its pessimistic airs, it works to undermine everything, uproot our illusions one by one. I often repeat to myself its famous line, "Vanity, vanity, all is vanity." Seeing that in this world, everything is precarious and fragile helps me move toward a more profound freedom. This is something that cures my soul of going for cheap consolations. Fundamentally it is in chaos that I can also discover peace. Everything passes but, to my great misfortune, I'm not able to let things pass. I get hung up and I suffer again and always . . . Fundamentally Ecclesiastes cured me of the very idea of being cured. Losing one's illusions and false hopes one by one opens the doors to a certain serenity. The struggle ends; the exhausting combat gives way to peace.

Developing one's spirituality at the crossroads of two traditions is not without risks. You have to keep yourself from absolutizing your path and avoid getting lost in syncretism and lack of focus. As for me, I try to follow Christ, and on this path Buddhism helps me to divest myself of ego and all its paraphernalia. Every day I try to keep company with the Gospels and nurture an authentic life of prayer. In my view, praying is stripping oneself bare once and for all, gradually leaving behind all one's roles in order to keep listening to transcendence and daring to let go into a confidence that is bigger than self. Here labels, representations, concepts, expectations explode into smithereens and the ego is eclipsed. It takes a lot of courage to let oneself lapse into the ground of all grounds, daring to do nothing, say nothing, want nothing, and to let God take care of God. Praying is saying yes to whatever happens, living without a reason. At that point, our defense mechanisms leave us, almost in spite of ourselves, along with rejections and the thirst to control everything. Here, stripped of everything, one can dare the unthinkable: call God, Father. Though the path is difficult, sometimes arid, because the ego never fails to resist, I find a tremendous joy in it, a freedom that invites me to drop my crutches and go forward, loving without a reason.

Obstacles to Practice

ALEXANDRE Among the thousand and one obstacles that arise on my path, I see one formidable one: worldliness. As soon as I am away from my master and my family, it doesn't take long before I'm caught up in a kind of agitation that distracts me from inwardness. Without speaking of the risk of malicious chatter, which is never very far away once you go through certain doors . . . How do we convince ourselves that we need a half hour of meditation when we are in an environment that is unwelcoming if not outright hostile to spirituality? How do we call up our faith in the God that nurtures us when so many taboos and prejudices prevent us simply from listening without judgment? I have reached the point of having to slip away on the pretext of exhaustion to spend a very cozy hour far from the mechanical lifestyle.

On the spiritual path, we have need of both flexibility and total determination. From morning till night, I make a ton of concessions. I don't even succeed in following this principle, as simple as it is: live in the here and now. So often I have to catch myself in the middle of taking a pee, brushing my teeth, or answering the phone—a dangerous piece of acrobatics.

When I arrived in Seoul, I had an enormous thirst for spiritual progress. I was ready to do anything to attain enlightenment, union with God. But my enthusiasm cooled after only a few weeks. "Father," I would say, "can't I just do retreat every other week?" And my conceptual mind doubled its tricks to get me away from the way of my heart. Then I admitted, so I could relax a little, "Father, the real challenge is to practice in daily life. Why withdraw from the world?" Every day we have to return to our profound inspiration and constantly engage further. Even if we haven't mastered much in life, every moment we can make the decision to engage fully on the spiritual path, where there is no instruction manual, no magical formula, no immediate consolation. The whole thing is to advance one step at a time, without being tied to the idea of progress.

What I Find Helpful

ALEXANDRE   In order to persevere and not make too many concessions, I committed myself to my master to meditate an hour a day. For five years, I have never failed to do this. And I really think that this has saved my life. The most curious thing in this business is that some mornings, I wake up stressed out by the idea of having to fit in my hour of meditation. Alongside this regular practice, I have my companions in the good and readings that convert me every day. When I get exhausted, thanks to my master, I always find the force to pick myself up and continue. Every time I come to him, he leads me back to the ground of all grounds. In talking to him, life becomes simple and light again, and I feel that I have *nothing else to do* but practice, again and always to dare to move forward in infinite surrender to God.

When I was a child, I went to Mass and all too often I found nothing there but flat sermons and a lot of ritualism, very far from my heart's inspiration. Today in Seoul, thanks to my spiritual father, I experience Mass as a place of total stripping, as an opportunity to reembark on life renewed. I found at the bottom of my heart that I could be pardoned, washed clean of the grip of ego, and that I could again find the force to go toward others—without always withdrawing into myself. Whether one is a Buddhist, a practitioner, or an atheist, in the end the essential thing is to choose a path and to devote oneself to it totally without falling into spiritual tourism. When one is digging a well, if one wants to reach water, one has to keep digging in the same hole.

A Typical Day

CHRISTOPHE   The various approaches we have talked about in this book are practices that we attempt to realize through a concern for consistency. To put this into more everyday terms, what is it that I do on a typical day, or an ideal day perhaps, that results from effort rather than chance or circumstance? Like you two, I begin my day with a period of mindfulness, at least ten or fifteen minutes, sitting and trying to focus my mind in being present to the moment, to life as it is second by second. Some days my practice is more compassion oriented, when one of my friends or acquaintances is suffering. Sometimes these are practices of compassion directed toward people who are suffering even if I don't know them, sometimes practices of altruistic happiness. There are also practices for regulating the emotions, in which I look for, as Matthieu puts it, antidotes to my painful and unpleasant emotions. If I don't do this practice of pacification and cleaning, these emotions will be parasitic weights on my day, on my relations with others, on my work.

After this, I get into my family life and, in general, especially these last few years, that begins with seeing my children, who get up early to go to their schools, which requires fairly long travel times. Before seeing my children, I try to remember the importance of being joyous, of starting the day with jokes, good humor, smiles. I have to remember to do that because I'm not biologically inclined to be enthusiastic in the morning.

Then my day continues. I make an effort to have little moments of contemplation to remember that what I am doing is not just for my bread and butter—something mechanical, an obligation—but a choice. The days I stay home to write, which I do whenever I find it possible, I first stand with my hands resting on the back of my chair. I remind myself that I have the good fortune to be writing books of psychology based on what I have learned and what I have heard. I remind myself that these books will perhaps do some people some good, will explain things to them that they have not reflected about, draw their attention to efforts they can make that are within their reach. When I get to the hospital, I try to take time to contemplate how fortunate I am to have this profession of teacher and doctor. When I have lectures to prepare or classes to give, I reflect on how I can transmit the desire to help and to give care. If I am speaking at a business, I concentrate on the fact that my words might perhaps help improve people's working conditions.

Another one of my objectives, which is an important one for many people in our society, is to remain centered and struggle against becoming scattered. I realized that if I didn't strictly regulate my digital life, I was a dead duck. So I try to look at my emails, my texts, and make my telephone calls only at certain fixed hours, generally in the morning, at noon, and in the evening. The rest of the time, I try not to get involved in the phone, not to answer, otherwise it's a considerable waste of energy, and one's attention gets scattered.

The presence of other people represents a practice about which I'm strict with myself. To the best of my ability, when I'm with someone, I try to really give them my attention, all the more so because I have a limited capacity to be available to others. After a while, other people tire me out. It's not that they disturb me but rather that I need solitude, quiet. That's why it's important for me to be completely with someone, even when it's for a short time. For example, when patients come to St. Anne's Hospital without an appointment and stand in front of my door trying to get one, I have them come in. They weren't on my schedule, so they throw it off. In the old days, that used to get me irritated. But now I say to myself, "You're with them, so give them what little you have. For these five minutes, be completely, absolutely, warmly with them." I tell them, "I can only see you for five minutes," and at the end of five minutes, I say, "I'm sorry, we're going to have to stop." I think that for this brief time, I am much more "there" than I used to be.

Then there's book signings, which used to upset me because I kept thinking about how little time I had for each person who came up for a signature. I had the impression of being a basket with holes in it, in which each person poured their expectations and their troubles without my being able to do anything for them. By now I understand that I can't do miracles, but if I make the effort to remain focused on them during the few moments the interaction lasts, I know that will perhaps give them a little bit of energy, courage, or consolation.

In the work I try to accomplish, of course I have to struggle against all the tendencies toward anxiety, discouragement, irritation, etc., which are the lot of all human beings, and perhaps more especially me, because I am emotionally sensitive and fragile. So I take the time to pause, as Alex was saying, over these emotional movements, if not to pacify them or suppress them then at least to verify where they come from and where they are leading me. Are they diverting me from where I want to go, from my values, from my objectives? Or can I continue on with them, and so take more time than I would have otherwise to compose myself with mindfulness and relate to this inner presence?

Another practice that I do quite regularly consists in setting aside some open time, time that is not spoken for. These are moments when I don't have to meet with anyone, to submit a manuscript, to edit an article or a lecture. It took me a long time to recognize the need for this. Even if I am only doing things I like, mostly with people I like, when it reaches the point where it's too much, where there's too much pressure, where it becomes a source of suffering or irritation, then it's totally absurd. So one of the things that I take great care to do—and it seems to me that a fair number of us are overloaded rather than lacking activity—is to take time to have open spaces where I can just breathe or perhaps respond to unexpected demands. In the past, there have been times that I had so much to do, I was so completely overloaded, that if a friend called me to tell me he needed some comforting, I would consider that yet another bother. It was ridiculous. That is why I try to allow time to deal with the unexpected.

I often observe at what moments I feel really right, in harmony with others, open, available, and ready to help. Basically, what are the days like, what are the activities like, that allow me to be both in a state of peace and a state of availability? To start with, I have great confidence in my positive emotions. They are a barometer that let me know if I am in the right space, if I'm doing the right thing, if I'm functioning well. And a piece of luck I've been the recipient of is that I don't have a lot of toxic positive emotions. I'm not very vulnerable to pride, to self-satisfaction. If I sense that somebody admires me, immediately I get a little alarm signal, something like a sense of awkwardness. On the other hand, I distrust my negative emotions, which often lie to me about the reality of my troubles.

The other practice, and much more than that, has to do with my connection to nature. Like most humans, I have a tremendous need to be connected with nature, and I have the good fortune to be able to walk for an hour in the woods practically every day. I almost always go the same way so I don't have to think about which route to take. Whenever I'm in a natural environment, major feelings of gratitude, thankfulness, and responsibility come up in me. My wish is that the greatest number of human beings possible, especially the ones that come after us, will be able to benefit from this. Causing nature to deteriorate is perhaps the greatest crime we are committing right now.

The day ends, and in the evening I have to reserve time for my relationship with my family, to check that everything's okay with them, to interact, to have some time for one-on-one contact with each one. It's also prayer time, when I want to ask for something for someone, pray for help, or pray for myself. Generally I ask for help for others, since for myself, it seems to me I can do the job all alone, and I give thanks. I give thanks for all the good luck I've had during the day, and when I go to sleep I practice an exercise from positive psychology: I remind myself of three pleasant events of the day. I attempt to let them pervade me physically, to connect them with a sense of gratitude, and to recognize that none of these happy events is due to me alone, that there is always someone who helped make it happen.

Looking at the Big Picture

CHRISTOPHE   Finally, to speak of my most all-embracing level of practice, I try to remind myself as often as possible that I could die in a year, two years, five years, and I try to live as though I'm going to die very soon. I say to myself, "If you were completely sure of dying in a year, what would you do?" Thinking you might die even tomorrow brings a very different kind of behavior. You say goodbye to all those you love. Dying in a year means continuing to live your life but in a much more intelligent way. Everything takes on more significance, more weight.

> I try to remind myself as often as possible that I could die in a year, two years, five years, and I try to live as though I'm going to die very soon.

Whenever you say goodbye to someone, you say it like maybe it's forever. This attitude has profoundly lightened my life and changed my relationship to everyday existence—but in a joyful way. Paradoxically, telling myself I might die tomorrow or in a year has put a great deal of joy and energy into my life.

For a few years now—thanks to you, Matthieu, and to all the masters you told me to read as well as to people you have introduced me to—I check much more regularly than before to see if I'm creating benefit around me. I try to think about that every evening, and in the morning, although I haven't ritualized it, it comes to my mind more naturally. Sometimes I think it's not terrific ("could do better"); sometimes it seems to me that it's okay. In that, I have benefited from considerable help from my friends, who have pointed out possibilities to me, and from readers who have written me, without knowing perhaps that their letters have a very powerful effect on my motivation to help others. Being able to provide help by means of words, sentences, and books is an amazing piece of good fortune.

In my books I try not to seduce, not to promise too much, and not to betray the hopes of others. That's why I sometimes seem a little cold, distant, cautious: I want to give just only what I can give. I do not have enough joy in being with others—I'm going to have to work on that—because sometimes people need you to reassure them by being attractive, pleasing. I succeed at being nice but not always warm.

Listening, Studying, and Assimilating Through Practice

MATTHIEU   Why practice? Because practice is the indispensable complement to study and reflection. Attentive reading and listening make it possible for us to increase our knowledge. We then have to reflect at length to examine the validity of the teachings we have read or heard. It is also helpful to consult people who possess the knowledge we need—scholars, experts, spiritual masters—and to clarify with them our doubts and uncertainties. According to Buddhism, we mustn't stop there because the most important step is the next one: assimilation through practice of all we have learned and studied, which should result in a change in our thoughts, speech, and behavior. So we give this the name *meditation*, a term that Buddhist texts define as familiarizing ourselves or learning to master the teachings we have received. If we omit meditation, all the knowledge we have acquired remains a dead letter. We will be like a sick person who keeps his doctor's prescription under his pillow without going ahead with the treatment; or like a traveler who reads the travel guides but never takes the journey.

Dilgo Khyentse Rinpoche used to say that we can judge the progress of our spiritual practice by seeing to what extent it manifests in

> Why practice? Because practice is the indispensable complement to study and reflection.

our being and in our way of reacting to the challenges of life. He also used to say that it is easy to be a good meditator when we are basking in the sun with a full belly, but it is in times of trial and troubles that our practice is "put on the pan of the scale."

One day, the great master Patrul Rinpoche, who lived as a wandering monk, went to visit a hermit who lived in a cave. He sat down in a corner with a sly smile and asked the hermit why he lived in such an austere and remote place. "I have been living here for many years," he replied with pride in his voice. "At this time, I'm meditating on the virtue of patience."

"Patience is really great!" exclaimed Patrul. "We old foxes are really good at deceiving everyone, aren't we?"

The hermit exploded with rage.

"So, so," cried Patrul Rinpoche, "where's your patience now?"

If I take myself to be a super meditator and after ten years people say I'm just as much of a grouch as I used to be, for sure that's a very bad sign. I'd better go back to the drawing board. If, moreover, I want to put myself at the service of other people, I absolutely must acquire the qualities needed for this vocation. Trying to bring about the welfare of others before having attained a certain level of freedom and inner strength, of discernment and compassion, is riding for a fall. We often see this in the humanitarian world. We go off to help others, and then, at a certain point, our project fails. Not because there's nothing left to do or because our funds have dried up. Most of the time it's the result of ego conflicts, not listening enough to the needs of others, and, in the worst cases, corruption. All that has happened because we weren't ready. The best preparation for humanitarian activism is to spend some time transforming oneself so that one is not thrown off balance by the challenges that will surely come.

The Infinite Transforming Power of Mind

MATTHIEU We all have a mixture of shadow and light within us, but that doesn't mean that we are doomed to stay that way forever. Our habits only remain the same if we do nothing to change them.

Saying, "I am the way I am, take it or leave it" is quitting the race before reaching the starting line. That approach comes from considerably underestimating the transforming power of our mind. Our ability to control the external world is, to be sure, very limited, but the same is not at all true of our inner world. What always amazes me is the incredible effort people make in everyday life pursuing goals that are as vain as they are exhausting, but they make no effort at all to find that which brings sure happiness.

Many people think that it's too long and difficult a project to train the mind. But by the same token, it takes years to learn to read, to write, to teach, to get an education, to learn a profession, or to master an art or a sport. For what mysterious reason should training the mind be an exception to that? If we want to become more open, more altruistic, less confused, and find inner peace, we have to show some perseverance.

On the physical level, athletic endeavors rapidly encounter unsurpassable limits. Through training, some people learn to run faster and faster and to jump higher and higher. But, in fact, they gain no more than a few hundredths of a second or a few centimeters. It is completely out of the question for a human being to run the hundred meters in four seconds, or jump higher than four meters. On the other hand, I don't see how there could be any limit to love and inner peace. Once our love for beings has reached a certain level, there is nothing to prevent it from becoming still more vast and profound. The natural limitations that are applicable to the quantitative are in no way applicable to the qualitative.

There is no other way to transform ourselves than persevering in daily practice. That might sound tiresome, but as Jigme Khyentse Rinpoche used to say, if you get bored in meditation, it's not meditation's fault. It's just simply that we have to deal with our old habits, our distraction, and our resistance to change. Buddhism puts the accent on repetition and regularity, on the analogy of water falling drop by drop that finally fills a big vase. It's better to do short but frequent meditation sessions than to do long sessions quite far apart. The neurosciences show clearly that regular training brings about change in the very functioning of our brains. This is what's called neuroplasticity.

So now, how can we maintain our meditation practice in the midst of life's daily activities? First, it's important to set aside some time every day, even if it's only a half hour. If we meditate early in the morning, that imparts a certain "fragrance" to our day, a fragrance that pervades our attitudes, our actions, and our interactions with others. We can also refer back at any moment to this first experience of our day. Any time we have a free moment, we can reimmerse ourselves in it and prolong the continuity of its beneficial effects. These moments help us situate the events of daily life within a vaster perspective and experience them with greater serenity. Little by little, by the force of habit, our manner of being will evolve. We will also be able to act more effectively in the world around us and contribute toward building a wiser and more altruistic society.

My Personal Practice

MATTHIEU   As for my personal practice, what can I say? The rhythm of my life varies a great deal according to circumstances. What could be more different than a hermitage in the Himalayas and the World Economic Forum in Davos? Ideally the body should be the hermitage of the mind. Ideally also, when our spiritual practice is sufficiently stable and profound, it can be maintained in all circumstances, in calm and chaos both, in sadness as in joy. This ability in turn depends on understanding, thanks to inner experience, that nothing can distort awakened mind, which has always been there and always will be there behind the curtain of ceaselessly arising thoughts and emotions. Personally I'm far from having reached this level, but my life spent in the presence of great spiritual masters as well as five years of solitary retreat, in periods of several weeks to a year, have at least given me a foretaste of it. Although I still have the greater part of the path ahead of me, the conviction I feel that the direction shown by my masters is the right one fills me with joy.

In conditions I consider optimal—that is, when I'm at my retreat place two hour's drive from Kathmandu—what is my typical day like? Since the small hours of the morning are propitious for mental clarity, I get up at four thirty and then do a practice session until sunrise. Then I take a simple breakfast on the deck at the front of the retreat house, contemplating the banks of fog in the valley, the birds flying in the forests below, and the majestic mountains, which some days you see clearly, some days less so. Then I do another practice session until noon. After the lunch pause, I generally read some Tibetan texts, or I work for an hour or two if I have a project in hand. Then I resume my practice until nightfall.

Tibetan Buddhism teaches a great number of practices corresponding to the needs and predispositions of each person. They generally begin with thorough contemplation on the unique good fortune of having a free human birth, on the impermanence of all things, on the ineluctable quality of the causality of our actions (if one wants to avoid suffering, one has to stop creating the causes for it), and on the numberless torments beings suffer when their vision of themselves and the world do not correspond with reality. These contemplations are followed by the so-called main practices, which end in a meditation on the ultimate nature of the mind, pure awareness beyond concepts. Days, weeks, months, and years go by in this way, in this regular discipline, which, far from being monotonous, generally fills practitioners with a serene joy and gives them the confidence that they are using the time they have left to live in the best possible way.

Some people think that withdrawing from the world in this manner is selfish. They're wrong, because the essential goal of these practices is to perceive clearly the falsity of ego and liberate ourselves from its grip. It leads to a benevolence and compassion that enable us truly to put ourselves at the service of others.

How do we find a balance between retreats and active life? In Tibet I met a Hungarian man, about thirty years old, who had worked in a lawyer's office in Beijing. One day as he was vacationing in eastern Tibet, he met a respected spiritual master. He stayed some time with this master, and after the latter's death, he spent several years in retreat in mountain hermitages. The nomadic herdsmen regularly furnished him with provisions, as is often the case in Tibet. Later, when I was coming back from Tibet and was about to leave China, a friend told me that this man had decided to go to a very isolated sacred place on the border of Tibet and India and spend the rest of his life there in retreat. Finding myself a few hours later in Hong Kong with its busy life, its luxury, its profusion of restaurants and stores, I felt a profound nostalgia and asked myself if I wouldn't have done better to have followed the example of this Hungarian.

It's a dilemma for me deciding how much time to devote to retreats and how much to the somewhat fast-paced activities I spend the rest of my time in. Once I posed the question to the Dalai Lama. He answered me that, at the end of twelve years, if I was sure to have attained the spiritual level of the great Tibetan hermit Milarepa, who lived in the twelfth century but whose life story is still today a great source of inspiration for most Buddhists, then I should certainly spend all my time in retreat. But if I was not sure of the result, it was perhaps better to devote six months of the year to retreat and the remaining six months to other activities, especially humanitarian projects. The second solution seemed to me to correspond better to my modest abilities! The circumstances of my life have not yet allowed me to set six months aside every year for retreats, but I do intend to remedy that as soon as I can. I'm getting close now to the end of my life, and in the best-case scenario—that is, if I don't die tomorrow—I only have a limited number of years to live.

So I deeply hope to be able to reconnect with the contemplative practice, which was, after all, the main reason for my first trip to India, when I went to seek out the spiritual masters who ended up being the inspiration for my whole life.

ALEXANDRE Thanks to you, I see clearly that it is important not to relegate spiritual practice to a secondary level of activity. What led the Buddha to enlightenment was his conviction, his determination. For reaching the end of suffering, or at least for accepting it, nothing rivals having a guide, a practice, and plenty of perseverance. Playing the dilettante here does not yield much in the way of results. Being constant, staying on course, is really what make a difference. That's why an authentic motivation that goes beyond the machinations of ego, a profoundly altruistic thrust, remains an unrivaled driving force. Thus the essence of ascesis can be summed up in just a few words: "Of your body, of your heart, and of others, you should take great care."

Advice for a Daily Practice

MATTHIEU Earlier I said that renunciation does not consist in depriving oneself of what is really good but in getting rid of what creates suffering. To do that, the first thing is to put aside activities that are constructive neither for oneself nor for others. In other words, one has to do a bit of housekeeping in one's life. Certain things look interesting to us, but they don't contribute anything to our inner peace and may even be an outright obstacle to it. The story is told of a Brahmin, very curious by nature, who often asked the Buddha a great number of questions: Is the universe infinite? Did it have a beginning? Why are flowers different colors? And so on. Sometimes the Buddha answered him, and sometimes he remained silent. One day when the Brahmin was pressing him once again, the Buddha picked up a handful of leaves and asked, "Where are there more leaves, in the forest or in my hands?" The Brahmin had no trouble coming up with an answer: "In the forest, of course." The Buddha then told him that, like leaves in the forest, the subjects of knowledge are number-less but that only a handful of them were necessary for enlightenment. Knowing the temperature of the stars or the manner in which plants reproduce is fascinating from many points of view, but it doesn't help us understand the nature of our minds, liberate ourselves from the mental poisons, acquire boundless compassion, and finally attain enlightenment. So everything, obviously, depends on what goal you set for yourself.

This explains the significance of our opening question in this book, "What really matters in my life?" Is it getting trapped in the smoke and mirrors of wealth, power, and fame? Or is it working for the benefit of others and myself? Real practitioners have no difficulty renouncing futile things because they feel as little interest in them as a tiger does in a pile of straw. So their approach is to "simplify, simplify, simplify," as Thoreau put it.

Finally, it is necessary to realize the value of time. Life passes extremely fast. Time is like water we can't keep from running between our fingers. But used intelligently, it permits practitioners to devote themselves to the essential. In the day of a hermit, every hour becomes a treasure. As Kahlil Gibran wrote, time is "a flute through whose heart the whispering of the hours turn to music."

Some people talk about "killing time." What a vacuous thing to say! There are so many worthwhile and engaging things to do. If we constantly put off doing the essential till tomorrow, this kind of hesitation might well accompany us all the way to our end. The right moment to start is *now*.

Epilogue

One clear winter morning, we reached the conclusion of our nine days of dialogue, in which we were able to fulfill a desire that we had been harboring for a long time—to have an open-minded exchange about what engages us, inspires us, preoccupies us, and sometimes torments us. Our friendship, already lively, has been reinforced and deepened, and our sense of mutual appreciation has become stronger.

We are only travelers in search of wisdom, aware that the path is long and arduous, and that we have so much still to discover, to clarify, and to assimilate through practice. The woodsmen of compassion, the junk dealers of ego, and the apprentices of wisdom have done their best, with joy and enthusiasm. Our dearest wish is to offer those who cast their eyes on these pages subjects for reflection capable of inspiring them and to brighten the light of their lives as much as they have brightened ours.

A Final Aspiration

When we reached the end of our conversations, Matthieu suggested that we come back to our original intention, that of being of use to others. The best way to conclude these lovely days spent together is to dedicate the benefit of them to all beings and to offer our wish that everything positive, helpful, and meritorious that comes out of these sessions may contribute to the relief, direct or indirect, of the suffering with which beings are afflicted. May they progress toward freedom, wisdom, and knowledge!

Acknowledgments

Three Authors and Some Inspiring Friends

Though planned for three, these conversations soon involved a whole little family of friends who came to listen, some for a few hours, others for the entire duration of our discussions. During the pauses, the meals, and the walks, they reacted to our remarks and offered their suggestions.

Sandra, who is so attentive and considerate, who prepared delicious vegetarian cuisine for us every day, suggested to us to talk about listening, which inspired us to produce the chapter that bears that title.

Our editors for the original French version of this book, Catherine and Nicole, attended all or part of our meetings, and illuminated us with their wise suggestions; while Guillaume and Sophie, who were unable to join us, guided us in giving the book its final form.

Working alongside Catherine, who played an essential role in the layout and formatting of the book, Christian gave us his precious help in making the text more presentable and readable.

Yahne, Matthieu's nonagenarian mother, offered us some of the gems of her creative and poetic mind, telling us to keep our hearts constantly open and available, and reminding us that "we are eternal every instant."

Our friend Yeshe painstakingly recorded and filmed all our sessions. He also did the portrait of the "three sailors of enlightenment" that's on the dust jacket of the French version of this book.

Anne and her daughters welcomed us into their beautiful and quiet house. Élie, Sandra, and Clara transcribed our dialogue.

Despite his tender age, Augustin, Alexandre's son, attended most of our conversations. His presence, calm and attentive, brought us back to clarity and simplicity. His affection and devotion to his papa inspired us all.

Patricia diligently helped us to organize the logistics of our endeavor, and then came to join us in the Dordogne.

Alexandre would be unable to write and speak without an extended network of support. All his thanks go to his wife, his children, and his spiritual father; to Romina Astolfi, his assistant, as well as to his companions in the good who surround and support him day after day. His thanks in particular to Justine Souque, Émilie Houin, Delphine Roché, Sandra Robbiani, and Baudouin d'Huart for their constant help all through the adventure of making this book.

Finally, a special mention for Delphine, who was initially to welcome us to her house in the Swiss Alps. For a few years, Alexandre and Matthieu would meet there for a period of time, and each time they would call Christophe on the phone to tell him how much they would like him to join them. It was Delphine's idea three or four years ago to bring us together at her house for some conversations. But for different reasons connected with the chance occurrences of our lives, we decided at the last moment to meet in the forests of the Dordogne. Delphine, who was then recovering from an illness, was able to come spend a few days here with her friend Mark and benefit from the lovely atmosphere that prevailed here throughout our exchanges.

Notes

Chapter 2. The Ego, Friend or Imposter?

1. Roy Baumeister, "The Lowdown on High Self-Esteem. Thinking You're Hot Stuff Isn't the Promised Cure-All," *Los Angeles Times*, January 25, 2005.

Chapter 3. Learning to Live with Our Emotions

1. Christian Bobin, *The Eighth Day: Selected Writings of Christian Bobin*, ed. Pauline Matarasso (London: Darton, Longman & Todd, 2015).

Chapter 4. The Art of Listening

1. Howard B. Beckman and Richard M. Frankel, "The Effect of Physician Behavior on the Collection of Data," *Annals of Internal Medicine* 101, no. 5 (November 1984): 692–96.
2. Shabkar, *The Life of Shabkar: The Autobiography of a Tibetan Yogin*, trans. Matthieu Ricard (Boulder, CO: Snow Lion, 2001).
3. Patricia L. Dobkin and Tom A. Hutchinson, "Teaching Mindfulness in Medical School: Where Are We Now and Where Are We Going?" *Medical Education* 47, no. 8 (August 2013): 768–79; Anjanette Ryan et al., "Therapist Mindfulness, Alliance and Treatment Outcome," *Psychotherapy Research* 22, no. 3 (2012): 289–97.

Chapter 5. The Body: Burden or Idol?

1. Richard J. Davidson et al., "Approach-Withdrawal and Cerebral Asymmetry: Emotional Expression and Brain Physiology I.," *Journal of Personality and Social Psychology* 58, no. 2 (February 1990): 330–41; Paul Ekman, Richard J. Davidson, and Wallace V. Friesen, "The Duchenne Smile: Emotional Expression and Brain Physiology II.," *Journal of Personality and Social Psychology* 58, no. 2 (February 1990): 342–53; Carroll E. Izard, "Facial Expression and the

Regulation of Emotions," *Journal of Personality and Social Psychology* 58, no. 3 (March 1990): 487–98.

2. Friedrich Nietzsche, *Thus Spake Zarathustra: A Book for All and None*, trans. Thomas Common (Edinburgh, 1909; Project Gutenberg, 2008), part 1, chap. 4, gutenberg.org/files/1998/1998-h/1998-h.htm#link2H_4_0009.

Chapter 6. The Origins of Suffering

1. Simone Weil, *La pesanteur et la grâce* (Paris: Librairie Plon, 1988), 223.

Chapter 7. Consistency: A Question of Fidelity

1. Friedrich Nietzsche, prologue to *Thus Spake Zarathustra: A Book for All and None*, trans. Thomas Common (Edinburgh, 1909; Project Gutenberg, 2008), gutenberg.org/files/1998/1998-h/1998-h.htm#link2H_4_0009.

2. Jules Renard, *Journal*, "25 Novembre 1895" (Paris: Gallimard, 1965).

Chapter 8. Altruism: Everybody Wins

1. Frans de Waal. *Le bon singe* (Paris: Bayard, 1997), 66–70; Frans de Waal, *Good Natured: The Origins of Right and Wrong in Humans and Other Animals* (Boston: Harvard University Press, 1997); Gershon Berkson, "Social Responses to Abnormal Infant Monkeys," *American Journal of Physical Anthropology* 38, no. 2 (March 1973): 583–86.

Chapter 9. The School of Simplicity

1. Meister Eckhart, *La divine consolation* (Paris: Payot & Rivage, 2004), 48.

2. Tim Kasser, "Can Buddhism and Consumerism Harmonize? A Review of the Psychological Evidence" (International Conference on Buddhism in the Age of Consumerism, Mahidol University, Nakornpathom, December 2008), 1–3.

Chapter 10. Guilt and Forgiveness

1. Jacques Lecomte, *La bonté humaine: Altruisme, empathie, générosité* (Paris: Odile Jacob, 2012).

About the Authors

Matthieu Ricard is a Buddhist monk and a photographer. A molecular geneticist, he has served as an interpreter for the Dalai Lama. He first became well known thanks to the book he wrote with his father, Jean-François Revel (*The Monk and the Philosopher*, 1997). The author of *Happiness* and *The Art of Meditation*, he devotes much of his time to humanitarian projects with the organization Karuna-Shechen.

Born in 1975, Alexandre Jollien spent seventeen years in a home for the physically disabled. A philosopher and a writer, his work has been attracting an ever-growing readership from *In Praise of Weakness* (1999, Académie Française Prize), *Le métier d'homme* (The task of being a man) (2002), *La construction de soi (Building the self)* (2006), and *Petit traité de l'abandon* (A short treatise on abandonment) (2012).

Christophe André, a psychiatrist, is one of the top French specialists in the psychology of emotions and feelings. He is the author of many successful books, including *Imparfaits, libres et heureux* (Imperfect, free and happy) (2006 Psychologies Magazine Prize), *Les états d'âme* (The soul's states), and *Et n'oublie pas d'être heureux* (Don't forget to be happy). His book *Looking at Mindfulness: Twenty-Five Paintings to Change the Way You Live* has become a popular introduction to meditation.

About Sounds True

Sounds True is a multimedia publisher whose mission is to inspire and support personal transformation and spiritual awakening. Founded in 1985 and located in Boulder, Colorado, we work with many of the leading spiritual teachers, thinkers, healers, and visionary artists of our time. We strive with every title to preserve the essential "living wisdom" of the author or artist. It is our goal to create products that not only provide information to a reader or listener, but that also embody the quality of a wisdom transmission.

For those seeking genuine transformation, Sounds True is your trusted partner. At SoundsTrue.com you will find a wealth of free resources to support your journey, including exclusive weekly audio interviews, free downloads, interactive learning tools, and other special savings on all our titles.

To learn more, please visit SoundsTrue.com/freegifts or call us toll-free at 800.333.9185.

SOUNDS TRUE
many voices, one journey